Secret Weapons
of World War II

Books by William B. Breuer

An American Saga
Bloody Clash at Sadzot
Captain Cool
They Jumped at Midnight
Drop Zone Sicily
Agony at Anzio
Hitler's Fortress Cherbourg
Death of a Nazi Army
Operation Torch
Storming Hitler's Rhine
Retaking the Philippines
Nazi Spies in America
Devil Boats
Operation Dragoon
The Secret War with Germany
Hitler's Undercover War
Sea Wolf
Geronimo!
Hoodwinking Hitler
Race to the Moon
J. Edgar Hoover and His G-Men
The Great Raid on Cabanatuan
MacArthur's Undercover War
Feuding Allies
Shadow Warriors
War and American Women
Unexplained Mysteries of World War II
Vendetta: Castro and the Kennedy Brothers
Undercover Tales of World War II
Top Secret Tales of World War II

Secret Weapons of World War II

William B. Breuer

John Wiley & Sons, Inc.

New York • Chichester • Weinheim • Brisbane • Singapore • Toronto

Published by John Wiley & Sons, Inc.
Published simultaneously in Canada

This publication is designed to provide accurate and authoritative information in regard to the subject matter covered. It is sold with the understanding that the publisher
is not engaged in rendering professional services. If professional advice or other expert assistance is required, the services of a competent professional person should be
sought.

Library of Congress Cataloging-in-Publication Data:

Breuer, William B.
    Secret weapons of World War II / William B. Breuer.
        p.   cm.
    Includes bibliographical references and index.
    ISBN 0-471-37287-0 (alk. paper)
    1. Weapons systems—History—20th century. 2. World War, 1939–1945—
Equipment and supplies. I. Title.

UF500 .B74   2000
623'.09'044—dc21

99-055653

Printed in the United States of America

10 9 8 7 6 5 4 3 2 1

Dedicated to
GENERAL H. NORMAN SCHWARZKOPF, III
A courageous warrior in Vietnam
and later the architect of
the brilliant Allied
victory in the Persian Gulf

Contents

Introduction

FEW PERSONS on Planet Earth today realize that the decisive factor in the outcome of World War II was not the brilliance of highly publicized Allied military leaders and statesmen. Rather, victory or defeat in the century's climactic struggle hinged on the secret war of wits between each side's ingenious scientists and cryptanalysts (codebreakers).

Famous personalities—Churchill, Roosevelt, Hitler, Mussolini, Eisenhower, Goering, Yamamoto, and others—appear often in this book. But the focus is on the high-stakes cat-and-mouse game waged behind the scenes in which first one side, then the other gained an advantage.

Both adversaries exerted gargantuan efforts to implement the often spectacular feats of the codebreakers and scientists through covert missions, plots, hoaxes, spying, conspiracies, and electronic sleuthing. The constant goal was to trick, foil, or outmaneuver the other side's armed forces.

This, then, is the incredible and little-known story behind the story that decided World War II.

Part One

War Breaks Out

German Invention
Triggers Global Search

WAR CLOUDS WERE GATHERING over Europe in mid-1938 when Stewart Menzies, the deputy chief of MI-6, the British secret intelligence service, had been laboring seven-day weeks in his office on Broadway, a side street near Westminster Abbey in London. These were fearful times among government leaders, because the nation's conventional defenses had been allowed to grow alarmingly weak. Now it seemed certain that Adolf Hitler was about ready to launch a war to gain the Third Reich "a place in the sun."

Menzies' special responsibility was collecting information about the secret plans of the German dictator and the strength and disposition of the Wehrmacht, his armed forces. Not since the conclusion of what was then called the Great War, in 1918, had British statesmen felt such a need for in-depth intelligence from inside Germany.

Britain had successfully intercepted and decoded German military and diplomatic telegrams for many years. But in 1934, two years after the German führer seized power, he installed a new and revolutionary communications system developed by Germany's foremost scientists. Since that time, Menzies had directed hundreds of agents in an exhaustive global search to establish the nature of Germany's new modus operandi. All the efforts were in vain.

The target of the ongoing MI-6 investigation was a compact (twenty-four inches square and eighteen inches high) electronic machine enclosed in a wooden box. Until the arrival of this device, encoding and decoding of messages had been done painstakingly for hours by human hand. Enigma (the ancient Greek word for puzzle), as the intricate machine was called, could accomplish the same thing in only two or three minutes.

Colonel Erich Fellgiebel, the Wehrmacht's chief signals officer, and his scientists had assured Hitler that Enigma would be unbreakable. It was capable of producing twenty-two billion different code combinations. If one person worked continuously day and night and tried a different grouping each minute, it would take him forty-two thousand years to exhaust all combination possibilities.

*Germany's "unbreakable"
Enigma coding machine.
(Author's collection)*

Even if an Enigma were captured by an enemy, it would be useless, Fell-giebel explained, because a foe would have to know the keying procedure, which was changed almost daily.

What Fellgiebel did not know was that agents of Department BS-4, the cryptographic (codebreaking) section of the Polish secret service, had "acquired" an Enigma. Two renowned Polish mathematicians, Henryk Zygalski and Marian Rejewski, managed to solve some of the Enigma mysteries and read intercepts. But their feat would be of minimal value in wartime, because it was mathematical and took several weeks to decipher even a short message.

In the meantime, a German in civilian clothes who claimed he was an officer in the Forschungsamt, the Third Reich's primary cryptanalytical agency, slipped into the French embassy in Berne, Switzerland. Historically neutral in European armed conflicts over the centuries, Switzerland had been a hotbed for espionage in the Great War, and spies continued to roam the mountainous country since that time.

The German told a top French diplomat that he could make a valuable contribution to the security of France against the Nazi government of his homeland. His motives, he stressed, were ideological.

After asking the mystery caller, who would be code-named "Source D," to return to the embassy in two weeks, the French military attaché immediately contacted "2 bis," the military cryptanalytical bureau in Paris. Secret Service officers were skeptical about Source D's true intentions. It was thought that he might be an agent provocateur sent by the German Abwehr (German intelligence agency) to infiltrate the French espionage apparatus in Switzerland.

After prolonged debate, however, 2 bis officers realized that the German could be an intelligence font of enormous magnitude. So Captain Ramon Navarre was rushed to Berne, where he questioned Source D for many hours.

Navarre's report to 2 bis was blunt: "'Source D' is a genuine German traitor acting out of a lust for money," the French captain declared. Moreover, he added, the German disclosed that Third Reich scientists had developed a coding and decoding apparatus of a completely new type. At the time, French intelligence did not know that the machine was code-named Enigma.

Although 2 bis was not completely sold on the true motivation of the German, Navarre was instructed to pay him a "modest compensation" and promise him a hefty amount of money if he were to provide 2 bis with detailed information about the communications machine.

Ten days later, Source D rendezvoused with Navarre at night in a small café on a quiet side street in Brussels, Belgium. The mystery German brought with him a monumental intelligence gold mine—a far richer lode than 2 bis officers had envisioned. There was a manual with the word "Secret" in large letters on the cover. The booklet contained detailed instructions on how to operate Enigma. The German also brought along a sample of a page of coded text together with its plain text match.

Navarre was both electrified and suspicious. Were these materials genuine, or a component of an elaborate Abwehr scheme to achieve some unknown objective? However, the Frenchman handed the other man a generous payment in German marks, with a promise that there would be much more cash for the traitor if French technicians in Paris found the information to be authentic.

Source D's data were, indeed, legitimate. French scientists found the materials capable of producing a working replica of Enigma. Source D continued to send invaluable information to 2 bis through Captain Navarre, including keying changes used by the Wehrmacht to stymie any outside entity that might try to crack Enigma.

Consequently, French intelligence was able to decode secret German communications. But this gargantuan espionage coup could last only as long as Source D retained his freedom and was able to furnish the keying changes.

In early 1939, the British were convinced that it would be essential to get hold of a genuine Enigma machine if there would be any chance of breaking into its mysteries. Consequently, British agents contacted the Polish Secret Service.

Polish and British secret agents knew the location of the German factory where the Enigmas were built and the security measures in place to protect the machines. Moreover, several Poles had been planted in the facility and were using German names. It was decided to have these undercover operatives steal an Enigma machine.

Almost in days, the Polish spies in the Enigma factory smuggled one of the devices out of the building and eventually to Warsaw—an incredible espionage feat.

Meanwhile, Commander Alastair Denniston, who had been involved in cryptography since serving in the British Admiralty in the Great War, slipped out of London in civilian clothes and traveled to Warsaw. Denniston's reserved demeanor in no way reflected his coolness in tight situations.

A few days after his clandestine arrival, Denniston rendezvoused with Polish Secret Service agents and was handed the genuine, brand-new Enigma machine stolen from the German factory. Then he sneaked out of Poland and arrived in London.

Now Menzies and MI-6 had an Enigma machine in their possession. But leading British scientists, mathematicians, and cryptanalysts concluded that there was only one method to penetrate Enigma and produce intelligence rapidly enough to be of use in wartime: develop another machine that could imitate the performance of the German device. The envisioned machine would have to be capable of making an almost infinite series of intricate mathematical calculations within a few minutes.

To tighten the security around efforts to penetrate Enigma, Polish, British, and French intelligence agents held the first of a series of top-secret conferences on January 9, 1939, at Château Vignolle, twenty-five miles from Paris. A crucial decision was reached: because Poland and France might be overrun by the Wehrmacht in the event of war, all vital papers, machines, and personnel connected with Enigma would be concentrated in England.

At a rendezvous in the Pyry forest near Warsaw, Polish intelligence officers handed over to British agents everything in their possession regarding Enigma. These precious documents were taken under heavy guard to London on July 24, 1939.

Five weeks later, Adolf Hitler unleashed his mighty Wehrmacht against Poland, whose armed forces were undermanned and ill-equipped. Despite heroic resistance by the Poles, the German Army conquered the nation in only six weeks.

With the capture of Warsaw, the invaders quickly collected all the intelligence documents they could locate. They most certainly would have learned that the two Poles, Henryk Zygalski and Marian Rejewski, had mathematically penetrated Enigma if British agents, a day earlier, had not sneaked the two men across the border into Romania. They were then escorted to Château Vignolle to work with the French on the Enigma-penetration project.

In the meantime, a team of Great Britain's foremost scientists and mathematicians, led by Alan Turing and Alfred Knox, began to develop the theoretical machine that, hopefully, would mechanically decipher Enigma in only minutes. They set up shop in a large, stone Victorian mansion forty miles north of London and just outside the serene little town of Bletchley Park.

Turing and Knox were as eccentric as they were brilliant. Fifty-six-year-old "Dilly" Knox, who seemed to be in a perpetual state of abstraction, was regarded as an exceptional mathematical logician. He was the son of the bishop of Manchester and had belonged to the Admiralty's cryptanalytical bureau in World War I. His first main success then had been solving a complicated German code while taking a bath.

After that war, the tall, gangling Knox spent eight years translating the seven hundred verses of Herodas, a third-century poet, working from the original papyri. It was an enormous cryptanalytical feat, and it gained him a wide reputation in the intellectual circles of Europe.

Turing, the younger of the two men, was also a mathematical genius. In the 1930s he attended the Institute for Advanced Studies at elite Princeton University in the United States, where his professor was a refugee from Nazi Germany, Albert Einstein.

Despite his recognized braininess, Turing had a childlike aspect to his personality. Each night at Bletchley Park, he listened avidly to *Toytown*, a children's series about Larry the Lamb on BBC radio. He kept the long-distance telephone line open to his mother so they could discuss each aspect of *Toytown* as the story unfolded.

When war threatened to erupt, Turing converted his money into silver ingots, buried them, then forgot where the precious bars were secreted. And, once, although there was no threat of gas warfare, he was arrested by a constable who found him strolling along a country lane near Bletchley Park at night while wearing a gas mask.

Periodically, Turing would be summoned to a conference in London. Instead of taking the automobile that was made available to him, he often ran the forty miles from Bletchley Park in a worn old flannel outfit with a large alarm clock tied with a rope around his waist.

Utilizing their own and Polish and French research information and the Polish-supplied Enigma machine, the intellectuals at Bletchley Park labored month after month, never knowing if the job could be done. Eventually they began to despair. Then, on the eve of Great Britain going to war against Nazi Germany on September 3, 1939, they hit the jackpot.

The Bomb, as its creators called their amazing creation, was able to match the electrical circuits of Enigma, permitting the device to imitate the daily change in keying procedures by the Germans. Information obtained by the system was code-named Ultra.

Development of the Bomb would prove to be a technological achieve-ment and an intelligence bonanza of unprecedented magnitude. From this point onward (not all the bugs would be eliminated until April 1940), the British (and later the Americans) would know the precise strength and location of German units and be advised in advance of enemy moves and intentions.[1]

Stealing America's Radar Secrets

AT CAFÉ HINDENBURG in the German-American section called Yorkville in New York City, a raucous celebration was ushering in New Year 1939. As the night wore on and as copious amounts of schnapps, cognac, beer, and wine were consumed, the din grew deafening.

At one table, Karl Schlueter, a steward on the German luxury ocean liner *Europa*, then docked in the Hudson River, was host to a group of friends and vying for the honor of being the drunkest and the loudest. Between hefty belts of schnapps, Schlueter pawed amorously at his attractive girlfriend, twenty-seven-year-old Johanna "Jenni" Hofman, a hairdresser on the ship.

Actually, Schlueter was a spy, the Orstgruppenführer (Nazi party official) who had total control of *Europa* under the cover of being a lowly steward. Jenni Hofman was his courier.

During the boisterous merrymaking at Café Hindenburg, Schlueter en-gaged in periodic conversation with a guest at his table whom he called Theo. A medium-sized man with black hair brushed straight back, Theo was the code name for Günther Gustav Rumrich, one of the slickest and most productive Nazi spies in the United States.

Rumrich was born in Chicago, where his father, Alphonse, had been sec-retary of the Austro-Hungarian consulate. When Günther was two years old, his father was transferred to a post in Bremen, Germany, and the boy grew up in a Europe ravaged by the Great War. At age eighteen he learned that because of his birth in Chicago, he was an American citizen. So on September 28, 1929, he arrived by ship in New York City to seek his fortune.

A curious mixture of shiftlessness, arrogance, cunning, and brilliance, Rumrich drifted from job to job around the country, including a hitch in the peacetime U.S. Army. Discharged from the service in 1936, he came to New York City and was recruited as an agent by the Abwehr, the German intelli-gence agency. Finally Rumrich had found his calling: he could live by his brains without having to exert much energy.

When Adolf Hitler had begun rearming Germany in the mid-1930s, he concluded that the United States, with its gigantic industrial potential, would be the "decisive factor" in any future war. So his secret intelligence service in the years ahead clandestinely established in America the most massive espi-onage penetration of a major power that history had known.

Ace Nazi spy Günther Rumrich sent this letter to a former
U.S. Army buddy, urging him to become a German agent.
(FBI)

In the late 1930s, the United States was a spy's paradise. No single federal
agency was charged with fighting subversive activities, so spies roamed at will.
Security at military installations was almost nonexistent. When one U.S. general commanding a large post in the East was asked what steps he had taken to
guard against espionage, he said with a snort, "Don't you think I'd know it if
there was a Nazi spy running around here?"

Now, amid the hubbub of the New Year's festivities at Café Hindenburg,
Orstgruppenführer Schlueter took Günther Rumrich into a side room and
handed him his new assignment: he was to obtain detailed intelligence about
secret research that scientists with the Signal Corps were conducting at Fort
Monmouth, New Jersey. Reputedly, these experiments involved techniques for
detecting aircraft at night, in fog, and through thick clouds—a process that later
would be known as radar.

Neither Schlueter nor Rumrich knew that German scientists in Berlin had secretly been making great progress in developing radar, so any information on the topic extracted from the American camp would be of enormous benefit. Already the international scientific coterie had become convinced that radar would play a decisive role in any future war.

A few days later, Rumrich crossed the Hudson River and drove up to the main gate at Fort Monmouth, where supposedly top-secret experiments were being conducted. A bored sentry simply waved the Nazi spy through the entrance and went back to reading a comic book.

Rumrich, a friendly, engaging fellow, meandered around the post unchallenged, striking up conversations with army officers and scientists alike. He had no trouble locating the site of the secret experiments: he had merely asked a captain where the radar tests were taking place.

Rumrich continued his sleuthing at Fort Monmouth in the days ahead, and he was able to collect an enormous amount of intelligence on radar research and experiments. Moreover, he obtained information on other secret tests: infrared detection, and an antiaircraft detector for searchlight control and automatic gun sighting.

When Karl Schlueter returned to New York City on *Europa* a month later, Rumrich handed him a thick packet of scientific intelligence he had collected at Fort Monmouth. Schlueter was delighted and handed over a present from the spymasters in Germany: a one-hundred-dollar bill, more money than Rumrich had made in an entire year as a soldier in the U.S. Army.[2]

History's Most Important Letter

THIRTY-SEVEN-YEAR-OLD Enrico Fermi, a professor of theoretical physics at the University of Rome, and his family were euphoric: he had just been notified of his selection to receive the Nobel Prize in physics for his work on nuclear processes. Established by a Swedish chemist, Alfred Nobel, who had invented dynamite, the prestigious awards go annually to persons who have made valuable contributions to "the good of humanity in their fields." It was December 1938.

A week later, Fermi; his wife, Laura; and the couple's two children arrived in Stockholm for the Nobel award presentation. Using his prize money, the renowned physicist was able to sail with his family to New York City, arriving there on January 2, 1939. America would be the Fermi family's adopted land.

What the Italian family kept to itself was that the entire trip—from Rome to Stockholm to New York City—had been carefully orchestrated to avoid trouble along the way, because the family was fleeing from Italy's newly decreed anti-Semitic laws. These oppressive regulations were regarded as a serious threat to Laura, who was Jewish, and to the couple's two children, who were half Jewish. Fermi himself was "pure" Italian.

In the United States, Fermi joined a distinguished coterie of physicists, all of whom were refugees from brutal dictatorships in Europe. They included Albert Einstein, who had fled Germany after Adolf Hitler came to power when the Nazi regime confiscated his property and ousted him as director of the Kaiser Wilhelm Institute for Physics because he was Jewish. In the United States, the famous physicist had accepted an appointment to head Princeton's new Institute for Advanced Study.

Other brilliant Jewish scientists who had immigrated to the United States were the Hungarians Leo Szilard, Edward Teller, and Eugene Wigner, and the Austrian Victor Weisskopf—all of whom had had personal experience with the barbarous conduct of nations headed by dictators.

At about the same time that Enrico Fermi had been in Stockholm to accept his Nobel Prize, two renowned German physicists, Fritz Strassman and Otto Hahn, who were considered to be far ahead of anyone else in the world in theoretical research into nuclear energy, split the atom when they bombarded uranium with neutrons. They called this process fission.

Neither Hahn nor Strassman, nor any other scientist, realized at the time that the two Germans were on a course toward developing the most powerful weapon that history has known. Fortunately for the free world, Adolf Hitler, who was drawing up plans to go to war in the fall of 1939, did not grasp the significance of nuclear energy as an ultimate weapon. So he raised no objection to Strassman and Hahn publishing their startling findings in scientific journals distributed around the world.

The electrifying news from Nazi Germany deeply worried the band of émigré scientists in the United States. They were haunted by the specter of the Germans developing an atomic bomb for which there would be no defense, a weapon that would give Adolf Hitler control of the world.

Consequently, these émigrés began an informal yet fervent campaign to encourage scientists in the Western democracies to cease publishing developments in nuclear physics that might assist Germany and Italy toward atomic explosives.

One leading American-born physicist, Harvard's Percy W. Bridgman, announced in *Science*, the publication of the AAAS (American Association for the Advancement of Science), that from that point onward he would no longer publicize or discuss his experiments with the citizens of any totalitarian state.

"A citizen of such a state is no longer a free individual, and he may be compelled in any activity including [building atomic explosives] to advance the purposes of the state," Bridgman explained.

Bridgman's announcement brought a shower of condemnation on him from other American scientists, and from several in Europe, including Niels

Bohr, a Danish physicist who was a sort of guru and confessor to the international scientific community. Bridgman, his critics charged, was guilty of betraying the basic principle of free inquiry for the benefit of all humankind.

Enrico Fermi and the others in the group of émigré physicists were also appalled and frustrated by the apathy toward and ignorance of the potential danger from the Hahn/Strassman experiments by leaders of America's armed forces. So Fermi obtained a letter of introduction from George Pegram, a noted physics professor and graduate dean at Columbia University, to Rear Admiral S. C. Hooper in the office of the chief of naval operations.

On March 17, 1939, Fermi entered the navy headquarters in Washington to sound the alarm to Admiral Hooper. But instead of an interview with this high-ranking officer, Fermi was ushered into a small room to tell his tale to two young lieutenant commanders. They listened politely as Fermi, handicapped by often faulty English, struggled to impress on the U.S. Navy the enormous significance of the new nuclear energy discoveries.

After the Italian émigré departed, it was later reported that one of the navy officers said to the other, "That Wop is crazy as hell!"

Whether or not that story was accurate, it reflected the officers' evident attitude toward the nuclear energy "nonsense." For his part, Fermi left the building fuming, feeling that he, a scientist of world renown who had been trying to alert his adopted country, had been personally insulted. He pledged never again to communicate with American military officers.

During the next few months, the coterie of refugee scientists watched helplessly as one clue after another indicated that Germany's leading chemists and physicists were being concentrated in the Kaiser Wilhelm Institute for Physics in Berlin, where they were involved with uranium, a key ingredient in the possible creation of a gargantuan explosive. Nazi officials were trying desperately to import the element from the Belgian Congo, the principal source of uranium.

In the summer of 1939, the Hungarians Leo Szilard and Eugene Wigner drove in a dilapidated automobile to a secluded cottage on the Long Island shore where Albert Einstein was taking a brief vacation. They were convinced that Einstein was the only physicist in the United States who had the prestige and the popularity to gain a sympathetic hearing from leading government officials. The two Hungarians persuaded the pacifist Einstein to agree to write, or to sign, a letter that might open a top-level door in Washington.

A few days after obtaining Einstein's pledge, Szilard was discussing the apathy toward the nuclear energy threat by the Roosevelt administration with Alexander Sachs, a Russian-born economist. Szilard had been introduced to Sachs by Gustav Stolper, a former member of the German Reichstag who had fled from Nazi Germany. Sachs always kept a close watch on scientific developments in Europe, Stolper had told Szilard, and was said to have access to the White House.

Albert Einstein wrote history's most important letter. (Author's collection)

In his conversation with Szilard, Sachs immediately grasped the potential danger if Adolf Hitler got his hands on an ultimate weapon resulting from the taming of nuclear energy. Moreover, the Russian émigré said that President Roosevelt should be informed at once.

Sachs told Szilard that if he, Sachs, were given a letter signed by Albert Einstein, he would make sure that it personally reached Roosevelt. Consequently, Einstein agreed with Szilard that Sachs was the ideal person to deliver a written message to the president.

Dated August 2, 1939, the clumsily composed letter signed by Einstein said in part:

> In the course of the last four months it has been made probably . . . to set up nuclear chain reactions in a large mass of uranium, by which large amounts of power and large quantities of new radium-like elements could be achieved in the immediate future.
>
> This new phenomenon would also lead to the construction of bombs and it is conceivable . . . that a single bomb . . . might very well destroy [an entire city] and some of the surrounding territory.
>
> In view of this situation, you may wish to speed up the experimental work, which is at present being carried out on limited budgets in university laboratories, by providing funds.

No one could know it at the time, but it would prove to be history's most important letter.

Now Alexander Sachs had the letter in his hand, but he was soon confronted by Washington stonewalling. He contacted Major General Edwin M. "Pa" Watson, Roosevelt's congenial military aide and confidant, and urgently asked for an appointment with the president, emphasizing that the secret information he wished to give him was of extreme significance.

However, Roosevelt was at the family estate at Hyde Park, overlooking the broad Hudson River north of New York City, and his time was fully occupied with signing or vetoing the blizzard of bills ramrodded through Congress during the final few days of the session recently concluded. Therefore, Pa Watson explained, the president could not work in an appointment with Sachs to discuss some vague subject referred to as nuclear energy and chain reactions.

Ten days passed. Leo Szilard and Eugene Wigner grew steadily more anxious and frustrated. Why hadn't their emissary given the Einstein letter to Roosevelt by now? Sachs counseled patience.

Then the two Hungarian refugees' patience was again put to the test. Sachs informed them that the president had boarded his private yacht and left for a vacation cruise.

Meanwhile, war had broken out in Europe on September 1, 1939, when Adolf Hitler sent his powerful Wehrmacht plunging into neighboring Poland. As a result, Szilard and Wigner grew even more restless. On October 3, 1939, Szilard wrote to Albert Einstein saying that "there is a distinct possibility that Sachs will be of no use to us," adding that he and Wigner had decided to "accord Sachs ten days' grace."

Curiously, on October 11, near the end of the "grace period," Alexander Sachs was finally granted an interview with Franklin Roosevelt, and he was ushered into the Oval Office by Pa Watson. Roosevelt, always "onstage," greeted the guest warmly. "Alex!" he called out as though Sachs's appearance was a pleasant surprise, "What are you up to?"

It was a meeting of two highly loquacious men. The forty-six-year-old Sachs asked for permission to read aloud three documents he had brought along to hand over to the president. No doubt Sachs knew that Roosevelt often liked to listen to verbal accounts as opposed to reading all of them. The chief executive nodded his approval.

The documents were Einstein's letter, a memo from Leo Szilard, and a letter from Sachs himself. Slowly, deliberately, emphasizing key points, Sachs read the materials aloud. In conclusion, Sachs quoted a remark from a lecture by the British physicist Francis Aston:

"Personally, I think there is no doubt that atomic energy is available all around us, and that one day man will release and control its almost infinite power. We cannot prevent him from doing so and can only hope he will not use it exclusively for blowing up his next-door neighbor."

These haunting words apparently echoed in Roosevelt's mind. After several moments of silence he said, "What you are after, Alex, is to see to it that the Nazis don't blow us up!"

"Precisely!" Sachs replied.

Roosevelt then summoned General Watson and handed over the Einstein letter and the two other documents. "Pa," the president said solemnly, "this requires action!"

Genial Pa Watson could be excused if the nuclear energy field eluded his mental capacity. Few others in or outside government could comprehend it either. And with Roosevelt swamped by countless other major problems, the "required action" evolved into a few tiny steps toward organizing an effective working relationship between the U.S. government and the scientific community.

Out of the Sachs presentation of Einstein's letter to Roosevelt there was established a presidential Advisory Committee on Uranium within the National Bureau of Standards.

When the eager physicists—Leo Szilard, Edward Teller, and Eugene Wigner—met with the panel for the first time on October 21, they were appalled to discover that the sense of extreme urgency, of potential fatal danger that they had tried desperately to instill in the federal government was absent.

The chairman of the advisory committee was the elderly director of the Bureau of Standards, Lyman J. Briggs, who had been in government service for more than forty years, usually in administrative posts. Although a physicist by training, his specialty had been soil physics—and it had been three decades since he had done research in that field. Established by an act of Congress in 1901, the bureau is the nation's physics laboratory, charged with applying science and technology in the national interest.

It was soon clear to Szilard, Teller, and Wigner that they were dealing with not a fellow physicist, but a long-entrenched bureaucrat who garbed himself in the protective coloration of not making decisive decisions.

Also on the Uranium committee were an army ordnance expert, Lieutenant Colonel Keith F. Adamson, and a navy weapons specialist, Commander Gilbert C. Hoover. These officers would prove to be especially offensive to the three Hungarians because of the crude manner in which they expressed their doubts.

Leo Szilard led off the discussion by stressing the possibility of a chain reaction in a uranium-graphite system. A large-scale experiment might be needed. He estimated the destructive power of a uranium bomb to be about twenty thousand tons of high-explosive equivalent.

Colonel Adamson loudly interrupted the speaker. "In Aberdeen we have a goat tethered to a stick with a ten-foot rope, and we have promised a big prize to anyone who can kill the goat with a death ray. Nobody has claimed the prize yet." (Aberdeen Proving Ground is a facility in Maryland where the U.S. Army tested new weapons and equipment.)

Referring to the twenty thousand tons of dynamite, Adamson declared contemptuously that he had once been standing outside an ordnance depot when it blew up and the blast hadn't even knocked him down.

Restraining their anger, Edward Teller and Eugene Wigner, both handicapped by language difficulties, did their best to support Szilard's arguments, but each was interrupted numerous times by barbs from Adamson and Hoover.

Despite the sluggishness and skepticism of the advisory committee, Chairman Briggs made a written report to President Roosevelt on November 1. Surprisingly, the document had a positive tone. It recommended the funding of research into the possibility of using a controlled chain reaction to power submarines, and that if the reaction resulted in being "explosive in character" it might "provide a possible source of bombs with a destructiveness far greater than anything known."

Albert Einstein's letter had finally paid off.[3]

A U.S. Foundation Funds Nazi Research

PETER DEBYE, a Dutch physicist who had received the 1936 Nobel Prize in chemistry, had spent most of his adult life working in Germany, and in late 1938 he was chosen to head the new Kaiser Wilhelm Institute for Physics in Berlin. Incredibly, at a time when the entire world knew that Adolf Hitler was rearming the Third Reich, funds for operating the institute were provided by the Rockefeller Foundation in New York City.

Chartered in 1913 as a nonprofit organization for "promoting the well-being of mankind throughout the world," the foundation had been provided an original endowment of $183 million (equivalent to some $2 billion in 1999) by the fabled John D. Rockefeller. Born in Richford, New York, in 1839, Rockefeller, the son of a peddler, became perhaps the world's richest man. A year after he died at age ninety-eight in 1937, his foundation's board of trustees apparently had concluded that Adolf Hitler was bent on "promoting the well-being of mankind."

Debye, who was widely known in the international coterie of physicists, didn't last long in that prestigious post. For six months he refused to join the Nazi Party and defended the independence of the institute from repeated efforts by the *Heer* (army) to take it over. The skirmishing had an inevitable conclusion: in October 1939, a month after Hitler had invaded Poland, Debye was granted "a leave of absence, effective immediately."

Seeing the proverbial handwriting on the wall, Debye accepted a professorship at Cornell University in Ithaca, New York. While preparing to leave, he met secretly with a Rockefeller Foundation official in Berlin, Warren Weaver, who told him the heer had finally taken control of the Kaiser Wilhelm Institute for Physics to develop an "irresistible offensive weapon," no doubt meaning an atomic bomb.

Then Debye learned from his good friend physicist Otto Hahn that large numbers of the Reich's foremost scientists had been persuaded or dragooned into joining the research program at the institute, which was only a few blocks from Adolf Hitler's Reichkanzlei (Chancellery).

A brilliant, ambitious young physicist, Carl F. von Weizsäcker, the son of Baron Ernst von Weizsäcker, who was second in command and reputedly the brains of the German Foreign Office, had taken the lead in coercing the intellectuals to participate. Even though the Reich's sweeping anti-Semitic laws had forced countless Jewish scientists to flee the country, some of the most talented physicists in the world were available in Germany.

In Berlin, the Education Ministry coined the name Uranverein (Uranium Club) to describe the physicists and chemists who were doing research in nuclear fission. But these scientists never worked in a common laboratory, never had a common chain of command, nor even shared a common agenda other than a vague understanding that they were to develop an "ultimate weapon."

In fact, the Uranverein consisted of a number of fiefdoms, with research and studies conducted in Hamburg, Heidelberg, Leipzig, Berlin, Cologne, and several other locales, each one under a different leader. The fiefdoms competed fiercely for funds, materials, and military exemptions for promising young students. Jealousies were rampant.

Despite this lack of a centralized bomb-development program operated with typical Teutonic efficiency, Adolf Hitler and his generals fervently hoped that an ultimate weapon would eventually be developed by the Uranverein. When a friend asked Otto Hahn whether a bomb was feasible, the famed physicist cagily replied with a question of his own: "My dear friend, do you really assume that I would blow up London?"

No doubt the most enthusiastic German physicist was Carl von Weizsäcker, who had strong-armed many scientists into joining the Uranverein. Only twenty-nine years of age yet respected by his colleagues, he sought wide recognition and immense political power in Germany, convinced that whoever developed an atomic bomb would achieve that lofty status.

Weizsäcker later wrote: "Scientifically I found other topics much more interesting. But I considered politics to be important. I believed that I might be able to gain political influence if I were someone with whom even Adolf Hitler had to speak."

Carl von Weizsäcker, like millions of other young Germans, idolized the führer, who had promised to restore the nation to her rightful glory after

Leaders in the German atomic-bomb project: Carl von Weizsäcker (left) and Otto Hahn. (National Archives)

her humiliating defeat in the Great War two decades earlier. "Not everything the Nazis are doing is wrong," the scientist told a Danish friend on a trip to Copenhagen.

On April 28, 1940, Peter Debye, who had been ousted as head of the Kaiser Wilhelm Institute for Physics because he opposed the German Army takeover, arrived in New York City on the way to his new job at elite Cornell University. A few days later, at a meeting of the American Chemical Society, he was collared by William Laurence, a reporter for the *New York Times*, widely recognized as the United States' most prestigious newspaper.

After much probing and digging, Laurence squeezed from a cautious Debye an admission that the German army had taken over the Kaiser Wilhelm Institute for Physics to conduct research on uranium.

Through previous study, Laurence knew that Germany had Europe's only source of uranium in Nazi-occupied Czechoslovakia, and Hitler's invasion of Norway had given him control of the world's only source of "heavy water" (deuterium oxide, or D_2O, used in connection with nuclear reactions).

Laurence had a blockbuster story: Adolf Hitler's scientists were developing an ultimate weapon, an atomic bomb. The article, along with illustrations, was plastered over most of the front page of the *Times* on Sunday, May 5, 1940.

Laurence and the *Times*'s editors waited anxiously for the expected alarmed reaction from Washington. They waited in vain: there was no reaction, only total indifference.[4]

"A Bunch of Crazy Scientists"

JUST PAST EIGHT O'CLOCK on the morning on May 7, 1939, Adolf Hitler was awakened in his apartment at the magnificent new Reichkanzlei in Berlin. Rain was beating onto the windows, and a cold wind was whipping through the capital city. The führer was in a foul mood. Much to his annoyance, he had been promised that he would watch a rocket-firing demonstration at the army testing grounds, Kummersdorf West, seventeen miles south of Berlin.

Hitler's grumpy disposition was compounded by several factors, one of which was that he had had only two hours' sleep. Essentially a "night person," he was accustomed to holding long and tedious conferences with his government and military leaders from nightfall to dawn. These discussions were largely Hitler monologues, with the others involved able to inject little more than monosyllabic comments.

Then the fifty-year-old leader of the Third Reich would sleep most of the day. Then, after a hot bath and vitamin injections by his personal physician, Dr. Theodor Morell, the führer was ready for another night-long round of discussions.

Other than for a lack of sleep, Hitler was agitated on this morning by the fact that he had monumental matters to address; only a handful of confidants knew that he planned to invade Poland in the fall. Now he was going to have to go into the field to watch a number of scientists "play" with some rockets.

Ninety minutes after being awakened, the leader of some eighty million German people stepped from his limousine at Kummersdorf West and was greeted by a clicking of heels and Nazi salutes from assembled military brass and scientists. After being escorted into a nearby building, Hitler was given a technical lecture on rockets by twenty-seven-year-old Wernher von Braun, who was widely regarded as Germany's—and perhaps the world's—foremost authority on rockets.

Although von Braun was an articulate speaker, his lecture seemed to bore the führer, onlookers noticed in quick glances. When the young scientist was finished, a thick silence engulfed the room as those there waited for Hitler to ask questions. Those present knew it had been his habit, when shown a new-model tank or airplane, to inquire about the smallest details. Now he remained mute.

Then Hitler and his entourage were escorted to a forest clearing where two small test rockets, their snouts pointed upward, rested on launchers. Suddenly there was a belching of smoke and fire, a roar, and the rockets zoomed skyward and vanished into low clouds. The führer watched expressionless and said nothing.

Hitler was then shown a model of the huge A-3 rocket, so constructed as to reveal the internal mechanisms. Without a doubt, the A-3 was the largest and most advanced missile that history had known. It was forty-six feet high, and if the model were perfected and went into mass production, it would carry a twenty-two-hundred-pound warhead.

The führer still made no comment. Von Braun and his rocket team were crestfallen.

A short time later at lunch, Hitler continued to keep his thoughts to himself. When he finally did say something about rockets, his remarks cast an even deeper gloom over the team of scientists and technicians. "Back in the early days [of the Nazi Party]," he said, "we knew a man in Munich who experimented with rockets but we looked on him as a *Spinner* [crackpot]."

Only when he was preparing to depart did Hitler give a cautious opinion on the rocket demonstration: "*Es war doch gewaltig!* (It was impressive!)"

Although von Braun and his team no doubt felt that they were pioneers in the field, rockets had been invented by the ancient Chinese, who used them to frighten their enemies in battle. It was not until early in the nineteenth century that a British artilleryman who had been in the Orient developed rockets into actual weapons. Their use against the Americans defending Fort McHenry during an all-night bombardment during the War of 1812 inspired Francis Scott Key's "Star-Spangled Banner" ("And the rockets' red glare").

Wernher was one of three sons of Baron Magnus von Braun, a wealthy descendant of a Prussian family that had served the Fatherland loyally and with distinction for seven centuries. Magnus had been a founder of the huge German Savings Bank, and later he was appointed minister of agriculture by President Paul von Hindenberg, a military legend of the Great War.

Although the baron had always been proud of his three sons, he was vaguely disappointed over the career route that the most intellectual of his offspring had taken—dabbling in rockets. Wernher could have assumed the dignified duties of a "landed Prussian gentleman," the father felt, but instead he was obsessed with rockets and space travel. "Utter nonsense, a classic way to waste one's life," the father told his wife, the soft-spoken Baroness Emmy von Braun, who had mastered six languages early in life.

In the wake of Adolf Hitler's visit to Kummersdorf West and his upbeat remark about the rocket demonstrations, Wernher von Braun and his team had been elated. No doubt German agencies now would provide ample funding for the ongoing tests. Soon the euphoria turned to anger and frustration. Instead of gaining more money, the rocketeers were being held back by the heavy hand of German bureaucracy, an impediment to scientific progress in any nation.

In Berlin, officials in the Bureau of the Budget regarded the rocketeers as "crazy scientists playing with their toys." Kummersdorf's spending was carefully audited at a time when Hitler was pouring huge amounts of marks into building up his armed forces.

Von Braun and his colleagues were not given an approval even to purchase needed office equipment. Undaunted, he used his ample ingenuity to circumvent the eagle-eyed auditors in Berlin. When ordering typewriters, the requisition request was filled out for "instruments for recording test data with rotating rollers." Pencil sharpeners were described as "appliances for milling wooden dowels up to ten millimeters in diameter." All such requests were promptly approved.[5]

Charles Lindbergh Helps the "Moon Man"

THIRTY-SIX-YEAR-OLD Gustav Guellich returned to his room at the Hotel Martinique, on New York's West Thirty-second Street, after a long and tiresome round trip by bus to New Mexico. It was late 1938.

Guellich, a native of Munich, had come to the United States in 1932 and was a metallurgist in the laboratories of the Federal Shipbuilding Company, a division of U.S. Steel, across the Hudson River in Kearny, New Jersey.

An emaciated bachelor who suffered from periodic seizures of depression, Guellich had been recruited as a spy by Ignatz Theodor Griebl, a prominent physician in Yorkville, a German-American neighborhood in New York City, and the chief German spymaster in that region.

Now, in the Martinique, Gustav Guellich was compiling for delivery to military intelligence in Berlin a four-page report titled "Experiments with High-Altitude Rockets in the United States." It contained details of the research that had been conducted by Robert H. Goddard, a professor at Clark University in Worcester, Massachusetts.

Goddard, Guellich stated, had made a "substantial breakthrough in the development of rocket-propelled missiles."

Then Guellich wrote about his long and hot bus trip to a barren locale in New Mexico. From concealment and without interference from anyone, he had watched as Robert Goddard and a handful of assistants scored a brilliant success by firing a rocket controlled by a gyroscope and by veins in the exhaust system.

The five-foot-long projectile had soared to an altitude of forty-five hundred feet, swung to a horizontal flight in response to its steering mechanism, reached an estimated speed of five hundred miles per hour, and continued for some three miles before plunging into the ground, Guellich stated.

More than twenty years before his modest success in New Mexico, Robert Goddard had published his first theoretical and speculative paper on rockets. Then he proceeded to actually design and build them. His first experimental

Robert H. Goddard, a pioneer American rocket innovator, was ignored by the U.S. military leaders in the 1930s. They regarded him as a crackpot. (National Archives)

missile, unique for its use of liquid rather than solid (gunpowder) fuel, soared two hundred feet from a pasture in Auburn, Massachusetts, in March 1926. The explosion was so ear-shattering that it terrified people for several miles around.

Other than for those frightened civilians, hardly anyone paid attention to the epic flight. For years, Goddard tried to interest large corporations into funding his experiments, but all of them declined to finance someone who was ridiculed as "the moon man."

When it seemed that Goddard's rocket experiment days had ended, he received a surprise visitor—Charles A. Lindbergh, the renowned Lone Eagle who had gained enduring fame by being the first person to fly the Atlantic solo. Lindy, as the tousle-haired, boyish aviator was known to millions, had read of Goddard's rocket work, and he came to Worcester to discuss developments.

Lindy was enthused about Goddard's experiments, and the celebrity, through his friendship with Peter Guggenheim, obtained for the scientist grant money from the Guggenheim Foundation for the Promotion of Aeronautics.

During the late 1930s the tall, shy Lindbergh made several trips to Germany, where the high and mighty Nazis laid out the red carpet for the international hero. Lindy became convinced that the Luftwaffe, by far the most powerful air force that history had known, was invincible.

Quite naturally, two fliers, Lindy and Reichsmarschall Hermann Goering, an ace in World War I, hit it off. They spent many hours together discussing the state of aviation. There is some evidence that during his visits to Germany, Lindy stimulated high-level interest in rocketry. As a result, conceivably, the Nazi regime supported limited rocket research.

Moreover, while the U.S. War Department stonewalled Goddard's efforts to convince the generals that rocketry had great potential, the Germans made "creative use" of Goddard's patents, which were easily obtainable by Nazi agents in Washington.[6]

An American Aids Japanese Nuclear Project

LIEUTENANT GENERAL Takeo Yasuda, a scientist and director of the Aviation Technology Research Institute of the Imperial Japanese Army, was under pressure from the warlords in Tokyo to develop an ultimate weapon from nuclear energy. Years earlier, the generals had drawn up a document called the Tanaka Memorial, which called for widespread conquest and driving the Americans and the British out of the Pacific. It was early 1939.

General Yasuda directed Lieutenant Colonel Tatsusaburo Suzuki, also a scientist, to prepare an in-depth analysis on the status of atomic-bomb progress in other nations, especially the United States. Suzuki had the background for the task because he had long been reading international scientific literature about nuclear energy experiments in the United States, Great Britain, and Germany.

Suzuki's comprehensive report concluded that Japan would have available in Burma and Korea sufficient uranium, a key ingredient to build an atomic bomb, and that other nations were working toward the weapon's development.

Yasuda passed the document to the head of the Physical and Chemical Research Institute, and then it was assigned to Yoshio Nishina, director of the Riken, a Tokyo laboratory. During the 1930s, Nishina had studied in Europe and had made friends with numerous British and American nuclear physicists.

In Japan, Nishina was regarded as the most logical choice to push a nuclear program. He and a young scientist, who had learned his trade as a student at the California Institute of Technology in the United States, were building a sixty-inch cyclotron, which accelerated nuclear particles in a circular magnetic field, a sort of nuclear pump. A cyclotron would be a major step in developing an atomic bomb.

A few years earlier, a noted American physicist, Ernest O. Lawrence, had developed a cyclotron, an epic feat for which he had been awarded the Nobel Prize in physics. In keeping with the doctrine of "open information" that then prevailed in the world's scientific coterie, Lawrence turned over his cyclotron plans to Yoshio Nishina, who used them to build a similar device in Tokyo.

Impressed by Nishina's brilliance in developing the cyclotron, the Imperial Japanese Army authorized and funded an extensive research program designed to develop an atomic bomb.[7]

Supersecret Station X

SOON AFTER Ultra became operational, British Rear Admiral John H. Godfrey, chief of the Naval Intelligence Division (NID) of the Admiralty, sent for Commander Ewen Montagu. Known as Uncle John, Godfrey was an energetic and impatient taskmaster. He drove everybody, including himself, to the limit—even beyond. But those serving under him admired and respected him. An aide to Uncle John was Lieutenant Commander Ian Fleming, who would gain postwar global fame as a novelist and creator of the British supersleuth James Bond. It was October 1939, one month after war broke out in Europe.

Commander Montagu walked into Godfrey's office with a degree of concern: Was he to be rebuked for some unknown delinquency? To the contrary, Uncle John advised Montagu that he was to handle all operational special intelligence. To get a grasp of the entire spectrum, Montagu was to go to the home of Ultra, Bletchley Park, now called Station X by insiders.

Station X was a supersecret operation, Godfrey stressed, so Montagu was to make his visit there in civilian clothes and not attract the attention of any spies who might be lurking around Bletchley Park.

Montagu hurried to his quarters and dug out an old civilian suit reeking of mothballs. Then he caught a train for the forty-mile trip. During the short ride he felt quite uncomfortable, sensing that other passengers in the packed coach were sniffing the man from whom waves of mothball scent emitted.

Reaching a railroad junction near Station X, Montagu got off the train, reminding himself that the utmost secrecy had to be maintained. He hailed a taxi and told the driver, "Take me to Bletchley Park."

"Oh, the cloak-and-dagger place, huh?" the cabbie responded.

The supersecret Bletchley Park mansion, headquarters for the Ultra operation. (Author's collection)

The masquerading Royal Navy officer winced.

That day, Commander Montagu had lunch with an old friend, Denys Page, an Oxford don, who had been involved in developing the Bomb. No sooner had the two men been seated than Page began wondering aloud about the source of the overpowering smell of mothballs.

Montagu relayed the warning he had received from Admiral Godfrey about the critical need to keep the utmost secrecy and how the taxicab driver had known that some clandestine function was being carried out in the old mansion at Bletchley Park. Page conceded that probably nearly everyone in the village knew that there were mysterious goings-on, even though the precise nature of the actual work did not leak to the townsfolk.

Page said that he was convinced that it would require a near-miracle to keep the German Abwehr (intelligence agency) from learning about the secret activities at the old Victorian mansion. Presumably there were Nazi spies skulking around the region—maybe even ones that had been "planted" right in Bletchley Park many years earlier.

Only a week before Commander Montagu arrived, Page said, the chief of the Imperial General Staff (Britain's top uniformed officer) and a large entourage, riding in a long, noisy convoy of vehicles with two motorcycle soldiers in the lead, roared into peaceful Bletchley Park to inspect the top-secret Ultra operation.

"All the bloody party came in wearing full uniforms, red tabs, cars flying the Union flag and all!" Page told his friend. "So much for secrecy!"[8]

Aspirins Foil the Luftwaffe

YOUNG PROFESSOR Reginald V. Jones, a member of the scientific and technical department of MI-6, the British secret service, was poised at a large table in his office. Spread out before him was a collection of documents and sketches. They included eight pages of typewritten text detailing innovative advances by German scientists and twenty sketches of what appeared to be revolutionary new weapons for the Wehrmacht. It was November 5, 1939.

A day earlier, a guard at the British embassy in Oslo had found a parcel with brown wrapping paper half buried in the snow on a stone ledge in front of the building. It was addressed to the Royal Navy attaché in the embassy and contained the amazing array of top-secret German documents. A slip of paper inside the package had these words: "A well-wishing German scientist."

Flown to London immediately in the sacrosanct diplomatic pouch, the parcel was assigned to Reginald Jones after reaching MI-6. A physicist, natural philosopher, and astronomer, he had joined the agency only six weeks before the arrival of what came to be known as the Oslo Report.

His first task at that time had been to study the files on German weaponry and make a report to Stewart Menzies, the deputy chief of MI-6. Bright and energetic, the forty-eight-year-old Menzies had been described by a close aide as having "a ready smile and the self-assurance which had come with the huge profits from the millions of gallons of whiskey distilled by his Scot ancestors."

Tall, solemn, and congenial, Reginald Jones was the son of a Grenadier Guards sergeant, and he received a doctorate from Oxford University when only twenty-two years of age. Because of his initial assignment with MI-6, he had been acquainted with the sum total of the knowledge available to British intelligence of German weapons programs. Therefore he was now in a unique position to study and evaluate the Oslo Report.

With an eagerness typical of his breed, Jones began examining the parcel's contents. It was clear immediately that the mystery man who assembled the report had an extensive technical and scientific background. Jones was startled by the extent of the disclosures: the Germans were developing long-range rockets, radio-controlled glider bombs, proximity fuses that would cause a shell to explode as it neared its target, a torpedo that homed in on its target acoustically, a system of radio range measurement that would permit German bombers to hit targets blind, and two radar systems (which would later appear with the code names Würzburg and Freya).

Jones and Robert Cockburn, the head of the radar countermeasures section of the Telecommunications Research Establishment (TRE) at Farnborough, England, argued at length about who in the Nazi hierarchy was in such an exalted position that he could obtain what seemed to be the entire German secret-weapons program. The true identity of the "well-wishing German scientist" would never be known for certain.

The lack of an identifiable source was perhaps the main reason that most British experts regarded the documents to be fakes and the entire episode a scheme by the Germans to cause British scientists to squander huge amounts of precious time pursuing technical developments that didn't exist.

Official interest steadily waned, and eventually the Oslo Report was pigeonholed and forgotten—except by Reginald Jones. As he continued to scrutinize the documents, he suspected that the Germans had developed a system for guiding airplanes by a series of radio impulses.

Then a small piece of paper recovered from a crashed Heinkel bomber reached his desk. The translation contained the words Radio Beacon Knickebein (Crooked Leg). That added evidence convinced the scientist-sleuth that the Germans had developed a radio-beam technique that could tilt the course of the war farther toward the enemy unless countermeasures were developed by the British. The Luftwaffe, with the new technology, would be guided to English targets in bad weather or blackness with devastating accuracy, while the RAF bombers, Jones knew, often got lost over Germany while trying to locate their targets at night.

On May 23, 1940, Jones submitted to the Air Ministry an official analysis of his investigation: "It is possible that the Germans have developed a system of intersecting radio beams so that they can locate a target within a half-mile [in darkness and bad weather]."

Jones had discerned the nature of Knickebein (two intersecting beams would mark the target), but crucial questions remained. Intersecting beams meant there had to be two German transmitters across the English Channel in France, Belgium, or the Third Reich. But where precisely were they? On what frequency did they operate? What was the technology of the system?

Partly because of Jones's relative youth (he was twenty-eight), but mainly because of hidebound viewpoints, brass in the Air Ministry were skeptical of his findings. Prior to the war, the Air Staff had flatly turned down proposals for a radio guidance system for RAF night bombers. In essence, the air leaders had held that what had been good enough for Christopher Columbus to navigate by was good enough today. So why would the Germans squander enormous amounts of money and time on these complicated contraptions for their bombers when using the stars would get the job done?

Undaunted, Jones continued to probe into radio beams. On June 12 he was summoned by Britain's most highly placed scientist, Dr. Frederick A. Lindemann (soon to be elevated to the peerage as Lord Cherwell), who was scientific adviser to Prime Minister Winston Churchill. Lindemann came from a wealthy family (his mother was an American), and he moved easily among the aristocracy but felt uncomfortable around the masses.

Big, broad-shouldered, a world-class tennis player in his youth, and an outstanding pianist, Lindemann was a nonsmoker and a teetotaler. Ironically, he had received a Ph.D. in physics, in 1910, at the Physikalisch Institut in Berlin.

Young scientific genius Reginald Jones (left) often clashed with Lord Cherwell, Churchill's scientific adviser. Jones was usually right. (Author's collection)

Never overburdened with humility, Lindemann was especially disdainful of the views of much younger scientists. Now he asked if Jones truly believed that the Germans had a radio beam to guide the bombers. Jones said he did. Lindemann vigorously disagreed with the other physicist, who was about half the age of the fifty-four-year-old Lindemann.

In an effort to demolish Jones's conclusions, the older man stressed that radio waves travel in a straight line through space rather than curving to follow the earth's surface. Therefore, Lindemann argued, it would be impossible for Knickebein beams to penetrate throughout the British Isles.

Jones returned the next day and showed Lindemann a graph and an analysis that had been produced by a respected scientist in the Air Ministry, Thomas Eckersley, a report that had been gathering dust for weeks in a bureaucratic pigeonhole: "There seems to be reason to suppose that the Germans have some type of radio device with which they hope to find their targets . . . It is vital to investigate and to discover what the wavelength is. If we knew this, we could devise a means to mislead them."

Lindemann glared at the younger man but made no reply.

A few days later, on the morning of June 20, 1940, a Heinkel was machine-gunned by a Spitfire, and the radio operator bailed out. Rapidly shucking his parachute on reaching the ground, the German's first action was to rip up his working notes into tiny pieces. While he was burying the fragments, a squad of the Home Guard, an organization of young boys and elderly men brandishing axes, swords, and a few ancient shotguns, rushed up and captured the German.

Scores of tiny scraps of paper were uncovered. They were put in a package and hurried to London, where technicians laboriously created a pasteup.

Reginald Jones was elated. Here was a wealth of highly significant information. It confirmed data taken from a downed German bomber that one beam transmitter for Knickebein was set up in the ancient town of Cleves, just inside the western border of the Third Reich, and a second beam transmitter was near the North Sea, in Schleswig-Holstein.

Amazing good fortune continued to smile on Jones—and Great Britain. Another shot-down Heinkel provided him with the pieces he needed to complete the intricate jigsaw puzzle he had been tediously assembling for six months. Notes found in the wreckage revealed that the Cleves Knickebein transmitter operated on a frequency of 31.5 megacycles per second and that the Schleswig-Holstein beam was at 30.0 megacycles.

On June 21 an urgent meeting was called at 10 Downing Street to discuss the alarming beam situation. Jones found himself seated among the high and the mighty of the British Empire: Churchill, puffing on a long, black cigar; the prime minister's scientific adviser, Professor Lindemann; Lord Beaverbrook, the aircraft production minister; a clutch of the nation's most distinguished scientists; and several air marshals. The conference was so secret that secretaries were not allowed to be present to take notes.

Jones felt ill at ease as all eyes seemed to be on him. Almost at once he grew alarmed, as a few of those present made remarks that indicated they had only a hazy grasp of the situation. Finally, Churchill began to direct questions at Jones, who asked, "Would it help, sir, if I told you the story right from the start?"

The implication of the question—that neither Churchill nor others in the room knew what they were talking about—caught the prime minister off guard. After a short hesitation, he cleared his throat and replied, "Well, yes, it would."

Although everyone in the room was Jones's senior by far in age and in every other way, the radio-beam threat was too serious for anyone to take exception to the Knickebein sleuth's seeming impudence. For his part, Jones drew strength from the fact that, judging by the earlier remarks of others, he knew more about the enemy's beam technology than did anyone else present.

When Jones had finished his presentation, a hush fell over the room. Finally Churchill asked Jones, "What can be done about it?" The prime minister was told that the first course of action would be to confirm the existence of the Knickebein beams, which were still only theory, by discovering the beams, then flying along them. Once that was done, countermeasures could be developed.

The conference broke up after Jones had been given the green light to try to locate the Knickebein beams—a task similar to finding the proverbial needle in a haystack.

Jones lost no time in launching his search. On the night following the Churchill meeting, Flight Lieutenant H. E. Bufton, an officer experienced in radio-guidance systems, and a special team lifted off in an Anson from Wyton airfield in Huntingdonshire in east-central England. Jones had calculated that a Knickebein beam—if there was one—could be found there. Bufton had been directed to search for the beam on the 30.0 and 31.5 megacycle bands (the bands mentioned in the notes recovered from the crashed Heinkel bomber).

As Bufton searched the sky, a sudden shout of exultation rang out in the Anson. Its radio band had picked up clear signals that told those aboard that they were winging through a narrow radio beam (some 400 to 450 yards wide). Later in the same flight, a second beam was detected, and the bearings on both beams were the precise locations of the transmitters thought to be at Cleves and at Bredstedt, on the North Sea in Schleswig-Holstein.

Under Robert Cockburn, a team of scientists plunged into the task of developing radio countermeasures (RCM). In a desperate emergency action, Cockburn commandeered diathermy sets from scores of hospitals and used them to distort Knickebein beams with sound. Then the team developed equipment that transmitted its own beam (code-named Aspirins) that jammed the Knickebein transmission.

Aspirins proved highly successful, as the garbled Knickebein signals confused German bomber crews, causing some aircraft to fly in circles through the black skies of England while seeking their target. One Heinkel, out of gas after a night of circling, crash-landed on a Channel beach in southern England in the belief that it was coming down in France.[9]

A Plan to Light Up the United Kingdom

AIR MARSHAL Hugh Dowding, chief of the Royal Air Force Fighter Command, anticipated heavy German bombing attacks throughout the United Kingdom after Great Britain had declared war on September 3, 1939, so he came up with a unique idea for the successful interception of the Luftwaffe bombers: all of the United Kingdom should be carpeted with searchlights.

Responsible for the possible implementation of the enormous lighting proposal was General Frederick "Tim" Pile, head of the Antiaircraft Command. He passed along the problem to a select group of scientists, who began by using simple arithmetic. The United Kingdom—England, Wales, Scotland, and Northern Ireland—total 93,347 square miles. Space between searchlights would be some 6,000 yards, with each beam covering about 10 square miles. That formula would require 9,300 sites, plus a need for 18 percent spares, for a total of some 11,000 searchlights.

Radar would be indispensable to find the German bombers, so 11,000 searchlight-control radars, plus spare parts, would have to be erected at each beam. A crew of seven men, plus a reserve force to replace those lost through attrition, would be needed at each site, or some 80,000 men in total.

A major support project would build living accommodations at each location, and rations, supplies, and spare parts would have to be trucked or flown to the often remote sites, requiring a few thousand more men.

There was no shortage of critics of the scheme. Many pointed out that the weather at all times would have to be closely coordinated with Reichsmarschall Hermann Goering, chief of the Luftwaffe, to make certain that his planes did not bomb through clouds and overcast when the searchlight carpet would be virtually useless. It was finally agreed that the grandiose idea would quietly be scuttled.[10]

Is a Death Ray Feasible?

FOR EIGHT MONTHS after Adolf Hitler's blitzkrieg had conquered Poland in only six weeks in September 1939, some 2.5 million German troops had been arrayed along the borders of France, Belgium, and the Netherlands. There the opposing sides sat. And sat. Hardly a shot was fired.

This eerie stalemate was known in the United States as the Phony War, in Britain as the Sitzkrieg, and in France as *la drôle de guerre.*

Suddenly, at 3:30 A.M. on May 10, 1940, the German armies plunged over the frontiers and surged ahead. The British and French had been warned that Hitler was about ready to launch Case Yellow, a massive offensive in the West, but the Allies were taken totally by surprise.

Across the English Channel later that morning, seventy-year-old Neville Chamberlain, who for two years had been trying to appease the führer, resigned as prime minister. A few hours later, King George VI summoned the first lord of the Admiralty, Winston S. Churchill, to Buckingham Palace and asked him to take over the reins of government.

Churchill eagerly accepted the challenge, and the two men held a brief discussion about the bleak war picture. Then the pudgy, energetic new prime minister withdrew with a series of bows.

There was nothing that Winston Churchill could do to halt the German tide. In only six weeks, Adolf Hitler rode triumphantly into Paris to accept the French surrender, and the British army that had been sent to France to whip the vaunted Wehrmacht was trapped at the small English Channel port of Dunkirk.

Under heavy pounding by the Luftwaffe, some 850 mostly small civilian vessels evacuated British soldiers to the ports of Margate, Dover, and Ramsgate in southern England. Left behind on the sands of Dunkirk were virtually all of the British army's machine guns, artillery, tanks, and other vehicles.

"If the Boches [Germans] come," Winston Churchill confided to an aide, "we'll have to hit them on their heads with beer bottles—we've got no other weapons!"

Contingency plans were drawn up to evacuate the British royal family and the government to Canada, to which some eighteen hundred million pounds sterling worth of gold ingots already had been shipped secretly on ships of the Royal Navy. Britain reeled in tumult and confusion.

One of Britain's top soldiers, highly decorated General Alan Brooke, penned gloomily in his diary: "The shortage of trained men and equipment is appalling . . . The ghastly part is that we have only a few weeks before the Boches [invade England]."

Spirits were high at the Oberkommando der Wehrmacht (German high command) headquarters at Zossen, twenty miles outside Berlin. In his personal diary, General Alfred Jodl, the führer's principal strategic adviser, declared: "The final victory [over England] is now but a question of time."

But Great Britain was a lion at bay. Her survival would depend on a revolutionary system of aircraft-warning and ground-to-air control unparalleled at the time anywhere in the world. Centerpieces of this complicated electronic mosaic were two technological miracles, Ultra and radar.

Radar is a procedure whereby an airplane in flight can be "seen" at night or through clouds at a distance of many miles by transmitting powerful radio waves toward it and reading the radio waves that bounce back.

Although the principle of radar had been discovered in the nineteenth century, it was not until 1935 that practical radar had its origins in Britain. At that time, physicist Robert A. Watson-Watt, a Scot who belonged to the family of James Watt, inventor of the steam engine some two centuries earlier, was summoned by Harry E. Wimperis, the director of scientific research at the Air Ministry.

In recent years, Watson-Watt, a heavyset man with a keen sense of humor, had been working as a meteorologist tracking thunderstorms, but he was now conducting experiments for the Radio Research Station at Slough.

Wimperis explained that he had warned the Air Ministry that "unless some new method of aiding our [air] defenses is evolved, we are likely to lose the next war if it starts within ten years."

Wimperis then asked Watson-Watt for his view on the possible development of some kind of damaging radiation as an aid to defending Britain from air attack. The idea was to create a strong beam of electromagnetic waves that would heat up anything in their paths to the point where enemy airmen and their planes would be destroyed. Quite aptly, the envisioned development was called a "death ray."

Watson-Watt returned to his laboratories and discussed the proposal with his colleagues. After exhaustive experiments it was determined that the amount of power that would be required to create a death ray would be far beyond current technology.

So Watson-Watt wrote a memorandum to Harry Wimperis stating that "we could not hope that an aircraft would linger so long, in the most intense beam of radio energy that we could produce, as to raise the pilot's blood temperature to an artificial fever level."

With the death ray ruled out, there remained the critical problem of defending Britain against air assault. What was needed, Watson-Watt stressed in a letter to the Air Ministry, was a system for combining direction-finding with range-finding to determine the flying height of an enemy plane. "It is not enough to locate an aircraft," he added, "but we ought to know whom we have located, so that we have to stop and think before we shoot."

That letter may well have been the birth certificate of British radar. Watson-Watt was instructed by the Air Ministry to proceed with his experiments, and he linked up with physicist Henry T. Tizard and other electronics experts to develop a practical pulse radar.

After several demonstrations of this primitive radar equipment to high government and military leaders, Watson-Watt was given the green light to develop an air-warning system. But first he and his colleagues sat down to hatch a label for the overall process.

"Let's think up something that doesn't merely conceal the truth but positively suggests the false," Watson-Watt said.

Finally, the initials R.D.F. were adopted, with a view that any enemy agent would think what the group was doing was merely Radio Direction Finding.

In early 1936, after the British scientists had continued to improve radar, a massive project got under way to erect a chain of 22 steel radar towers, each soaring 350 feet, along the southern and eastern coasts of England. Within two years, invisible walls 12 miles high would confront hostile air intruders.

Even though the construction of the towers had to be funneled through public firms, contractors, power and telephone companies, and the bureaucracies, Adolf Hitler's customarily highly efficient Abwehr would learn nothing about the revolutionary detection system.

A string of 350-foot steel towers provided a radar "fence" around southern England. (Author's collection)

A clever two-year campaign by deception agencies was launched to "hide" the huge towers. Along the British coasts, undercover agents circulated in pubs and other gathering places to subtly spread the word that these were radio spires to provide ground-to-air communications with fighter pilots. At least two Nazi spies were known to have been planted on farms along the coastline months earlier, and they hopefully would pick up the fake information and pass it on to Berlin—which indeed would be the case.

At the same time, a global dissemination of *sibs* (Latin, to hiss) by British diplomats and military officers made it known in foreign embassies and to Nazi sympathizers that England was spending millions of pounds sterling to erect a chain of radio towers.

German radar experiments had begun in late 1934, two years after Adolf Hitler had gained absolute power, and it was known as Dezimeter Telegraphie. To mask its development from foreign eyes, the system was placed under cover of the German post office department.

A few years later, a large German commercial firm, Telefunken, got into the Dezimeter Telegraphie field and began producing devices called Freya and Würzburg. Far ahead of its time, the Würzburg could track a swiftly moving airplane with great precision many miles away.

At the Oberkommando der Wehrmacht on July 16, 1940, Adolf Hitler signed General Order Number 16:

> Since England despite her hopeless military situation still shows no sign of any willingness to come to terms, I have decided to prepare for, and if necessary carry out, an invasion of England. . . . Preparations for the entire campaign must be completed by mid-August.

Code name for the looming cross-Channel attack would be Seelöwe (Sea Lion). Estimated time to conquer England: sixty days.[11]

A Hassle with British Bureaucrats

WITH THE ARRIVAL of 1941, fresh problems in the operational use of the British radar early-warning chain kept surfacing as German scientists developed new tactics to try to outsmart the system. At Royal Air Force Fighter Command headquarters at Bentley Priory, a staff of technicians had the sole function of studying the results obtained by the radar chain and, where needed, implementing improvements or remedial actions.

One of the more serious defects discovered was that the radar did not detect the approach of low-flying German planes until they were too near their targets to be intercepted. Consequently these sorties inflicted heavy loss on merchant shipping along the coasts, even when the vessels were sailing close to RAF fighter bases.

Air Marshal Philip P. Joubert, a burly man who was assistant chief of the British Air Staff and adviser on the use of radar, realized that a new technique against low-flying planes would have to be developed to provide early warning to RAF fighters. He assigned that crucial task to John D. Cockroft, who was recognized as one of Britain's foremost experts on radar.

Remarkably, within a few weeks Cockroft and his assistants created an effective new technique. Then, by speedy cars and transport aircraft, they dashed from radar station to station up and down the coastlines to install the new equipment.

These innovations solved the problem because RAF fighters scrambled on time to pounce on approaching low-flying German aircraft.

Now Cockroft was hit by a lesson in dealing with the British bureaucracy. Because of the urgency involved, he and his team had paid their own living and traveling expenses to the radar stations, many of them in remote regions. Now they asked payment to recover their personal costs while on duty for the Crown, but the Finance Department of the Treasury balked.

General Joubert was irate. The expenses totaled only a modest amount, yet Cockroft and his team had to duel with the Treasury for five months before they were begrudgingly reimbursed.

"I could go to the Treasury with a single sheet of paper covered with figures and get authority in ten minutes to spend four million pounds sterling," Joubert howled to aides. "Yet Professor Cockroft and his men saved a large number of ships and lives and they couldn't even get back their expenses without a knock-down-and-drag-out fight!"[12]

Conjuring Up Wild Theories

IN THE FALL and early winter of 1940, both the Luftwaffe and the Royal Air Force were bombing targets in England and Germany almost exclusively at night because daylight assaults had proven to be too costly. Under the relentless stress of creating innovative measures and countermeasures against one another, German and British scientists began conjuring up wild theories as to what device or technique the other side might have developed.

In early December, the Germans became convinced that the British were switching on red lights along the coast when Luftwaffe bombers were heard approaching. So the commander of an airfield outside Vannes in German-occupied France was ordered to investigate the red-light technique.

For three weeks, German bomber crews flying northward over the English Channel to hit targets in England studied the red-light warning system and reported that, based on their eyewitness observations, the British indeed had installed a new electronic aircraft-detection network.

When Ultra, the supersecret British monitoring system, decrypted a Luftwaffe report, British scientists were hilarious. There had never been a red-light warning system. So many red lights along the Channel shore had been winking and blinking in violation of strict blackout regulations that German aircrews and the scientists in Berlin had concluded that this was a sophisticated, coordinated operation.

During this same period, the tables were turned. Ultra unbuttoned a chilling German message that stated that a certain region in France across from Great Britain would be ideal for storing Flak Gas. Another Ultra decrypt indicated that the Germans were filling antiaircraft shells with gas.

Now the British scientists became jittery. They theorized that the shells were intended to explode in front of Royal Air Force bombers, and the released clouds of gas would paralyze engines as the planes flew through the thick condensation.

After a flurry of investigations it was discovered that a single missing letter in the German messages had caused the commotion that had reached the upper levels of the British government. The letter *t* should have been at the end of *Gas,* as it had been meant to read *Gast* (for *Geräte Ausbau Stelle*), merely a depot for antiaircraft shells.[13]

Part Two

Great Britain Stands Alone

A Nation's Survival at Stake

KROLL OPERA HOUSE in Berlin was decorated in dazzling colors on July 16, 1940, the same night that Adolf Hitler had ordered an invasion of England. The cavernous hall was filled with bemedaled generals and admirals and the Nazi Party hierarchy, together with exquisitely groomed and gowned wives. It was a gala affair: Adolf Hitler, who had planted the Nazi swastika over much of western Europe, would speak and bask in the type of worship and adulation once showered on his idol Frederick the Great, as well as on Napoleon and Julius Caesar.

Thunderous applause rocked Kroll as the führer strode briskly to the rostrum. Speaking in a calm, almost pious tone, he said, "It almost causes me pain to think that I should have been selected by Providence to deal the final blow to the edifice that these men [Winston Churchill and King George] have already set tottering by their warlike actions. . . . In this hour I feel it is my duty before my conscience to appeal once more to reason and common sense in Britain. I see no reason why this war must go on!"

In London, Prime Minister Churchill ignored Hitler's "final offer of peace." This silence treatment infuriated Nazi leaders. Hitler told the chief of the German Navy, Grossadmiral Erich Raeder, "We are confronted by an utterly determined enemy" who "will stop at nothing to prevent an invasion."

The führer directed Reichsmarschall Hermann Goering, leader of the Luftwaffe, to wipe out the Royal Air Force to pave the way for the invasion. Goering (Fat Hermann to his subordinates), the most pompous of the Nazi bigwigs, was delighted. His Luftwaffe alone would bring Great Britain to her knees, he assured Hitler.

Goering set August 13, 1940, for Adlertag (Eagle Day) to launch massive air assaults on England. The Luftwaffe chief and his top commanders were confident that the Royal Air Force would be rapidly destroyed. Possibly the only man in the German armed forces not radiating confidence was General Wolfgang Martini, the Luftwaffe signals head. He was a worried man.

A month earlier, Martini had gone to the Channel coast in France and set up several electronic monitoring stations. All through July, the German Air Force had been bombing English Channel shipping and pounding British targets inland. What made Martini nervous was the fact that the monitors in

43

France had steadily been picking up signals beamed from the chain of 350-foot "radio" towers along the southern and eastern coasts in England.

It appeared to the general that the RAF was "seeing" German warplanes as they lifted off from airfields behind the Channel coast in France, Belgium, and the Netherlands, and then Hurricanes and Spitfires soon congregated at the locales where they could intercept the intruders as they approached the British coast.

Martini, realizing that the British had developed some kind of an innovative technique of air defense—possibly radar—promptly conveyed his concerns to the Luftwaffe high command. "Tut, tut," said the brass. On the threshold of Eagle Day, General Martini had simply come down with a bad case of the jitters.

Major Beppo Schmid, chief of Abteilung 5 (Luftwaffe intelligence), hurried to pitch cold water on Martini's gloomy analysis. Schmid fired off to Goering an appreciation of the British air-defense system, as he viewed it from six hundred miles away in Berlin.

RAF fighters, Major Schmid trumpeted, were controlled from the ground by standard radiotelephones, a process that restricted the planes' operations to the sky above their respective radio towers. He concluded: "The forming of a strong [RAF] fighter force at crucial points at crucial times is unlikely. There will be confusion in the defense during massed [German] air attacks."

These were fearful times in the higher echelons of the British armed forces and government. Those in the know about the forthcoming clash between the Royal Air Force Fighter Command and the Luftwaffe were aware that the odds against the British would be enormous and the stakes infinite—the survival of England.

Through Ultra (electronic monitoring) intercepts, it was known that Goering would have 3,358 bombers and fighters ready to hurl at Great Britain. It was a force unprecedented in numbers and striking power. Against this mighty sky armada would be some 700 Spitfires and Hurricane fighters, whose pilots would be outnumbered four or five to one.

These odds would be balanced to a degree, however, because British scientists had provided Air Marshal Hugh Dowding, chief of the Fighter Command, with the gargantuan advantages of Ultra and radar, facts about which Adolf Hitler and Hermann Goering knew nothing.

"Stuffy" Dowding, a reserved, contemplative man, would direct what became known as the Battle of Britain from an underground chamber called The Hole in Fighter Command headquarters in Bentley Priory, a huge old mansion in Middlesex.

At dawn on August 13, 1940, Dowding was in The Hole after being forewarned by Ultra intercepts that Reichsmarschall Goering was ready to launch the mighty Luftwaffe. Across the Channel, and stretching from France up into Norway, thousands of German airmen climbed into Junkers, Dorniers, Heinkels,

A *British Women's Auxiliary Air Force technician plots German airplanes on a cathode-ray ube of an early radar set. (Smithsonian Institution)*

Stukas, and Messerschmitts. Morale was high. Crews had been told the RAF could last only a few weeks.

Through radar, Dowding "saw" the Luftwaffe flights winging toward targets in southern England. In The Hole, German aircraft positions were plotted on a huge map table, then disseminated to the operations rooms of the various fighter group headquarters.

Ultra decrypts kept The Hole informed of Luftwaffe targets and tactics each day, permitting ground controllers to gather fighter squadrons at the right places, times, and altitudes to meet the major threats. This technique prevented precious Spitfires and Hurricanes from being frittered away by chasing madly across the skies after secondary or decoy German flights.

For four weeks, fierce, murderous clashes raged over Britain and the Channel. The bright blue skies were laced with white contrails, and the silence of the hot days was broken by the eerie sounds of straining engines and the angry mutter of machine-gun fire at high altitudes.

Both adversaries suffered horrendous losses. In only a two-week period between August 23 and September 6, the RAF reported the loss of 466 fighter planes and 231 pilots, while the Luftwaffe had 214 fighters and 138 bombers shot down.

Steadily the scales turned against the Fighter Command. There was deep anxiety in official British circles. Surviving RAF pilots were nearly exhausted from almost continuous dogfights. A few more weeks of this carnage and Britain would be doomed.

In Berlin, Adolf Hitler was both puzzled and furious at Goering. Why hadn't the reichsmarschall destroyed the British Air Force in a few weeks, as he had boasted? The führer ranted, "The enemy [RAF] recovers again and again. . . . They seem to know when and where we are coming!"

On September 17 Winston Churchill, at his bombproof headquarters beneath the pavement at Story's Gate in London, was handed an Ultra intercept. For the first time in months, the British Bulldog allowed himself the luxury of a beaming smile. It was an order from Berlin: Adolf Hitler had canceled Sea Lion.

England had endured because of her two secret weapons—Ultra and radar—along with the courage and stamina of the Fighter Command's pilots, whom Stuffy Dowding affectionately referred to as "my chicks." These fighter pilots were a breed apart—brash, scrappy, courageous, the elite. A few years earlier, many had been avowed pacifists. Some had signed the controversial Oxford Pledge, in which they swore they would never fight "for king and country." But with the existence of the empire at stake, they fought—and hundreds gave their lives.

Air Marshal Dowding, the victor in the Battle of Britain, soon suffered an ignominious blow. His air tactics had displeased someone in the British hierarchy. On November 25, 1940, without preamble, Air Chief Marshal Charles F. Portal, the RAF's top officer, curtly ordered Dowding to relinquish his post immediately.[1]

A Little Black Box of Secrets

ON AUGUST 30, 1940, a highly secret and dramatic episode was unfolding in the United States. American science, spurred on by urgent British appeals, was finally gearing up for war.

A group of Britain's foremost scientists, headed by Henry Tizard, arrived in Washington with a black-enameled metal steamer trunk (called "our little black box") full of military secrets. The delegation had been sent by Prime Minister Winston Churchill to disclose "unilaterally and unconditionally" everything the visitors knew about science in war.

Tizard had been told by Churchill to put all of Britain's cards face up on the table—except for Ultra. But before the delegation had departed from London, Churchill had been under heavy pressure to call off the plan to give treasured and closely guarded secrets to a still officially neutral nation, where freedom of speech might be stretched into a license to publicly reveal this crucial information.

Disclosures by the Tizard mission would indeed be unilateral; military scientific research and development in the United States had been virtually nil during the previous two decades. Most Americans had been preoccupied with their homegrown problems, so they felt the nation was protected by two broad oceans. At the time the Tizard mission had reached Washington, some seven hundred citizens committees in the United States were loudly opposing America's "drift into other people's wars."

Curiously, when word had circulated through Washington that Churchill was going to send a tell-all scientific delegation to the United States, many in the Roosevelt administration were skeptical. Was this some sort of machination hatched by the cagey prime minister to somehow drag the scientifically and militarily unprepared United States into the "European war"?

Henry Tizard and his colleagues began holding a series of meetings with members of the National Defense Research Council (NDRC). Its chairman was Vannevar Bush, president of the Carnegie Institution, and members included James B. Conant, the young president of Harvard University; Karl T. Compton, president of the Massachusetts Institute of Technology (MIT); and Frank B. Jewett, head of the National Academy of Sciences and president of Bell Telephone Laboratories.

The NDRC had been formed only two months earlier by President Franklin Roosevelt, at the instigation of Vannevar Bush, who had earned doctorates in engineering from both Harvard and MIT during one intense year just prior to America's involvement in the Great War in 1917. At that time he had gone to work for a corporation that was developing a magnetic submarine detector.

Van Bush and his colleagues had succeeded in producing an effective device, and one hundred sets were rapidly built. Then the enthusiastic scientist had gotten his first exposure to bureaucratic confusion: these submarine detectors no doubt would have saved many lives, but they had never been put to use against German U-boats.

That shocking and galling experience etched into Bush's mind the dangers of the total lack of proper liaison among the armed forces, the government, and the civilian sector in the development of weapons in time of war. So more than two decades later, when Adolf Hitler's potent Wehrmacht began conquering much of western Europe, Bush resigned his post as vice president of MIT and moved to Washington, D.C., to take direction of the Carnegie Institution, and to be closer to the federal government. Carnegie conducted fundamental scientific research.

After the Germans had invaded Poland in September 1939, Bush called together a group of leading scientists, and they agreed that the United States was going to get involved in the conflict one way or another sooner or later. This bloody struggle would feature high technology, they concurred, and the United States was woefully unprepared in this regard. What was especially frightening, Bush and the others were certain, was that the structure of America's armed forces, as it then existed, would never be able to develop and produce the scientific instruments of war that they would so desperately need.

Leaders of wartime U.S. science projects. Left to right: Ernest Lawrence, Arthur Compton, Vannevar Bush, James Conant, Karl Compton, Alfred Loomis. (National Archives)

As a result of the lengthy discussion in Washington, Bush and the others envisioned a national group to do the needed job. Because he had learned about the Washington political minefields and the key to getting things done, Bush was named to spearhead the project. It was agreed that the group would have independent authority so that its recommendations and needs would not get bogged down in the capital's bureaucratic maze.

Moreover, it was agreed, the organization would report directly to President Roosevelt rather than go through military channels, and it should have its own source of funds. It was a tall order, but Bush plunged into the task. For a few weeks he dashed about Washington, making obligatory calls on the army, navy, Congress, and the National Academy of Sciences. The idea was to ruffle as few feathers as possible once the secret plan became known.

Finally, the Carnegie president visited the centerpiece of his selling project—Harry L. Hopkins, a onetime Iowa farm boy who was Roosevelt's closest civilian confidant. Tall, a chain smoker, and emaciated, Hopkins usually worked out of one of America's most hallowed chambers—the Lincoln Bedroom in the White House.

Although Hopkins was a Democratic liberal and Bush was a Republican conservative, the two men's personalities meshed from the beginning. Hopkins tried to sell Bush on his own idea for an Inventors Council, but when the Carnegie head counterattacked with his more comprehensive National Defense Research Council, Hopkins readily agreed that it was much the better plan.

On June 10, 1940, Van Bush was ushered into the Oval Office of the White House. It was the first time he had met Franklin Roosevelt. After a few moments of chitchat, the scientist handed the president a sheet of paper on which the plan for the NDRC was described in four short paragraphs.

The entire interview lasted fewer than ten minutes. Bush knew that his new crony, Harry Hopkins, had already paved the way. The president scrawled on the sheet of paper, "OK—FDR." Those few initials would set the scientific wheels in motion and open doors all over Washington.

Now, eleven weeks after the White House meeting, Bush, Frank Jewett, James Conant, Karl Compton, and other members of the NDRC were conferring intently with the Tizard mission. Any suspicions the American scientists may have harbored about Winston Churchill's motives steadily melted as the visitors brought out a wide array of British scientific developments from their figurative "little black box."

John Cockroft explained the high-powered generator. Even these brainy, sophisticated Americans were awed: They had never seen anything like it. Some of the exhibits were in drawings and written descriptions, but most were the items themselves. There were rockets, predictors, gyro-gunsights, jet propulsion devices, radar, and the "micropup" valves that made airborne radar practicable.

Perhaps the featured attraction was the high-power resonant magnetron, a diode vacuum tube in which the flow of electrons is controlled by an externally applied magnetic field to generate power at microwave frequencies.

An American scientist would later write: "When the Tizard mission brought a magnetron, it carried the most valuable cargo ever brought to our shores. The magnetron sparked the whole development of microwave radar [in the United States]."

One weekend, Britain's John Cockroft (a future recipient of a Nobel Prize) and Ernest O. Lawrence, a product of small-town South Dakota who had paid his way to earn a Ph.D. peddling aluminum kitchenware door-to-door, were guests at the palatial private laboratory of Alfred Loomis in Tuxedo Park, a New York suburb. Loomis was known whimsically as the last of the gentlemen scientists—indeed, he was a multimillionaire and a physicist.

As a result of the two days of discussions at Tuxedo Park, the groundwork was laid for a major new NDRC laboratory at MIT, in Cambridge, Massachusetts, near Boston. To keep its work secret, the MIT facility was named simply the Radiation Laboratory.

With war clouds from Europe and the Far East starting to drift toward the United States, radar research and development began in earnest at the Radiation Laboratory. With a few months, advanced-type radar was installed on twenty U.S. warships in the Pacific, where the Japanese were about ready to strike at a place few Americans had ever heard of—Pearl Harbor.[2]

A Huge Mousetrap in the Sky

ALTHOUGH HERMANN GOERING had been defeated in his attempt to gain aerial superiority over England in the fall of 1940, he promptly changed the Luftwaffe's tactics and resorted to bombing London and other major British cities. Each night 150 to 250 Heinkel and Dornier bombers cut through the skies over England. Destruction and civilian casualties reached a horrendous plateau.

Early in November, means for striking down the black-bodied German bombers were high on the priority list of Prime Minister Winston Churchill, so he called a midnight meeting at his official residence, 10 Downing Street. Among those present was a small group of naval scientists who operated in a semisecret agency called the Directorate of Miscellaneous Weapons Development (DMWD). Its chief and guiding spirit was Lieutenant Commander Charles F. Goodeve, a Canadian in his midthirties, who had been a civilian scientific consultant before the war.

As a temporary agency manned mainly by reserve officers, the DMWD was far from touchy about stepping on the toes of hidebound generals and admirals if the brass was holding up its work. No scientist was concerned about postwar promotions. They called themselves the Wheezers and Dodgers, and the "miscellaneous" in the organization's title provided Goodeve and his freewheeling men with the wide latitude they needed to develop innovative, unorthodox, and sometimes bizarre weapons to help thwart the ambitions of Adolf Hitler.

Now, at the midnight meeting, Winston Churchill, waving a cigar for emphasis, was explaining a pet weapons project: a gigantic mousetrap in the sky to snare Luftwaffe bombers. Then he listened impatiently as Commander Goodeve and his scientists and others argued back and forth over the technical difficulties involved.

Churchill was not concerned with problems. "I want a square mile of wire in the sky as big as the Horse Guards Parade, with parachutes holding it in place," he declared. "Just think of the difficulties of an aircraft trying at the last minute to avoid a thing that large."

Continued discussion around the table produced a vague concept of the "mousetrap in the sky." Wire cables would have to be shot into the air by rockets, it seemed, and held there by parachutes. High-explosive mines would be attached to the cables.

At dawn, the conference adjourned. The Wheezers and Dodgers were directed to solve the technical problems and report back to Churchill at a later date.

Intense experimentation was conducted, and a device called the Free Balloon Barrage was developed. The apparatus had a few hundred components, and each one had a large balloon filled with hydrogen. Suspended below each balloon was a metal container, a wooden spool with two thousand feet of piano wire, and a parachute.

The operating procedure for the device was simple—in theory. The balloons would be sent aloft in an area about two miles square, and when they reached a specified height a mechanism would release the two thousand feet of thin, sturdy piano wire under each balloon. A parachute at the bottom of each wire would hold it taut. Moments later, the metal containers that held bombs and that were dangling beneath the balloons became activated.

Theoretically, at the split second that a German bomber struck a wire, things would happen in rapid-fire order. Air blasts pouring into the parachute would cause the wire to tighten and the dangling bomb to slide down the wire and detonate on impact with the hostile aircraft.

The DMWD scientists conducted a number of tests and worked feverishly to iron out numerous kinks in the apparatus. On December 29, 1940, orders came down for the Free Balloon Barrage to be given its first full-scale tryout. Ultra, the supersecret British procedure that intercepted and decoded German wireless messages, learned that the Luftwaffe was going to hit London with a mighty firebomb attack that night.

In a colossal expenditure of effort, hundreds of Royal Air Force and Royal Navy men transported the balloons, hydrogen, bombs, explosives, and other components to the windward side of London. More than eight hundred trucks and trailers were used in the project. This logistics operation was conducted in as much secrecy as could be gained.

Charles Goodeve, the DMWD chief, and his scientists feared a disaster, as they were convinced that much more testing and refinement were needed on the Free Balloon Barrage. But British leaders, from Winston Churchill on down, were desperate. London was steadily being pulverized. Any device that might bag even a few German planes had to be used.

When Luftwaffe bomber streams neared London at about midnight, some two thousand of the bomb-laden balloons were launched in fewer than three hours. Reports reached the DMWD control center confirming the fears of the Wheezers and Dodgers. Balloons broke loose or leaked, coming down with their lethal explosives at many points in southern England. One landed on the grounds of Buckingham Palace, the home of Britain's kings and queens since 1837, in the West End district of London.

Balloons straying across the English Channel into France caused a major flap in that country. One balloon-carried bomb exploded near a German army barracks, and the remains of the strange device were rushed to intelligence officers in Berlin with the suggestion that the British may have developed a secret weapon with which to bombard German military facilities and troop units on the Continent. French newspapers reported "mysterious objects" in the sky.

The first major Free Balloon Barrage results cast a thick layer of gloom over Goodeve and his men, even though few, if any, of them had expected the apparatus to work. Experimentation continued, however, and future trials resulted in what was described as 80 percent efficiency, although it could not be determined if any German bombers had been snared by the mousetrap in the sky.

In the meantime, the Wheezers and Dodgers were developing another unique scheme to thwart Luftwaffe navigators: "hiding" the moon. Railroad tracks, bridges, and roads were used by the airmen as orientation points, so many of these landmarks were camouflaged. However, the Luftwaffe could count on one unfailing aid to pinpoint English targets: the iridescence of the moon reflecting on rivers, lakes, and canals.

Goodeve's project-development team first considered using large nets held up by floating corks to mask the bodies of water. This technique proved to be applicable only on small lakes and ponds. After weeks of diligent effort, a mixture of coal dust and fuel oil was concocted to spray onto bodies of water. The sticky substance would cling to the surface, resulting in a dark, nonreflecting coating, thereby "hiding the moon."

Now came the trial. The majestic Thames River in London was selected. Winston Churchill, drawing on a long cigar, showed up unannounced and stood on nearby Westminster Bridge to view the novel demonstration.

As the prime minister watched intently, four launches carrying spraying apparatus sailed into view and began depositing huge amounts of the oily concoction onto the surface. But it was not just the Thames that was being coated with the sooty substance; so were the men on the launches.

Then Mother Nature got into the act. The wind began to gust, the current grew brisk, and the oily substance on the Thames began to break up and dissolve. Matters went from bad to worse. A disappointed Churchill, flicking specks of oil from his face and clothing, strolled off the bridge and departed.

A naval craft had to be dispatched to pick up the dead dogs and cats floating in the river after the animals had drunk the contaminated water. Housewives downstream complained bitterly that the oily substance had blown from the river and ruined washing hanging on outdoor lines.

Commander Goodeve's team of ingenious minds would go on to develop numerous offbeat items that helped greatly in the prosecution of the war, but they had to admit defeat on the moon-hiding project on the Thames. However, outside Coventry, where they did not have to contend with the ocean tides, they camouflaged a canal that the Luftwaffe was using as an orientation point. So realistically had Goodeve's men done the job that an elderly man and his dog, out for an evening walk, fell into the canal, having mistaken it for a newly built road.[3]

Americans Break the Purple Code

IN THE FALL OF 1940, the American people were still peacefully preoccupied at home, just as they had been during the 1920s and 1930s. True, a madman with a comic opera mustache named Hitler had overrun most of Europe and was threatening further conquests, and the Japanese Army was brutalizing ancient China. But there were two broad oceans to protect the United States from those unpleasant affairs, so why worry? America's motto was: "Keep out of other people's quarrels!"

As a result of this national attitude, the United States' defenses had been allowed to slip to those of a third-rate power. America was the only major nation that had no global intelligence apparatus. Only the dedicated efforts of a hard core of professional military officers and a small group of scientists would keep the United States from conceivable conquest by seemingly invincible hostile war machines.

A team supervised by William F. Friedman and headed by a former schoolteacher, Frank B. Rowlett, had first discovered that the Japanese were using a diplomatic code called Purple on March 20, 1939. Since that time, these cryptanalysts had been laboring diligently to crack Purple. But their efforts had been in vain.

Friedman, the son of a Russian Jew, was born in 1891, and he came to the United States with his family a year later. The Friedmans settled in the Pitts-burgh region, where the father sold Singer sewing machines door-to-door. The son, a brilliant scholar, graduated from Cornell University in 1914.

After the United States entered the Great War in 1917, young Friedman, who had long had an interest in cryptology, was employed by the army. His first target was to decipher the code of a group of Hindus who were agitating in the United States for Indian independence. Friedman easily broke the code, and there were mass arrests and trials of the group's members for illegally trying to buy firearms.

Meanwhile, Friedman had married Elizebeth [*sic*] Smith, and on January 1, 1921, they both became cryptographers in the War Department's so-called Black Chamber (officially the Code and Cipher Solution Section). His task was to devise cryptosystems, and he wrote a standard work on the craft, *Elements of Cryptanalysis*.

In 1930 Friedman was appointed chief of the army Signals Intelligence Service, which a tightfisted Congress supported with only niggardly funding. His staff to break codes from around the world consisted of three young crypt-analysts and two clerks.

During the 1930s, while Nazi Germany and imperial Japan were build-ing monstrous war machines, the Signal Intelligence Service (SIS) and the Naval Code and Signal Section (CSS) were supposed to be cooperating to break codes of foreign powers. However, the two entities were not speaking to one another. Army and navy cryptanalysts worked separately on the same codes to try to gain sole credit in the event of a breakthrough.

In 1939, the army's SIS scored a major triumph: it cracked Red, code name for the Japanese diplomatic cipher. A few months later, for the first time in U.S. history, foreign intelligence decrypts were being circulated to the White

House and to other top branches of the government and military—a procedure other nations had been following for centuries.

Although the sleeping giant known as America was edging into the twentieth century as far as cryptanalytic intelligence was concerned, President Roosevelt displayed minimal interest in the Red decrypts, even though they often contained startling disclosures.

Then Red revealed that a new Japanese machine, Purple, had been developed and would replace the Red system.

On the afternoon of September 20, 1940, Frank Rowlett, who had led the eighteen-month attack on Purple, suddenly leaped from his chair and shouted: "That's it!"

Rowlett's principal assistant, Robert O. Ferner, also customarily reserved, called out in a loud voice: "Hooray!" A junior cryptanalyst, Albert W. Small, was too choked up to speak; he merely ran around the room with his hands clasped above his head, like a victorious boxer after a bout.

Breaking Purple had been the greatest success in the history of U.S. intelligence, and it called for a celebration. So the four men sent out for bottles of Coca-Cola, drank them, and quietly returned to work.

Major General Joseph Mauborgne, the army's chief signals officer, began referring to the cryptanalysts as "magicians." The name stuck, and intelligence gathered from Japanese decrypts was code-named Magic. (The term would also be used on occasion for high-grade intelligence in general.)

Among those in the higher councils in Washington enthralled by the breaking of Purple was Secretary of War Henry L. Stimson, regarded by many as having one of the more astute minds in the capital. Stimson was no newcomer to armed conflict. During the Great War, he had seen action as a colonel in command of a field artillery outfit in France.

After serving as governor general of the Philippines in 1929, Stimson had been appointed secretary of state by President Herbert Hoover. At that time, Stimson felt that there was a great amount of "international goodwill" and therefore no need for the United States to have a codebreaking agency. So he ordered the Black Chamber, which had been deciphering foreign messages since the Great War, to close down.

"Gentlemen simply do not read other gentlemen's mail," Stimson explained with incredible naïveté for a man of his global experience.

Now, eleven years later, Secretary of War Stimson had flipflopped on his view of codebreaking. Clearly, with Adolf Hitler, Benito Mussolini, and the Japanese warlords pillaging much of the world with their powerful armed forces, there was now a critical need to read "other gentlemen's mail."

In his daily diary, Stimson spoke glowingly of the achievements of America's codebreaking geniuses. "I cannot even in my diary go into some of the great things they have done," he wrote.

With Purple broken and U.S. officials reading Tokyo's most intimate secrets, the SIS and the OP-20-G (formerly the Naval Code and Signal Section) began the painstaking task of intercepting and unbuttoning (deciphering) a blizzard of Japanese diplomatic messages.

At a time when the world was aflame, interservice rivalry reared its ugly head, however. Both the army and navy signal intelligence agencies were fearful that the other side might gain an advantage. So after lengthy discussions between the two branches, a bizarre formula was adopted: the army would receive all diplomatic traffic on days with an even date, and the navy would handle the signals on days with an odd date.

"This arrangement is intended to give both services equal opportunities for training, recognition, 'credit,' and the like," a report stated. The outlandish and unworkable system would result in serious flaws in ascertaining Japan's warlike intentions in the Pacific within a year.

In August 1940, Brigadier General George V. Strong, head of a U.S. military mission that would meet soon with the British chiefs of staff to discuss mutual military assistance, proposed to Secretary of War Stimson that the United States and Britain engage in a "free exchange of intelligence," which would include all decoded messages and codebreaking techniques.

Stimson, now an enthusiastic supporter of the cryptanalysis field, thought General Strong's idea was a great one. However, the navy was bitterly opposed. Stimson met with Secretary of the Navy Frank Knox, a former Chicago daily newspaper publisher, and won him over to the plan for cryptanalytic cooperation with the British.

Stimson told Knox that the British were willing to take part, but he proved to be overly optimistic. While the Americans proposed including all information received through Magic, the British would not even disclose that Ultra existed.

Strong's recommendation, which had the strong support of President Roosevelt, was politely sidetracked by the British chiefs of staff. Winston Churchill no doubt had made that decision. He feared, with considerable merit, that the most closely guarded military secret in the history of the British Empire might not be secure in the United States.

"Washington leaks like a sieve!" one British security officer stated.

British concerns about "leaks" in the United States were intensified when it was learned about a flagrant security breach by Major General Edwin "Pa" Watson, a longtime Roosevelt crony who served as the president's military aide.

Part of Watson's job was to furnish Roosevelt with Magic decrypts. One day, security officers were highly alarmed to discover that a top-secret summary was missing. An exhausting and frantic search of the White House finally turned up the documents—in Pa Watson's wastepaper basket.[4]

The Mystery Truck from Mars

LATE IN SEPTEMBER 1940, the British codebreakers at Bletchley Park north of London decrypted a chilling message and rushed it to Prime Minister Winston Churchill. It stated that Benito Mussolini, the bombastic dictator of Italy who had declared war on Great Britain three months earlier, had assembled a three-hundred-thousand-man army in Libya, North Africa, and that it was preparing a massive offensive.

Under Marshal Rodolfo Graziani, the Italian force's objectives were the British naval base at Alexandria, Egypt; the capital of Cairo; and the Suez Canal, a few hundred miles to the east. Graziani would be confronted by only thirty-six thousand ill-equipped and largely untrained British soldiers scattered throughout Egypt in packets and vaingloriously called the Army of the Nile.

Control of the three-thousand-mile-long Mediterranean Sea, whose entrance is at Gibraltar on the west, was crucial to Great Britain, because through that vast body of water ran the empire's "lifeline," the short route from England to her dominions at the eastern end of the sea.

At the time Churchill received the decrypt, the Battle of Britain was still raging, and the entire world thought that the prime minister would need every soldier in the Home Army. However, thanks to Ultra, Churchill was privy to a German secret: Hitler had canceled Sea Lion, a looming invasion of England. So two divisions of British troops and their tanks sailed for North Africa to reinforce the Army of the Nile.

As soon as the new troops arrived in Egypt amid great secrecy, Archibald Wavell, one of Britain's most highly regarded generals and commander in the Middle East, began infiltrating them westward at night to edge into position opposite Marshal Graziani's force. Although the British would be outnumbered eight to one in the looming battle, Lieutenant General Richard J. O'Connor, leader of what was called the Western Desert Force, would have one enormous advantage: Ultra.

Because of the extreme fluidity of desert fighting—the front was usually only a line on military maps—and the omnipresence of German and Italian radio intelligence eavesdroppers, Winston Churchill and his intelligence officers had decided that none of the generals in the forward fighting would be allowed to see, possess, or even know about Ultra.

At Middle East headquarters near Cairo, only General Wavell and his intelligence chief, Brigadier Francis "Freddie" de Guingand, were allowed to read Ultra decrypts. These two officers received their information from Bletchley Park by way of a newly formed Special Liaison Unit (SLU).

This top-secret detachment consisted of Royal Air Force officers of proven discretion, and radio technicians and cipher experts from the Royal Signal Corps. Their task was to provide a continual flow of details on the enemy's com-

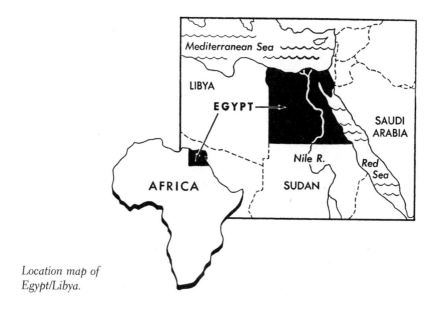

Location map of
Egypt/Libya.

mand structure; tactical plans; and the strength, location, and morale of opposing units, often down to battalion and even company levels. Although pleasant
to those not in the know, these men were tight-lipped and casually aloof, as
though they wanted to avoid conversation.

Shrouded in a thick cloak of intrigue, the SLU operatives and their
curious-looking truck with a twenty-six-foot antenna protruding skyward from
the roof were a constant topic of interest and speculation. The vehicle was
always parked just outside General Wavell's headquarters.

"I say, old fellow," a Tommy (British soldier) would inquire of an SLU officer, "pray tell, what is that absolutely weird-looking lorry [truck], and what are
all you chaps doing?"

"Haven't you heard the latest form?" the other might mock good-
naturedly. "That bloody lorry was shipped in from Mars. It's Winnie's [Chur-
chill's] 'secret weapon,' don't you know."

The bewildered outsiders would have been even more mystified had they
known the code name of the unit's base in England—Station X—the Ultra center at Bletchley Park. The truck was in radio contact with Station X on a round-
the-clock basis.

Royal Air Force officers, sworn to secrecy under pain of a long prison sentence for violation of security, perused each message that came in from Station
X. Each decrypt was marked with a symbol from Z to ZZZZZ, designating the
degree of importance. The more Zs, the greater the significance.

After each message arrived, an officer would clasp the decrypt in one
hand and slip out of the truck. He lifted one of his flying boots and glanced at

"Mystery trucks from Mars," like this one at a British battle headquarters, played a major role in the outcome of the war. (Author's collection)

the sole, then repeated the process with the other boot. He could not risk the off chance that bits and pieces of Ultra materials in the wireless truck had stuck to the bottoms. These scraps might shake loose and be found by unauthorized persons.

Reaching General Wavell's office, the RAF officer would enter and hand him the decoded message from Station X. As the SLU man stood by silently, Wavell would read the signal, then hand it back to the courier.

None of the British brass were permitted to retain copies of SLU signals. In accordance with standard procedure, the RAF man returned to his truck with the secret message and burned it. Nor could the generals or their top aides take notes, which might carelessly go astray and find their way into hostile hands.

If the contents in an Ultra message would be of importance to General O'Connor's battle planning or during the actual fighting, Wavell would acquaint him with the hot intelligence in a letter sent by a courier. The message did not reveal the source, but O'Connor was instructed by a separate memo to destroy the first message by fire after reading.

On occasion, Brigadier de Guingand would personally call on O'Connor and give him the Ultra intelligence, again without disclosing the source. These procedures were the only ones available at the time, but they carried the danger that O'Connor might reject the information from the unknown (to him) source, believing that his own local intelligence was more accurate and up-to-date.

On December 9, 1940, General O'Connor struck. He held the gargantuan advantage of knowing Marshal Graziani's troop positions and those of his supporting forces, such as artillery. Taken by total surprise and racked by low morale, the Italians were soon fleeing westward in disarray. The Desert Rats, as the British fighting men now proudly called themselves, advanced 650 miles westward into Libya.

By February 7, 1941, the Western Desert Force had taken 130,000 prisoners and destroyed or captured 400 tanks and 1,290 guns. British losses were 506 dead and 1,400 wounded. It had been a colossal triumph for O'Connor's soldiers—and for the mystery truck from Mars, which had kept him informed of Graziani's plans in advance.[5]

Churchill's Agonizing Decision

SHORTLY BEFORE MIDNIGHT on November 5, 1940, Kampfgruppe 100 (Battle Group 100) bombers took off from their base near Vannes, France, and winged northward over the dark waves of the English Channel toward the large industrial city of Birmingham. Aboard the black-coated heavies was sophisticated new navigational equipment called X-Gerät (X-Apparatus). Developed by German scientists, the new technique could guide bombers to targets at night and in cloudy weather. The equipment was so complicated that only the elite Kampfgruppe 100 had been trained in its use.

X-Gerät worked according to expectations and took Kampfgruppe 100 directly to Birmingham, which was bombed heavily. Then, on the way back to France, a Heinkel crashed on a beach in southern England, and from the wreckage the X-Gerät was salvaged. It was rushed to the Telecommunications Research Establishment (TRE) near Swanage.

Less than an hour after the secret device arrived it was being intensely studied by Reginald Jones, Robert Cockburn, and other scientists, who had been and were engaged with their German counterparts in a twilight war of measure and countermeasure, parry and thrust. Neither scientific adversary could let down its guard for a minute. The immutable law of challenge and response was almost constant.

Jones and the others had been aware from German POWs' conversations the previous March that the Luftwaffe was developing X-Gerät. Now they determined that it consisted of a primary radio beam aimed at a target and three crossbeams. The main beam (code-named Weser by the Germans) was transmitting from Cherbourg on the Channel coast of France, and the three crossbeams (Oder, Elbe, and Rhine) were being sent from Calais, opposite Dover.

As a result of the scientists' findings, an alarmed Dr. Frederick A. Lindemann sent Prime Minister Churchill a memorandum on X-Gerät's capabilities: "Bombing accuracies on the order of twenty yards are expected."

While Churchill was pondering suggested countermeasures to the X-Gerät threat, including a commando raid on Kampfgruppe 100's base at Vannes, Ultra intercepted signals that revealed the Luftwaffe would launch a massive assault (Operation Moonlight Sonata) to wipe off the map three British cities code-named Einheitspreis, Regenschirm, and Korn. Moonlight Sonata would be launched on November 14–15 and continue on successive nights. But which were these code-named cities?

There was a sinister motive behind Moonlight Sonata: revenge. On the night of November 8, at the time Adolf Hitler had spoken before the Nazi Old Guard in the Löwenbräukeller in Munich to commemorate the seventeenth anniversary of the Beer Hall Putsch, the führer's first attempt at revolution, the Royal Air Force winged over and dropped a few bombs on the city.

Although Hitler had addressed his diehard supporters ninety minutes earlier than planned and had already left the beer hall when the British bombs burst, he was infuriated. Munich had a holy aura with Hitler: it was the cradle of Nazism.

The German propaganda genius Josef Goebbels issued a communiqué on the raid, claiming that Winston Churchill had deliberately targeted women and children to be killed to spite the führer. "There will be particularly heavy retaliation against England," the communiqué concluded.

That retaliation would be Moonlight Sonata.

After receiving the Ultra decrypts, frantic activity erupted as British scientists and others tried to determine which cities were going to be hit. Speed was essential: the massive blow would strike in only five days. Reginald Jones's view was that the targets were the Midlands cities of Coventry, Wolverhampton, and Birmingham. All sorts of wild guesses came out of the Air Ministry.

Suddenly the gods of war smiled on the British. No doubt an Enigma operator transmitting orders from a high Luftwaffe headquarters slipped up and instead of a city with a code name, Coventry was spelled out. Ultra also discovered that the famous Kampfgruppe 100, equipped with X-Gerät, would fly to Coventry along a radio beam, and it would bomb with incendiaries to start fires that would act as beacons for the main bomber force.

When the Ultra decrypts reached Winston Churchill in his battle dugout in London, the prime minister was confronted by an agonizing decision: at all costs, the security of Ultra had to prevail. From any extra actions taken to defend Coventry, a city of a quarter of a million people about ninety miles northwest of London, the crafty German intelligence might deduce that the British had received foreknowledge of the raid, possibly through cryptanalysis. That deep suspicion might lead Adolf Hitler to conclude that Enigma had been penetrated by the British and cause him to change to another communications system.

Was the security of Ultra more important than the security of a large British city? While the defenses against night bombing were primitive, there

German Gerät beams target Coventry. (Courtesy Prof. R. V. Jones)

were several measures that Churchill could take to minimize the massive destruction and loss of lives that were certain to occur.

Through Ultra, the British had detailed an accurate intelligence on the location and strength of the German air squadrons in western Europe. Therefore the prime minister could give the green light for the Royal Air Force to launch Operation Cold Douche. That plan called for frustrating the Coventry raid before it got started by launching all available fighter planes to attack the German bombers when they were most vulnerable—heavily laden with bombs and fuel, assembling above their airfields.

Antiaircraft guns—some four hundred were available in England—and smoke-screen and searchlight defenses could be rushed to Coventry. A combination of withering antiaircraft guns and searchlights might cause the Luftwaffe bomber streams to break up and throw off their aim. Fire-fighting and ambulance units from around southern England could be sent to Coventry.

Could a confidential warning that the Luftwaffe was about to hit Coventry be given to city officials there? Should not the elderly, the children, and the ill in hospitals be evacuated?

Churchill anguished over these options. Few, if any, leaders in history had been required to make such an excruciatingly painful decision. Finally, to all these propositions, the prime minister replied no. German intelligence could not be alerted to the fact that the British had foreknowledge of Moonlight Sonata. It was a tragic decision, but it was the only way to protect the Ultra secret for the long and bloody war ahead before Adolf Hitler would be brought to his knees.

Soon after dusk on November 14, Churchill, with his confidential secretary, Jock Colville, rode off from the prime minister's residence at 10 Downing Street to spend the night at a retreat outside London. During full-moon periods, the prime minister's country home, Chequers, would be a clear and tempting target to German bombardiers, British counterintelligence officers insisted.

At the same time as the heavy-hearted Churchill was rolling through the streets of London, swarms of German bombers were taking off from airfields in France, Belgium, and the Netherlands. An hour later, masses of flame leaped high into the black sky over Coventry after a visit by Kampfgruppe 100, whose planes followed the X-Gerät beam to the target. The inferno served as a beacon that could be seen fifty miles away by approaching German bomber crews. One hundred fifty thousand incendiaries and fourteen hundred high-explosive bombs were dropped.

Historic Coventry had been pulverized. Sprawled in death beneath the rubble were 1,554 men, women, and children. Nearly 5,000 others were injured or burned. A horrendous price had been paid, but the secret of Ultra remained secure.[6]

Duel of the Radio Beams

BAD WEATHER largely protected the British Isles from heavy German bombing raids during the last few weeks of 1940, a pause that permitted scientists at the Telecommunications Research Establishment (TRE) near Swanage to try to develop countermeasures to X-Gerät. Code-named Wotan 1 by the Germans, the device was the most accurate and sophisticated airplane electronics guidance system yet devised by either side.

Working feverishly night and day, the British scientists came up with a technique for jamming X-Gerät, thereby making it almost useless to the Germans. But there was no time for celebration in the British camp. Through the snooping apparatus Ultra, the British learned that German scientists had come up with an even more precise night-bomber radio beam, code-named Wotan 2.

Wotan 2 was a remarkable invention. The beam not only guided the bomber to its target but also told the bombardier when to release his cargo. However, scientists at TRE were soon eagerly inspecting this new electronic guidance equipment, which had been salvaged from three Heinkels that had been shot down over England.

Wotan 2 proved to be remarkably easy to jam, and the BBC radio transmitter at Alexandra Palace in London was ideal for the task—it worked on the right frequency band. This countermeasure was code-named Domino.

British scientists employed subtle means to cause hostile bombers to stray slightly from their courses and drop their explosives off-target. The trick was to hoodwink the Luftwaffe without its discovering that it was being bamboozled. During the first few nights of the BBC transmitter's use, a minimum of power was injected into the Wotan 2 system, just enough of a signal to give approaching bomber fleets a slightly false course without arousing the suspicions of crews. Gradually the BBC power was turned higher to deflect German bombers even farther from their targets, and eventually the Luftwaffe realized that Wotan 2 had been compromised and was useless.

The rapid jamming of Wotan 2 had been one of British scientists' most notable achievements. But this did not stop the bombing of London, a target so huge that German bombers could find it without radio beams. Nor did it halt raids on ports in southern England, which the Luftwaffe could reach before the British had time to jam their guiding devices.[7]

Enigma Betrays the Italian Fleet

ABOARD A BATTLESHIP anchored in the harbor at Alexandria, Egypt, Admiral Andrew B. "ABC" Cunningham, the Royal Navy commander in the Mediterranean Seas, was handed an Ultra decrypt of a message sent on the German encoding machine Enigma. It disclosed that the Italian Navy and the German Luftwaffe were about ready to launch combined heavy assaults against British convoys in the Mediterranean. It was March 20, 1941.

Cunningham, a tough-minded old sea dog, had a daunting mission second in naval importance only to the Home Fleet's guarding of the British Isles. Although he had mainly old ships and too few of them, the Dublin native was expected to protect convoys along the eastern half of the three-thousand-mile-long Mediterranean Sea.

Now Cunningham immediately sprang into action, ordering the three battleships, nine destroyers, and an aircraft carrier in Alexandria Harbor to raise steam. Then, to disguise the fleet's preparations to sail from the prying eyes of German and Italian spies—of whom there was no shortage in Egypt—the admiral conspicuously came ashore in broad daylight dressed in casual civilian clothes with a bag of golf clubs slung over a shoulder.

Soon after nightfall blanketed the Middle East, Cunningham stole back to his battleship, and his flotilla steamed out of the harbor. In the Mediterranean, the battle group was joined by four cruisers and four destroyers.

Cunningham knew from Ultra decrypts that the Italian fleet had sortied from Naples, but, above all, he had to protect the secret of the greatest intelligence means that history had known. So after daylight, the admiral dispatched a Sunderland flying boat, a type customarily used for wide-ranging patrols at sea. It "discovered" the Italian fleet, flying just close enough to be seen by those on board.

This ruse was intended to make the Italians and the Germans believe that it had been aerial reconnaissance, not the cracking of the Enigma code, that had been responsible for the Royal Navy's attack on the Italian fleet.

Reichsmarschall Hermann Goering, chief of the Luftwaffe, had promised the Italian admirals that his warplanes would be out in force to cooperate with the Italian Navy in the assault of British convoys. But on March 28, when Cunningham's force caught two Italian squadrons off Cape Matapan, Greece, there was not a single German aircraft in the sky.

Planes from the Royal Navy carrier *Formidable*, aided by heavy gunfire from the destroyers and cruisers, badly damaged an Italian battleship and sank three cruisers and two destroyers. What remained of the Italian fleet limped back to Naples and went into hiding.

In the wake of the disaster, an inquest was held in Rome to try to learn how the British had located the marauding Italian warships. It was concluded that the Sunderland flying boat had been the culprit.

Once again, Ultra had provided the British with a crucial strategic advantage, at this critical time in the eastern Mediterranean.[8]

Code Names Rebecca and Eureka

BY EARLY 1941, Special Operations Executive (SOE), the supersecret British espionage and sabotage agency created by Prime Minister Winston Churchill with the stirring exhortation "Set Europe ablaze!," was in trouble. SOE had been parachuting a large number of spies, radio operators, and couriers "blind" into German-held France, Belgium, and the Netherlands, and many had fallen into the hands of the Gestapo.

The principal cause of these human disasters was that Royal Air Force pilots were finding it almost impossible to locate a drop zone for the parachuting spies at night. Lifting off from secret bases in southern England, the pilots navigated mainly by using rivers, roads, and towns as guiding landmarks. However, in the blackness and often under German antiaircraft fire, picking out the right landmarks was a perplexing task.

Most drop zones were in meadows, but from the dark sky one meadow looked much like any of a million others in Europe. Consequently, Charles Hambro, the SOE chief known by the cipher "D," put in an urgent call to Britain's electronic experts. Could an apparatus be developed that would permit a pilot or a navigator to locate a drop zone at night without unduly attracting the attention of the Germans? John Pringle, a skilled scientist and also a pilot, was assigned to lead a team to work on the complicated project.

SOE, under Charles Hambro, had taken its first wobbly steps less than a year earlier by settling into sparsely furnished offices at 64 Baker Street in London. From its birth, the agency had been cloaked in the tightest secrecy.

At this stage of the war no one knew if German spies had infiltrated the British high command. So SOE handed out different names and addresses to the chiefs of the British armed forces. The Air Ministry knew SOE by one set of initials, the Admiralty by another set. Both commands thought the covert organization was located at addresses other than the correct one. There were no markings or signs anywhere in the building at 64 Baker Street to indicate that SOE was located there.

Prime Minister Churchill's goal, even when a German invasion of the British Isles had still been a threat in late 1940, was to organize in Nazi-held Europe a large and sophisticated secret alliance of zealous, well-trained spies and saboteurs. When England (hopefully with some allies) would eventually invade the Continent, a clandestine army would rise up to assault, disrupt, and bedevil the Germans. Until that time, SOE's covert force in Europe would provide intelligence and keep the German Army in a constant state of jitters.

Even as the first secret agents had been parachuting into western Europe, D was diligently expanding the organization. Each country that had been conquered and occupied by the Wehrmacht had its own section in SOE, designated as F for the French Section, B for the Belgian, D for the Dutch, N for the Norwegian, and P for the Polish. Each section was to direct secret operations in its own country, and recruit and train its own agents. If the agents parachuted safely and escaped capture, they in turn would organize their own *réseaux* (secret cells).

Chief Hambro and his officers recruited anyone who showed an inclination to kill or torment Germans—a curious mixture of Catholics, Communists, capitalists, paupers, Protestants, royalty, artisans, lawyers, and factory workers. They were largely ordinary men and women who barely knew how to fire a pistol or to lay a charge of plastique.

After being selected as SOE agents, they were trained and assigned to secret houses near secluded airfields, mainly in southern England. There the agent was given a cover story and forced to repeat it endlessly while British security men, playing the role of brutal Gestapo interrogators, browbeat and threatened them.

When an agent was notified at about noon that his or her mission was to be launched that night, SOE officers provided forged identification papers, a radio set, and a parachute. At a hangar at the dark airfield, the escorts made certain once again that there was nothing about the agent to indicate that he or she had ever been in England. Clothes, shoes, hats, cigarettes, money, toilet equipment—all were painstakingly inspected. A forgotten English bus or theater-ticket stub, a grocery receipt, or a handwritten note could doom the agent to death after a horrible grilling by the Gestapo.

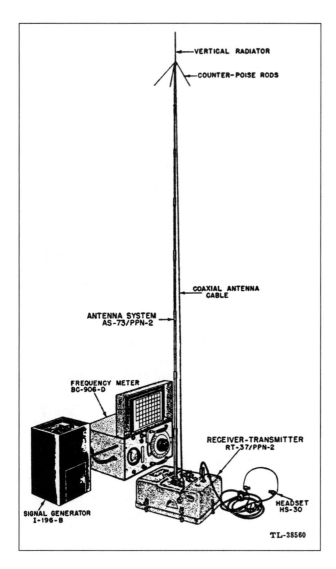

A *Eureka is set up on the ground. Aircraft carrying spies or paratroopers home in on Eureka with its Rebecca. (Author's collection)*

After the agent climbed aboard the airplane, the RAF crew barely acknowledged his or her existence. For security reasons, the airmen would never know the real or code names of the passenger they were to ferry across the English Channel and watch parachute to an unknown fate. These faceless figures were known merely as "Joes" or "Janes."

Elsewhere in England, meanwhile, the electronics specialist John Pringle and his team developed a system that would permit a pilot to find the drop zone at night in hostile territory. The revolutionary apparatus was code-named Rebecca and Eureka. Rebecca was short for "recognition of beacons," and its smaller sister, Eureka ("I have found it!"), was to be sought by Rebecca.

Eureka was a portable beacon, weighed only fourteen pounds, and could be strapped to the leg of a parachutist. Once the Eureka was on the ground, the agent or members of the underground would set it up with its telescopic antenna extending upward.

Rebecca was a device fitted into an airplane, and as the craft drew closer it sought out the Eureka and homed in on its beam to the drop zone. Eureka had a trait that was crucial to clandestine operations. Instead of being activated hours ahead of a parachute drop, thereby giving Gestapo mobile electronic monitors time to locate the device, Eureka "spoke" only when "asked" to do so by Rebecca.

The new homing apparatus was soon put into use, and both parachuting spies and RAF pilots reported that it was producing the desired results. The scientific development would play a tremendous role in building a widespread clandestine army ready to rise up against the Wehrmacht when the Continent of Europe would be invaded.[9]

A Dying Genius "Sinks" the *Bismarck*

SPRING WAS BREAKING OUT over Europe on May 1, 1941, when Adolf Hitler and a large entourage arrived at Gotenhafen, a port on the Baltic Sea, to inspect the monstrous new battleship *Bismarck*, the pride of the Kriegsmarine (navy). She was a grimly spectacular floating gun platform, heavily armored, and secretly far exceeding in tonnage limitations set by international treaty when her keel had been laid in 1936.

The battleship was named in honor of a legend, Prince Otto Eduard Leopold von Bismarck, a Prussian statesman who had united the German people under the government of one empire in the nineteenth century. Known as the Iron Chancellor, he had declared that great problems had to be settled by "blood and iron" instead of by speeches and resolutions.

Now the führer, piped aboard the battleship with great pomp and circumstance, reviewed the crew, which was mustered on the upper deck. Trailing him as he trod the boards was the ship's skipper, Kapitän sur See (Captain) Ernst Lindemann. Because he was not strong physically, he had been accepted into the imperial German Navy in 1914 at the beginning of the Great War "on probation," a status that remained unchanged when he had taken command of the *Bismarck* in the spring of 1941.

It was ironic that Lindemann received the choice appointment to command the huge battleship. Since his days as a naval cadet twenty-seven years earlier, he had lived by the motto of the Iron Chancellor: *Patriae inserviendo consumer* ("I am consumed in the service of the Fatherland").

The Bismarck, *pride of Nazi Germany, heads for the Atlantic to attack Allied convoys bound for England. (U.S. Navy)*

As Lindemann was escorting Hitler through the ship, Lindemann pointed to a large portrait of Prince von Bismarck by Franz von Lenbach, the leading German portraitist of that era. It was hanging just outside Lindemann's stateroom. He remarked to the führer that he was concerned that something might happen to the priceless painting during combat action.

Hitler shook his head. "If anything happens to this ship," he said, "the picture might as well be lost, too."

Four years of planning and four more years of construction at Hamburg's Blohm & Voss shipyard produced the heaviest warship (over fifty thousand tons) ever launched by a European nation. With a maximum speed of thirty-two knots, she was one of the fastest battleships afloat in the world.

There was an imposing array of armaments. The ship's four main turrets, two fore and two aft (named Anton, Bruno, Caesar, and Dora), each housed twin fifteen-inch guns with a maximum range of more than twenty miles. Three armored control stations directed their fire, using sophisticated stereoscopic range finders and radar mounted on rotating cupolas. Fifty-two smaller guns bristled from the monster battleship.

On May 17, fewer than three weeks after Hitler had departed from the ship, liberty for the *Bismarck's* crew was suddenly canceled. At noon the next day, the ship left the wharf at Gotenhafen on a three-month secret mission code-named Rheinübung (Exercise Rhine). Accompanied by the powerful new cruiser, *Prinz Eugen*, the *Bismarck* was going to prowl the North Atlantic to shut off the convoys of war accoutrements that were flowing from the United States to England.

A few months earlier, President Franklin Roosevelt, aware that the United States itself would be in grave danger of invasion should Great Britain fall, had declared America to be "the arsenal of democracy." He had ramrodded through

Congress a program called Lend-Lease, in which Britain would be provided with airplanes, tanks, trucks, jeeps, guns, and munitions in return for only nominal payments.

Meanwhile, in early 1941, several high-ranking officers in Swedish intelligence had secretly concluded that a weakened Third Reich would be to the advantage of their officially neutral country. They began to work closely with the Norwegian underground, represented in Stockholm by Colonel Roscher Lund, who had become a friend and trusted informant of the British naval attaché in Stockholm, Captain Henry W. Denham.

On the night of May 20, Lund was tipped off by the chief of staff to the head of Swedish intelligence that the *Bismarck* and the *Prinz Eugen* had left their Baltic Sea port under heavy air cover. Lund rushed to the British embassy, where he was told that Captain Denham was at a certain restaurant in the city. He pursued him there and gave him the electrifying news. Denham left his meal, hurried back to the embassy, and sent the alarming message to London.

The high-grade intelligence triggered a rash of nervous tics in the Admiralty. There were even hushed whispers in dark corners that unless the *Bismarck* was dealt with, she might create such carnage in the North Atlantic that Britain would be strangled for war materials and supplies and might even have to seek peace terms.

As the two German warships headed up the coast of Norway before turning sharply westward into the Atlantic, they were picked up and shadowed by two aircraft of the RAF Coastal Command. Soon the British Home Fleet based at Scapa Flow in northern Scotland set sail and moved toward the German marauders.

At Bletchley Park in England, Ultra was decrypting a series of radio messages between the *Bismarck* and the Admiralstab, the navy headquarters in Berlin. As a security measure, the German signals were not being sent in the regular Enigma code, but in a special cipher created for Exercise Rhine.

Alfred Knox, who, along with Alan Turing, had created the Ultra system, was at his home in Hughenden in the Thames valley when he received word of the sorties of the two great German warships, and he ordered the decrypts to be sent to him for decoding.

Known as Dilly to his friends, Knox had been diagnosed with cancer a year earlier, but he had insisted on keeping his job as chief cryptographer at Bletchley. Now he was very weak and in pain. Propped up in bed and using paper and pencil, he attacked the special code being used by the *Bismarck*.

Perhaps because of his declining health, he was unable to crack this code. However, he did decipher a raft of Luftwaffe and diplomatic codes relative to *Bismarck*'s mission so the British could keep track of the dreadnought.

Based on information from Alfred Knox's decrypts, the British cruisers *Norfolk* and *Suffolk* emerged from fog and mist and spotted the *Bismarck* and the *Prinz Eugen* only about six miles away, a dangerously close range to German guns that could shoot more than twenty miles. Both British ships rushed back into fog banks, but they began shadowing the German leviathan, keeping contact by radar.

In the meantime, the British cruiser *Hood* and the battleship *Prince of Wales* steamed up and opened fire on the *Bismarck*, which returned the salvos. Several shells struck the *Hood* and she exploded, taking all but three of the fifteen hundred men aboard to their doom.

During the savage encounter, the bridge of the *Prince of Wales* became twisted wreckage from a direct hit, killing or wounding every officer or crewman except the ship's skipper, Captain John C. Leach. Other shells pierced the battleship below the waterline, and Leach broke off the engagement.

Miraculously, perhaps, the *Bismarck* had escaped the duel of the big guns unscathed, and she continued onward at full steam. This news shocked the Admiralty. There were ten large convoys on the ocean heading for England at the time, so within six hours of the *Hood's* destruction, two more battleships, an aircraft carrier, four cruisers, and nine destroyers from throughout the vast Atlantic were ordered to join in the chase.

All the while, the *Suffolk* continued to shadow the German behemoth at a safe distance and report her location. Within hours, nine planes from the carrier *Victorious* swooped down and dropped their torpedoes, but only one "fish" struck the *Bismarck*, and she wasn't even slowed.

Five hours later, a grim message reached the Admiralty: in the darkness the *Suffolk* had lost the mighty ship, and for nearly thirty hours, the *Bismarck* was loose in the North Atlantic and presumably heading for the oncoming convoys of merchant ships.

Captain Ernst Lindemann was apparently confident that he had shaken off the pursuing British ships, because he radioed a long message to the Admiralstab detailing his current situation and future plans.

At his home in Hughenden, Alfred Knox, racked by intense physical agony and after almost constant deciphering of the *Bismarck's* radio traffic for five days, decoded an order from the Admiralstab instructing the *Bismarck* to head full steam for the sanctuary of the naval base at Saint-Nazaire, in western France.

This crucial information was rushed to the Operational Intelligence Center of the Admiralty, which was able to roughly determine the course the battleship would take to reach the French port. Coastal Command aircraft fanned out, and one of them spotted the *Bismarck*.

Within hours, British warships were swarming around the German ship. A torpedo plane from the carrier *Ark Royal* scored a direct hit, which apparently damaged the rudders, causing Captain Lindemann to lose control of the vessel. Then the battleships *Rodney* and *King George V* opened fire with their sixteen-inch guns. Several shells, each weighing more than one ton, scored numerous hits on the pride of the Kriegsmarine.

The *Bismarck*'s top deck became an inferno. Men's clothes were ripped off by the explosions. Ghastly wounded crewmen were shrieking, and the dead lay everywhere.

Then the mighty ship began to list. She had no stability left, her stern sank deeper, and her bow reared steeply out of the water. Crewmen began leaping overboard, and they were bouncing up and down like corks.

When swimmers close to the bow of the ship looked back, they saw Captain Lindemann standing on the deck. Soon he began climbing a steadily increasing slope of the bow. Then the skipper who lived by Prince von Bismarck's creed "I am consumed in the service of the Fatherland" saluted the battered bridge.

Stabsobermaschninist Wilhelm Schmidt struggled away from the doomed vessel, not wanting to be sucked under when she sank. He saw air bubbles rising from under her, then she rolled over on her side like a great wounded beast.

Only six days after the giant ship had been spotted heading into the North Atlantic and less than a year after she had been commissioned, the *Bismarck*, a smoking ruin, slipped below the waves. In the finest tradition of the old imperial navy, Ernst Lindemann, instead of trying to save himself, deliberately went down with his ship.

Nearly two thousand *Bismarck* crewmen lost their lives. Some one hundred Germans were rescued from the water by British warships. These men were haggard and hollow-eyed. Days later, after they had been put to bed and given medical treatment and hot food, they were still dazed. They hardly spoke, not even to one another.

It was more than physical shock they had suffered. There had been a shattering of faith. The *Bismarck*, they had always believed, was indestructible.

Late in the morning of May 27, only a few hours after the *Bismarck* had sunk, Prime Minister Winston Churchill announced the feat in the House of Commons. Cheers and shouts erupted.

Several hundred miles away, in Berlin, Grand Admiral Erich Raeder, chief of the Kriegsmarine, received the news with shock and dismay. He was deeply suspicious. How had the British Navy managed to locate and track the *Bismarck* in the vastness of the Atlantic Ocean?

Raeder felt that the special Exercise Rhine code must have been broken by the British. A board of inquiry was convened by Raeder. "There was no breach of security as regards the code and cipher tables," the panel reported.

Then who or what might have been helping the British Navy? Possibly a traitor at Kriegsmarine headquarters? The board pointed out that the navy's telephone line between Berlin and Paris ran through boosters that were not always manned by Germans. Therefore, the tapping of these lines by British spies was quite probable.

Neither the Admiralstab nor the *Bismarck's* survivors would ever know that the fate of their warship had largely evolved through the deathbed crypt-analytical exploits of a British genius. Later, the family of Alfred Knox would be told that his efforts had enabled the Admiralty to locate and eventually sink the magnificent battleship.

For his colossal contributions to Great Britain in developing Ultra and in the *Bismarck* action, Knox was made a companion of the Order of St. Michael and St. George by King George VI. The codebreaker was too ill to go to Buckingham Palace, however, so the monarch sent a top emissary to his home to make the formal presentation.

Despite his weakened condition, Knox insisted on getting out of bed and dressing. He appeared on the balcony overlooking his drawing room, his clothes hanging in folds over his emaciated frame. Refusing helping hands, he managed to descend the staircase for the ceremony, for which his family had gathered.

After the Saxon blue and scarlet ribbon with gold and white star was placed around his neck, Knox was so weak he had to be half carried back up the stairs to his bedroom.

No one was more aware of the crucial significance of Knox's contributions to the war effort than was Winston Churchill. At a time when every warship was needed in the fight to keep the Atlantic shipping lanes open, the prime minister offered Knox's family the services of a destroyer to carry him to the warm climes of the Caribbean to hopefully help his recovery. Knox was too ill to be moved.

Churchill then obtained special medical treatment for him through his own personal physician, Lord Moran. Arrangements were also made with the U.S. embassy in London to obtain supplies of fresh tropical fruit, a rare delicacy in wartime England and for which the cryptanalyst had cravings.

A few months later, Alfred Knox died.[10]

Cryptographic Sleuths
Silence the Red Orchestra

ALTHOUGH A SAVAGE WAR had been raging in Europe for more than twenty months by the spring of 1942, Polish-born Leopold Trepper was getting richer from his far-flung business enterprises. Suave, articulate and impeccably dressed (his expensive suits were bought on the black market), he operated in Nazi-occupied countries, providing construction materials to Organization Todt—German paramilitary construction engineers and workers who built fortifications and facilities for the German armed forces.

Trepper had two business firms: Simex on the Champs-Élysées in Paris, and Simexco on Brussels' Rue Royale. He and his top executives carried special passes that permitted them to enter and move around nearly every German military facility.

Citizens in Paris and Brussels were infuriated to know that the Pole was not only raking in huge profits by dealing with the Third Reich, but also that he was entertaining his Nazi friends to gourmet black-market meals in expensive restaurants. What was not known to the Germans or the Belgians or the French was that Trepper was a cagey master spy for the Soviet Union.

For two years, the Pole had been building a widespread espionage network later to be known to the Gestapo as the Rote Kapelle (Red Orchestra). His cover was almost foolproof: How could a businessman be more pro-Nazi than to supply building materials for Adolf Hitler's war machine?

Trepper had been so clever in organizing his two "fronts," Simexco and Simex, that nearly all of his many employees thought they were working for a legitimate firm. One clerk, a Nazi zealot, unaware that his company was a cover for spying against the Third Reich, unknowingly lent credibility to the sham by barking *"Heil Hitler!"* each time he answered the telephone.

As the Rote Kapelle began to expand throughout much of the führer's European empire after Trepper had established the first cell in Brussels, he was joined by Victor Sukolov-Gurevich, a Russian-born secret agent who went by the alias of Edward Kent.

Kent posed as a Uruguayan businessman, and to enhance his cover, Trepper "hired" him to head Simexco, ostensibly an international importer, while Trepper continued as head of the sister firm, Simex, in Paris. Kent spent little time in his office, however. Using the special pass provided by German security services, the "Uruguayan" freely roamed around Europe, recruiting agents for the Rote Kapelle.

Among members of the Soviet spy ring, the two leaders were known as le Grand Chef et le Petit Chef (the Big Chief and the Little Chief). The heavyset Trepper was the Big Chief and the wiry Kent was the Little Chief.

In March 1941 Trepper radioed a blockbuster report to his contact in Moscow, the Gosudarstvennoye Politischeskoye Upravleniye (State Political Administration), commonly known as the GPU. Many German infantry and tank divisions were being withdrawn from France and Belgium, where they had been poised for months to invade England, and sent eastward into Nazi-occupied Poland near the Soviet frontier.

A few weeks later, the Big Chief reported that Adolf Hitler was about to invade Russia, and he was even able to provide the approximate date of the offensive.

Soviet dictator Josef Stalin, who had signed a "friendship" pact with the führer a year earlier, was unimpressed. He wrote on the margin of one Trepper report: "This is merely an English provocation. The perpetrator should be sought out and punished."

During the first three weeks of June, various secret radio sites of the Rote Kapelle sent Moscow some 250 transmissions, most of them detailing plans for the German invasion.

Before dawn on the morning of June 22, 1941, German armies of three million men poured across the Soviet border on a two-thousand-mile front, from Finland southward to the Black Sea. Josef Stalin and the Red Army had been taken totally by surprise.

On the morning of June 26, four days after the invasion, a German radio-intercept station at Cranz on the Baltic coast picked up a coded message from a clandestine transmitter with the call sign PTX. Bearings taken by long-distance direction finders indicated that the radio was located somewhere in Belgium.

During the next several days, signals were intercepted from three other secret transmitters in Berlin, and it was indicated that they were beaming their messages to Moscow.

Despite the high priority assigned to wiping out the espionage radio sites, the search was slowed by the intramural skirmishing that usually afflicted German counterintelligence. The Luftwaffe possessed the most powerful direction-finding equipment, but it refused to lend it to the Funkabwehr, the signals security branch of the armed forces high command. Only after much wrangling did Luftwaffe agents and their equipment join the search in Berlin.

Now began an electronics cat-and-mouse game between the pursuers and the pursued. The German radio sleuths cruised around Berlin in unmarked vehicles, wore the uniforms of telephone repairmen, and concealed their equipment in street shelters used to cover work done on underground cables.

The Rote Kapelle radio operators changed frequencies and schedules often and kept their broadcasts short so the Germans would not have time to take bearings on the signals.

It was not until late October 1941 before the German sleuths closed in on three buildings in Berlin that held the covert transmitters. But Lady Luck came down on the side of the Soviet agents. A radio operator from the Red Orchestra named Hans Coppi happened to pass one of the equipment-carrying vehicles and noticed its license plate had the telltale letters WL—for Wehrmacht/Luftwaffe.

Coppi rushed to the three buildings, and the operators gathered up their transmitting equipment and fled. Within an hour, heavily armed Germans barged into the structures.

Foiled in Berlin, investigators of Abwehr Section IIIF, the German counterespionage branch of military intelligence, under Captain Henry Piepe, focused on the original transmitter, PTX. The search centered on Brussels.

Berlin sent Piepe, a forty-eight-year-old retread from World War I, the latest portable direction-finding equipment developed by German scientists. This unobtrusive gear could be carried in an ordinary suitcase and had a built-in aerial.

In early December, Piepe and his men pinpointed a house on the Rue des Atrébates. On a dark night, they surrounded the three-story structure and charged inside. Taken into custody was a Soviet radio operator and two badly frightened women. On the premises were found two photographs, and one of the women identified them as the leaders of the espionage ring—Leopold Trepper and Edward Kent. She claimed she knew them only as le Grand Chef and le Petit Chef.

Piepe studied the photographs intensely. He felt that he had seen the two men before. Then it dawned on him: they were his next-door neighbors.

When Piepe had taken over the investigation in Brussels, he had donned civilian clothes and assumed the cover of a jovial Dutch businessman named Otto Riepert. Then he rented an office on Rue Royale. Incredibly, the firm next door was a company called Simexco—the cover for Edward Kent (the Little Chief). Piepe had often passed both Kent and Leopold Trepper in front of their building, and the three men had tipped their hats pleasantly to one another.

Still the Red Orchestra continued to operate. But on the night of July 30, 1942, Piepe led a raid on a Brussels house harboring the Red Orchestra's last piano, as the Germans called the individual transmitters. Among those apprehended was a prize catch: Johann Wenzel, a Soviet spy long sought by the Gestapo, which had dubbed him the Professor in admiration of his daring and accomplishments.

In the meantime, codebreakers in Berlin had long been struggling to identify other players in the Red Orchestra. The codes the pianos had been using were so complicated they had defied solving. So a team of ten experts in linguistics and mathematics had been assembled under Wilhelm Vauck, a schoolteacher and reserve army lieutenant.

Vauck concentrated on a charred document covered with ciphers that Captain Piepe and his men had snatched from a fireplace when they raided the piano site on the Rue des Atrébates in Brussels the previous December. In six weeks of intense effort, Vauck's codebreakers managed to reconstruct a single word: *proctor*.

The Soviets were known to base their codes on sentences in obscure fiction books, and one of the women arrested in the Rue des Atrébates raid had recalled the titles of five works of fiction kept on a desk there. Her information touched off a hunt for the titles in bookstores, and Vauck's agents came up with four of the novels. Elation rapidly turned to despair: the word *proctor* was not mentioned in any of the books.

Further scouring of bookstores in several European countries proved to be fruitless. Then, in mid-May 1942, an agent happened to be browsing in a secondhand bookshop in Paris when he came across the wanted novel. In the book was a character named Proctor.

Now Vauck's codebreakers plunged into the burdensome task of studying some three hundred intercepted messages between the GPU in Moscow and the pianos in Brussels. The sleuths detected that one-third of the messages contained a clue that pointed to a sentence in the Proctor book.

Based on the key sentences, Vauck's cryptanalysts were able to decode the messages, which included a wealth of pilfered intelligence on German troop units, their strengths, and war production figures. But there was not a hint in the three hundred messages concerning the identity of the Red Orchestra "musicians."

A month later, Vauck's men hit the proverbial jackpot. They deciphered a message sent the previous October by the GPU in Moscow to the Little Chief, Edward Kent. The Soviets had wanted Kent to travel from Brussels to Berlin to find out why the three pianos there had shut down. In an amazing breach of security, the GPU had listed the names and addresses of the Rote Kapelle's three leaders in Berlin.

Within hours, the Gestapo had the three men under surveillance. All were prominent in the Third Reich: a top official in the Reich Economics Ministry, an author, and a socially eminent lieutenant in the Luftwaffe.

The Orchestra leader in position to pilfer the most sensitive German information was the Luftwaffe officer, thirty-two-year-old Harro Schulze-Boysen, who was assigned as an intelligence analyst with almost constant access to top-secret documents and other materials. During the previous year and a half, Schulze-Boysen and his colleagues had radioed the GPU in Moscow more than five hundred messages detailing the development of new weapons by German scientists and a wide array of other military secrets.

For several weeks, Gestapo agents shadowed the Orchestra leaders, tapped their telephones, and opened their mail in an effort to snare as many members of the Soviet espionage ring as possible. Finally, on the night of August 30, the telltale black automobiles of the Gestapo fanned out in Berlin. Before dawn, Schulze-Boysen, the other two leaders, and numerous Orchestra members had been taken into custody.

At first the prisoners indignantly denied any knowledge of or connection with a Soviet spy ring. All claimed to be loyal to Adolf Hitler. But after two weeks of brutal interrogation, tongues began to loosen. By late October 1942 more than one hundred Orchestra members were in jail, and the Berlin espionage apparatus had been wiped out.

Now the energetic Captain Piepe and his agents focused on Paris in pursuit of the Big Chief and the Little Chief. Several traps were laid for the Big

Chief—Leopold Trepper—but the slippery Orchestra leader avoided each one. However, the Little Chief—Edward Kent—was captured in Marseilles, in southern France, when betrayed by an Orchestra member.

Aware that the Rote Kapelle had been nearly decimated and that German agents were hot on his trail, the clever Trepper concocted an ingenious plot: he arranged to "die" and have his own funeral, together with a fake death certificate, staged in a small town outside Paris. He had even prepared an obituary to be sent to local newspapers after his "death."

Before being "buried and forgotten," however, Trepper kept an appointment with his Paris dentist. A terrified wife of an Orchestra member, under heavy grilling, disclosed that Big Chief had complained of a severe toothache and that her husband had recommended a certain dentist.

On the afternoon of November 24—a day before Trepper's "funeral"—the Big Chief was in the dentist's chair when Captain Piepe and a squad of men, weapons drawn, burst in.

As handcuffs were clamped on the unflappable Trepper, he merely remarked to Piepe: "You've done your work well."

Trepper was treated with respect in the hope of extracting important information. Each day, Piepe or another German counterintelligence officer sipped cognac and coffee with the Pole, swapped spy stories, and cleverly pried loose the names of more Rote Kapelle members.

In January 1943 Piepe reported to Berlin that the final remnants of the Soviet spy ring had been rounded up.

Meanwhile, Trepper agreed, or pretended to agree, to cooperate with a German intelligence scheme. Using the captured transmitters and their operators, a fake Rote Kapelle began sending carefully concocted messages to the GPU in Moscow. To an extent, the GPU was foolish enough to send back information on other Communist espionage networks in France and Belgium.

On September 13, 1943, ten months after his apprehension, the Big Chief, while in a Paris pharmacy, tricked his German escort and vanished.

The final curtain had been brought down on the Rote Kapelle, which had been tripped up by the painstaking efforts of the schoolteacher, Lieutenant Wilhelm Vauck, and his gifted codebreakers.[11]

A Miraculous Escape from Denmark

EARLY IN THE SUMMER OF 1941, Reginald Jones, chief of intelligence on the British Air Staff, received a telephone call from Squadron Leader S. D. Felkin, who was in charge of England's Royal Patriotic School, a center for interrogating prisoners of war and suspected enemy agents.

Jones was told that a Dane who had just arrived in England under mysterious circumstances was being held, and his story was so bizarre that the interrogators were highly suspicious. They wanted Jones to come to the school to check the technological aspects of the Dane's story.

Moreover, the Dane had brought with him some undeveloped film that, he said, he had taken of a radar station on Fanø Island in Denmark. Jones was eager to see the evidence of what could have been an advanced German radar code-named Freya. The sleuth was already involved in trying to determine what progress German scientists had made with radar aids to the German night-fighters that were taking a heavy toll of Royal Air Force bombers.

From various intelligence sources, Jones and his colleagues knew that the Germans' basic radar unit was the Freya, and if the Brits could study a photograph of the device they might be able to understand its performance and limitations. That information, in turn, could prove to be the key to unbuttoning the entire system of German night defenses against RAF bombers.

After Reginald Jones arrived at the Royal Patriotic School, he listened to the amazing story of the Dane: His name was Thomas Sneum, and he had been a lieutenant in the Royal Danish Air Service. He had escaped from Denmark after the German Wehrmacht seized the country in early 1940, but a few months later he decided to return to his estate on Fanø Island.

Sneum and a friend had discovered that another friend had a dismantled small airplane lying in a barn in the city of Odense, on Fyn Island in central Denmark. By that time, Sneum was anxious to get back into the war, so he and his first friend hatched a scheme to escape to England.

Based on the skills he had learned while in the air service, Sneum and the other man, working inside the barn, reassembled the plane, using bits and pieces of wire instead of fasteners. Then they stole from the Germans enough fuel to get them to England, which was beyond the range of the rickety aircraft's tank. So the Danes would carry extra gasoline in cans.

Now the two men were ready to depart. The plane was sitting inside the barn. As the coughing engine finally started (it had not functioned in a year), one man climbed into the front cockpit, and the other flung open the barn doors, then scrambled into the second cockpit. The plane taxied outside, charged straight ahead, and lifted off.

Sneum and his companion knew that a freight train passed nearby each morning at almost the same time and that it sounded its whistle at a road crossing. So the takeoff had been timed to coincide with the passing train, thereby masking the noise of the airplane engine from a nearby German headquarters.

The two men, both experienced pilots, set a course for England, a few hundred miles to the southwest across the North Sea. When they were about halfway to their destination, a cockpit instrument revealed that the fuel tank was nearly empty. Now came the most critical—and hazardous—part of the escapade. Sneum edged out of the cockpit and gingerly began inching along

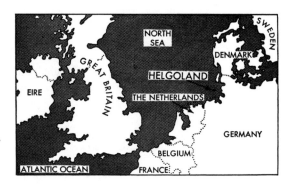

Two Danish patriots flew across the North Sea in an "impossible" feat to bring important intelligence to British scientists.

the wing, which was slippery with moisture. He hoped to insert the end of a hose into the tank, while his companion in the cockpit poured gasoline from the reserve cans into the hose.

Neither man knew if the procedure could be accomplished. Perhaps Sneum would fall off the wing and plunge to his death in the North Sea. In that case, his companion would also perish when the plane plummeted for lack of fuel. But the delicate technique did work, and the aircraft flew onward. Near England, they were intercepted by Royal Air Force fighter planes, which escorted the old aircraft to a landing field.

Now, after Thomas Sneum had told his story at the Royal Patriotic School, Reginald Jones was incredulous. None of the Britons could believe that the little aircraft had flown such a long distance, even after the refueling procedure was explained. Why weren't the extra fuel containers and the hose in the plane when it landed in England? Because they had pitched the items out after the transfer of the gasoline, Sneum explained.

Interrogators from MI-5, the British counterintelligence service, felt that Sneum and his companion had perpetrated a hoax hatched by the German Abwehr espionage agency to infiltrate two highly intelligent spies, whose mission was to gain the confidence of the British.

Despite his own skepticism, Jones withheld judgment until he had seen the undeveloped film Sneum said he had taken of the Freya back on Fanø Island. Jones was frustrated to learn that MI-5 agents had taken the film to a government agency to be processed and nearly all of it had been ruined.

Only two frames remained, but Jones was electrified when he saw them. The photos definitely were of a Freya in operation. Now the scientist was convinced that Sneum was a genuine patriot who had risked his life to snap pictures of the closely guarded German radar and to fly to England against all odds.

Jones clashed with the MI-5 men. They still thought Sneum was a spy and wanted to lock him up. But Jones extracted the Dane from their clutches and did his best to make up for the horrible treatment he had received since arriving in England.

Soon the film brought by Sneum helped Jones and his colleagues to unlock the mysteries of Freya and create countermeasures for jamming the German radar that was taking such a heavy toll on British bombers.[12]

Bright Ideas for Winning the War

IT WAS THE JOB of Great Britain's operational research scientists to come up with ingenious ideas for inflicting greater mayhem on the enemy, to save as many friendly lives as possible, and to eventually win the war against Nazi Germany and Fascist Italy. Often this coterie of gifted men (and a few women) received bizarre suggestions from journalists and the public at large. No matter how outlandish the ideas seemed for wiping out Adolf Hitler, Benito Mussolini, and their regimes, they received attention.

One scheme targeted Vesuvius, the only active volcano on the European mainland. It rises about seven miles southeast of Naples, Italy, and has erupted frequently over the centuries, spouting steam, cinders, and lava into the air. The greatest loss of life in recent years had occurred in 1906, when several entire towns were buried under countless tons of lava.

From Australia, South Africa, and the United States numerous highly educated people proposed that a deluge of bombs be dropped into the "throat" of Vesuvius, thereby "exploding southern Italy."

Other contributors from the civilian sector proposed ideas to abruptly halt advancing German or Italian soldiers. British bombers would drop "enormous quantities of sticky stuff," such as molasses, in front of the enemy troops. If that technique failed to halt them, follow-up flights of bombers would drop coils of barbed wire to "trip up and entangle soldiers."

A citizen in Durban suggested that "millions of poisonous snakes" be shipped from South Africa and released at night over Berlin and other major German cities. Yet another contributor proposed that millions of cabbage leaves be saturated with a lethal poison and dropped among livestock in German and Italian pastures, thereby creating famines in those two nations.

Numerous idea donators devised schemes for use by the Royal Air Force. A fleet of thirty or forty fighter planes would pretend to flee when confronted by enemy aircraft. While presumably hightailing it away from combat, these British planes would "squirt out from their rears" a spray of chloroform. Pursuing German pilots, sensing a British disaster, would fly into this concoction, lapse into unconsciousness, and their planes would crash.

Yet another proposal contemplated fitting "long projecting knives of razor sharpness" to the underbellies of airplanes. Thus equipped, "they could chase the enemy airmen who bailed out of disabled aircraft and fly over them in such

A British idea was to "wipe out southern Italy" by dropping bombs down Mount Vesuvius near Naples. (Author's collection)

a way that the knives would cut their parachute cords." This would cause the Germans to plunge to their deaths.

One contributor of a freakish scheme for defeating the Germans and Italians concluded his presentation by predicting: "The war will finish at 2:30 P.M. on May 4, 1945, with Britain on top."

Amazingly, nearly four years in advance of the actual German surrender, the man had missed the conclusion of the conflict in Europe by only seventy-two hours.[13]

Operation Jay: An Intricate Hoax

SOON AFTER Winston Churchill had been appointed as prime minister in the spring of 1940, he promptly took steps to launch an air offensive against the Third Reich. At the time, Great Britain had been hanging on by her fingernails and under a dire threat of imminent invasion by the German armed forces.

Churchill, known as the British Bulldog, had sent a letter to Lord Beaverbrook (born William Maxwell Aitken), a wealthy newspaper baron who had accepted the crucial post of minister of aircraft production:

> Without an army capable of confronting the Germans on the Continent, there is only one way that we can defeat the Third Reich. And that is an absolutely devastating, exterminating attack by heavy bombers from this country upon the Nazi homeland. We must be able to overwhelm him by this means, without which I do not see a way to [win the war].

By mid-1941, Bomber Command of the Royal Air Force had been sending raids over Germany for nearly a year and a half. But only now did Churchill get around to ordering an official study to assess the true accuracy of the bombing missions.

Handed the task was Davis Bensusan-Butt, a member of the War Cabinet Secretariat. Over a period of weeks, he and a team of experts evaluated some six hundred photographs taken from bombers equipped with cameras at night over the targets.

On August 18, 1941, Butt submitted his shocking report. On raids over the Third Reich in June and July, only 25 percent of the crews claiming to have hit their targets had actually done so. In attacks against the region known as the Ruhr, where the industrial might of Germany was harnessed to supply the Nazi war machine, only one bomb in ten had fallen within five miles of the target. Numerous flights had gotten lost in the black skies over the Third Reich.

Bomber Command's primary problem lay in navigation. Radio beams from England provided a fix for the bombers for only two hundred miles or less. Once past that limit, a navigator had to plot his course based on the airplane's speed and the estimated wind velocity.

The Butt report triggered an uproar in the high circles of British government. Influential critics called for disbanding Bomber Command and assigning its aircraft and crews to the army and the navy. Winston Churchill, too, was stunned by the report. Yet he backed Bomber Command and directed Britain's scientists to develop sophisticated navigational aids as rapidly as possible.

Soon engineers led by R. J. Dippy at the Telecommunications Research Establishment put the final touches on a new and vastly improved radio navigational aid known as Gee, named for the first letter in the word "grid."

Gee divided Europe into a radio grid, theoretically enabling bomber navigators using special Gee charts and cathode-ray tubes to fix their positions without visual landmarks. The system involved sending synchronized radio pulses from three ground stations in England, guiding bombers to targets more than four hundred miles from their bases.

Secret trials of Gee were conducted over England and far out into the Atlantic Ocean. But the chiefs at the Air Staff were dubious, even though the results were encouraging.

Consequently, Gee receivers were covertly fitted into three bombers, which were sent over Germany without Air Chief Marshal Charles Portal, the RAF's top uniformed officer, and his Air Staff being notified in advance. Crews returning from the mission were unstinting in their praise for how Gee had helped the flights to find their way to the targets.

Now it was decided at Bomber Command to continue to use these three Gee-equipped aircraft as pathfinders to mark the targets with flares for the main armadas on several missions over the Third Reich.

On the night of August 13, 1941, a haunting message reached England. One of the three Gee bombers had been shot down over Germany. Wreckage of the airplane could provide German air intelligence officers with stark evidence that the Royal Air Force was adopting a new technique for finding targets at night or in cloudy weather. Armed with this information, the Germans could then develop countermeasures to thwart Gee, which would not be available for general use in the RAF for another seven months.

News of the incident set off a major flap at the Air Staff's headquarters because the RAF was either going to be committed to using Gee for most of 1942, or it would have to continue using the existing primitive techniques, which had proven so inaccurate.

Air Chief Marshal Portal, who had been hailed by Winston Churchill as "the accepted star of the RAF," was livid over the top-secret Gee receiver falling into German hands and the fact that he had not been informed about the trial air missions.

Now he directed Henry Tizard, scientific adviser to the Air Staff, to convene a meeting of the experts to decide what was to be done about the Germans presumably having a Gee receiver in their hands.

At the solemn conference, Reginald Jones, the Air Staff's intelligence chief, expressed the opinion that there was only one chance in three that the Germans could have extricated a functioning Gee receiver at the crash site. The device may have been damaged by the impact or by the demolition charge with which it had been fitted for just such an emergency.

Jones felt that the main danger lay in the fact that some seventy-five RAF bombers had been shot down or crash-landed over Germany since the first Gee receiver had been installed in a bomber and the device had been lost. Consequently, an unknown number of British airmen (perhaps twenty or thirty) who knew about Gee were now in German prisoner-of-war camps.

What especially worried the scientists was the fact that the Germans might have overheard some reference to Gee when eavesdropping on the POWs' conversations, and this would provide a clue for them to closely investigate the wreckage of any bomber from that particular squadron in the future.

Tizard instructed Reginald Jones to create a scheme that would "throw the Boches [Germans] off the track" until Gee would be fitted in most bombers seven months later. Jones eagerly accepted the challenge. With such enormous stakes involved (the long-range bombing campaign that might decide the war), he was assured that he could draw on almost any of Great Britain's resources within reason.

Jones's first step was to "erase" the word Gee from the German scientists' lexicon. To achieve that goal, he planted clues to coerce his opposite numbers in Berlin into deducing that Bomber Command was introducing an entirely different type of navigational system, a tactic to detract the Germans' focus from Gee.

Jones located a few radio-beam transmitters that had been used to guide Bomber Command raids across the Channel to Brest, France. Using his new-found clout, he ordered these beams to be relocated on the eastern coast of England.

Making certain that the highly efficient German Y Service, which monitored British radios, believed that a new (phony) navigational system was being installed, he gave the setup the name Jay Beams, or Jay for short.

There had been good reason for selecting the title Jay. Jones and his colleagues hoped that it would mislead the Germans in the event they had bugged an RAF POW camp and overheard British airmen referring to Gee. Again, hopefully, the Germans would believe that they had misheard the prisoners and that the Britons had actually been talking about Jay. German translators would reason that the British dialect had caused them to hear Gee when they had really heard Jay.

Knowing that German electronic monitors would pick up the Jay beams, RAF bombers were urged to use the beams while going and coming on missions, a subtle touch to add to the authenticity of the hoax.

At the same time that these machinations were unfolding, German spies who had been captured in England since the outbreak of war provided Jones with a channel to send fake information to the Third Reich. Within hours of Britain's declaration of war on September 3, 1939, agents of MI-5 (the counterespionage agency) and sleuths from Scotland Yard had fanned out over the British Isles in a mammoth roundup of German spies. The British spybusters had their hands full: there had been 365 names on their Class A espionage list.

Some of the German agents had been deep under cover after having been planted in England four or five years earlier by German intelligence. After the nationwide dragnet had hauled in nearly all of Hitler's spies, many of them went to the gallows. Scores more were now awaiting execution.

What an enormous waste of potential benefit to the British Empire, thought twenty-nine-year-old Major Thomas A. Robertson, who had served with distinction while fighting on the Continent with the Seaforth Highlanders in 1940. After being evacuated from Dunkirk, Tar, as he was known to friends, had mysteriously vanished. Actually, he had joined MI-5, and his name had been stricken from British Army rolls, as though he had never existed.

Major Robertson conceived an idea for a deception scheme whereby German spies captured in England, instead of being hanged, buried, and forgotten, would be put to work double-crossing their former Nazi handlers. Using his ample charm and eloquence, Robertson convinced the Air Staff and Air Intelligence that a live double-crosser would bolster the war effort far more than would a dead spy.

All captured spies would be given two choices. They could be hanged within a few days, or they could radio phony information to their former masters in the Third Reich. Nearly all of them quickly decided they would do the bidding of their captors.

These double agents would be orchestrated by a top-secret British deception group quite appropriately named the Twenty Committee. Twenty in Roman numerals is XX, so the panel was usually called the XX Committee (Double-Cross Committee).

When collared, the spies had been taken to the XX Committee's interrogation center at Latchmere House, a former convalescent home for "shell-shocked" British officers in World War I. After learning that they could save themselves from the gallows, the captives eagerly told their British controllers (also known as case officers) where they had hidden their Afu shortwave radios and disclosed their secret codes for sending messages to Germany.

As yet another key component of Operation Jay, Reginald Jones got in touch with a friend at the XX Committee and suggested that turned spies, whom the Abwehr in the Third Reich would believe were still roaming freely in England, be used to radio back misleading information.

With Jones's aid, scripts were carefully prepared by clever minds in the XX Committee. The scriptwriter had to be exceptionally careful to make certain that a lone German agent could not have gathered information that was too detailed and difficult to obtain, or his German controllers would have grown deeply suspicious and concluded that the agent had been captured and turned.

Using their own suitcase-size Afu transmitters and personal codes, the spies radioed the specified phony information while XX Committee case officers sat at their elbows to make certain that the Germans, not the British, were double-crossed.

The first transmission Jones had suggested involved a nonexistent conversation the spy would claim he had overheard between two RAF pilots at the bar in a posh London hotel. A touch of authenticity was injected into the message by situating the two Britons in a place where it could be expected that their tongues had been loosened by alcoholic drinks.

In the prepared script, one RAF officer was to be projected as quite angry, complaining: "Why did Colonel Blank get a high medal? All he did was copy the German beams—and a year after they came out with them!" Replied his drinking partner: "Well, you'll have to admit that we now have the Jay beams to get us to our targets. They worked fine for us at Brest [France], and we'll soon have them over Germany."

In another fake transmission hatched by Jones, a turned German spy was supposed to have been talking with an RAF junior officer who told him that a "Professor Ekkerley" had been giving lectures to Bomber Command units on the new "Jerry" navigational system. Again, a lone spy could not be totally accurate. XX Committee case officers hoped that the German controllers would deduce that "Ekkerley" was Professor T. L. Eckersley, who was Great Britain's foremost expert in radio waves. Moreover, the idea was for the Germans to conclude that "Jerry" actually meant "Jay."

A few days later, the Hamburg branch of the Abwehr, which was responsible for espionage in Great Britain and the United States, radioed enthusiastic praise to the two German agents who had risked their lives for the führer and produced such high-grade intelligence.

Reginald Jones would never know for certain if his Operation Jay had paid off. However, much concrete evidence would surface in the months ahead that the intricate deception scheme had bamboozled the Abwehr and the German scientists. Ultra picked up a report that an air signals experimental regiment had been set up by the Germans along the English Channel coast in France to investigate the Jay beams.[14]

England's "Kamikaze" Pilots

In mid-1941 a group of experienced Royal Air Force pilots from Fighter Command congregated at an airfield in England's Northwest for an assignment cloaked in deep secrecy. For nearly two hours, the airmen, in the words of one, "wandered around the mess, trying to decide which chap appeared to be so intelligent that he would know something about the job for which we had volunteered."

That afternoon, the curious pilots gathered to hear their commander, Squadron Leader Louis Strange, explain their unique—and hazardous—duty. He pointed out that heavy convoy losses came not only from U-boats and occasional surface raiders but also from long-range Luftwaffe aircraft in the Atlantic and standard bombers along the Arctic route carrying accoutrements of war to the Soviet Union.

To combat these Luftwaffe planes, the volunteer pilots were being formed into one of the strangest outfits in the Royal Air Force: the Merchant Ship Fighter Unit (MSFU). Centerpiece of the innovative operation was a fascinating apparatus new to warfare and developed by British scientists and aeronautic engineers.

Designed to protect the convoys, thirty-five vessels were fitted with catapults on the bows. The catapult consisted of an eighty-five-foot runway, along which a trolley carrying a Hurricane (later Hurricat) fighter plane was forced

A Royal Air Force "kamikaze" pilot is catapulted by a newfangled rocket-power device. (National Archives)

by a battery of three-inch rockets over a diameter of sixty feet. Using thirty-degree wing flaps, a pilot could make a perfect takeoff without losing height.

These specially designed vessels were called Catapult Aircraft Merchant ships (CAM ships, for short). Although engaged in normal cargo-carrying duties, they would provide protection for the convoy against Luftwaffe bombers.

It soon became obvious to the MSFU pilots that they were to be the Royal Air Force's version of what the Japanese would later call kamikaze (suicide) pilots. Every launching from a CAM ship was a one-way ride. Usually the Hurricane was so far from land that the pilot had to bail out over the ocean or try to stay with the plane as he ditched it. If all went well—a big "if"—the pilot would ride the waves in an inflatable dinghy until picked up by a passing ship—if any.

On one occasion, Flying Officer Alastair Hay catapulted from a CAM ship while traveling in a convoy bound for the Soviet Union north of Norway in the Arctic. He was credited with destroying a Heinkel bomber and damaging two other German planes. During the encounters, Hay was wounded in the thigh, and his Hurricat was badly damaged. But he parachuted to the ocean and found himself in luck: he came down almost next to a friendly vessel and was fished out of the water within minutes.

By the time the CAM ships were replaced on convoy duty by new escort carriers in 1943, the Hurricats had bagged seven Luftwaffe aircraft and chased away scores of others.[15]

Part Three

Thrust and Counterthrust

Could Pearl Harbor
Have Been Avoided?

IN WASHINGTON, D.C., early in the afternoon of December 7, 1941, Admiral Harold Stark, chief of naval operations, bolted into the office of Secretary of the Navy Frank Knox.

"The Japs have hit Pearl Harbor!" Stark blurted.

"My God," replied the stunned Knox, "this can't be true!"

Two hours later, Prime Minister Winston Churchill in London placed a telephone call to Franklin Roosevelt. "Mr. President, what's this about Japan?"

"It's quite true," was the reply. "We're all in the same boat now!"

"This actually simplifies things," the prime minister declared. "God be with you!"

Churchill, knowing that he now had a potentially powerful ally in the shooting war, went to bed and slept soundly.

Within hours, Washington learned the full extent of the disaster at Pearl. Except for two aircraft carriers and some twenty warships that were at sea, almost the entire Pacific Fleet and the air corps in Hawaii had been virtually wiped out.

Edward R. Murrow, a CBS correspondent who had gained fame during the past year by sending back to the United States on shortwave radio eyewitness accounts of the Luftwaffe Blitz of London, had been invited with his wife to dinner with the Roosevelts that evening. His wife phoned the White House: Were they still expected?

Eleanor Roosevelt replied, "We all have to eat. Come anyway."

After dinner, President Roosevelt pounded the table in his study as he described to Murrow how the U.S. ships had been caught sleeping and scores of airplanes were destroyed "on the ground, by God, on the ground!"

Could the Pearl Harbor debacle have been avoided or a heavy toll taken on the Japanese? Months later, American codebreakers would discover that could have been the case.

Between the time that Adolf Hitler had plunged Europe into war in 1939 and late 1941, Congress ladled out codebreaking funds by the spoonful. In that two-year period, usually only two, and never more than five, cryptanalysts were assigned to try to crack Japanese naval codes. At the same time, the Germans and the Japanese had assigned hundreds of specialists to try to break enemy ciphers.

During the last half of 1941, the codebreaking staff in the Navy Building in Washington, D.C., had in its hands hundreds of messages in the Japanese naval code, known as JN25. But this raft of potentially crucial intelligence had to be filed because there were not enough cryptanalysts to work at unlocking its secrets.

After the United States was bombed into war, the navy cryptanalyst staff was beefed up and JN25 was eventually solved. There were shocking disclosures. In the intercepts just prior to the sneak attack on Pearl Harbor, there were details of a powerful Japanese naval force, including six aircraft carriers, that had steamed from the home islands in the direction of Hawaii.[1]

The British Invade Washington

FIVE DAYS after the Japanese wreaked havoc on the U.S. Pacific Fleet, Hans Thomsen, a zealous Nazi and chargé d'affaires at the German embassy in Washington, received a cable from his boss, Foreign Minister Joachim von Ribbentrop, in Berlin. Thomsen's title was a cover for his true role, chief masterspy in the United States. It was December 12, 1941.

Thomsen was warned in the cable not to "commit some indiscretion" that might tip off Washington leaders what Adolf Hitler planned to do the next day: declare war on the United States.

"We wish to avoid under all circumstances," Ribbentrop stated, "that the government there beats us to such a step."

When the führer called the Reichstag into session to rubber-stamp his intention to go to war against the United States, he thundered to the cheering deputies, "We will always strike first! We will always deal the first blow!"

Hitler spent most of his speech hurling insults at President Franklin Roosevelt. "This man alone, backed by the millionaires and Jews, is responsible for the Second World War!" he thundered.

A day later, Hitler's crony Italian dictator Benito Mussolini also declared war against the United States.

A week before Christmas 1941, British Field Marshal John Dill arrived in grim, snow-blanketed Washington to take up his new duties as senior liaison officer. Dill was shocked.

"This country is the most highly organized for peace that you can imagine," Dill cabled London. "This country has not—repeat not—the slightest conception of what war means, and their armed forces are more unready for war than it is possible to imagine. . . . The whole organization belongs to the days of George Washington."

Soon after Christmas, Washington was "invaded" by the British for the first time since the Redcoats burned and sacked the capital one hundred and thirty years earlier in what was known as the War of 1812. This time, the English, led by Prime Minister Winston Churchill, came as allies. The purpose of the "invasion" was to integrate the war interests and operations of the two English-speaking nations.

President Roosevelt and Churchill hit it off well. Both were outgoing, expansive men who enjoyed hearing an occasional risqué joke and imbibing during cocktail hour—and at other times. It was perhaps at one of these relaxing sessions at the close of the workday that Churchill disclosed the existence of history's most colossal intelligence bonanza: Ultra. And Roosevelt, no doubt at the same time, revealed the secret of Magic, code name for the decrypts of the Japanese Purple Code.

Royal Air Force Squadron Leader Frederick Winterbotham, whose sole function was to protect the security of Ultra, had strongly questioned the wisdom of disclosing the secret to anyone, including the Americans. They were incredibly lax in such matters, he argued. However, after assurances were sought and pledged that neither the British nor the Americans would employ Ultra-Magic decrypts in circumstances that might cause the Germans or the Japanese to suspect that their secret messages were being read, a pact was reached.

The British would concentrate on penetrating Germany's Enigma code, while the Americans would focus on the Japanese ciphers. To hide even the existence of Ultra, it was agreed that all of its signals disseminated to various commands for operational purposes would be called Magic. So if German intelligence became suspicious through American security lapses that Enigma had been penetrated, the Germans would conclude, hopefully, that it was the fault of the Japanese and continue to use Enigma.

After the Ultra-Magic agreement had been reached and the British delegation returned home, Alan Turing, one of the two men who had spearheaded the creation of Ultra, came to the United States to demonstrate to his American counterparts how his complex machine worked. In return, the Americans carried to England a copy of the device that had helped penetrate the Japanese Purple Code. At the same time, American cipher clerks and cryptographers began to descend on Bletchley Park, the supersecret base of Ultra north of London.

Despite these cooperative actions, the British continued to remain apprehensive about the agreement. With its huge land area and a population several times as large as that of England, along with the unbridled media, the United States would not be able to enforce the same tight degree of security that was possible in Britain.

However, the die had been cast. For better or for worse, the United States was now a full partner in the two nations' cryptographic operations.[2]

A Scheme to Bomb New York

NOW THAT the sleeping giant the United States was directly involved in what was being called World War II, Nazi bigwigs in Berlin were anxious to strike a blow against the newcomers. So Field Marshal Erhard Milch, Reichsmarschall Hermann Goering's deputy in the Luftwaffe, consulted with his scientists and came up with a fantastic scheme that he was convinced would please Adolf Hitler. Milch planned to bomb New York City, which was nearly four thousand miles from the Third Reich.

German engineers and designers had developed an airplane that theoretically could fly that far, but could not return. So the portly, energetic Milch, who loathed his boss Goering and idolized Hitler, conceived a plan to compensate for the lack of technology with regard to distance.

Milch had his scientists attach a light bomber under the belly of the new long-range airplane. Once the piggyback tandem flew to a point a short distance from New York City, the smaller aircraft would disengage from its parent and cover the remaining distance until it was over Manhattan's forest of skyscrapers. Then the plane would drop its single bomb, turn, and fly back out to sea. At a designated point, the aircraft would ditch in the ocean and its crew would be picked up by a waiting U-boat.

In typical bureaucratic style, Milch's plan was bounced from one department to another within the German high command. It eventually died for lack of nourishment, partly because the Kriegsmarine was reluctant to part with one or more U-boats for what its leaders considered to be a crackpot scheme.[3]

Five U.S. Scientists Killed

ADMIRAL KARL DOENITZ, *führer der U-Boote* (leader of submarines), launched on January 12, 1942, Operation Paukenschlag (Roll of the Drums), which was designed to knock the United States out of the war by blockading her ports along the eastern seaboard. Doenitz selected eleven of his ace skippers to create havoc.

As reports flowed in from Nazi harbor spies in the United States and from the B-Dienst (a German wireless monitoring network), Doenitz, like a chessmaster adroitly moving pawns, shifted his underwater craft up and down America's Atlantic coast.

Just before midnight on January 16, blond, handsome Leutnant Reinhard Hardegan boldly surfaced his U-boat off the port of New York. Through highpowered infrared binoculars, he was mesmerized by the dazzling sight before him. Although the United States had been at war for more than a month, Manhattan was aglow with thousands of lights that twinkled in the night like fire-flies.

"It's unbelievable!" Hardegan exclaimed to his second officer, Horst von Schroeter.

In a whimsical radio signal to Admiral Doenitz in France, Hardegan stated that he could discern couples blissfully dancing the night away on the roof of the ornate Astor Hotel in Times Square.

During daylight hours, Hardegan's *U-123* nestled silently at the bottom of one hundred feet of water off Wimble Shoal outside of New York City. His radioman reported sounds of ships overhead.

"*Mein Gott!*" the skipper exploded. "Can you imagine what we could do with ten U-boats here [New York Harbor]?"

The U-boat campaign was devastating. The loss of Allied merchant vessels and hundreds of crew members along the Atlantic coast of the United States during the next few months was a national disaster comparable to saboteurs blowing up eight or ten of America's largest war plants.

Soon the U-boats became bolder. Instead of attacking only at night, they now sank ships by daylight, often within view of shore. Thousands of bathers at Coney Island in New York City, Virginia Beach, Virginia, and Miami Beach, Florida, looked on in horror as Allied ships were torpedoed and sunk.

In Berlin, Nazi propaganda minister Josef Goebbels boasted over the radio: "German heroism conquers even the widest oceans!"

The U.S. high command was stunned by the carnage along the eastern seaboard. There were no means to counter the threat. Years of American apathy toward its armed forces had left the navy, like the army, ill prepared for war.

Worse, the catastrophe on what Hitler called the "American Front" was inflicted by only a handful of U-boats; no more than twelve had been in action at any one time. Each undersea craft carried fourteen torpedoes, many of them a revolutionary electrically propelled type that left no wake or air bubbles, a contribution to the führer by German scientists. Often the first indication that a merchant ship was under attack was the concussion of a direct hit.

Nervous admirals in Washington enlisted the aid of several scientists, who concluded from operations analyses that airplanes and blimps could be more effective than surface craft in knocking out U-boats.

When a patrolling aircraft detected a submarine, studies disclosed, the U-boat left the scene before planes could be called to bomb the underwater craft. So the scientists developed float lights that marked the spot where the U-boat had been so that when a bomber rushed to the scene, it could track and destroy the intruder.

Experiments also were conducted of underwater flares to be dropped by blimps or planes to illuminate submerged U-boats at night. While two U.S. Navy blimps were operating off the New Jersey coast testing the underwater flares on the night of June 8, 1942, there was a collision in midair. Both blimps crashed into the sea, killing all on board except for one navy officer.

Among the casualties were five scientists of the National Defense Research Committee: Israel H. Tilles, Lawrence S. Moyer, Arthur B. Wyse, Franklin C. Gilbert, and Charles R. Hoover. They had died for their country as surely as soldiers in the front lines, pilots in air combat, or sailors in a sea battle.[4]

Mystery of the Vanishing U-Boats

DURING THE FIRST six months of 1942, German submarines sank 585 Allied ships. Only six U-boats had been lost. It had been a magnificent hunting season throughout the Atlantic Ocean for the energetic U-boat skippers, but then Admiral Doenitz, the submarine service leader, began to detect strange happenings.

Doenitz's first clue came when the *U-82* was on its way back to its base in France from an extended Atlantic patrol. Its skipper sighted a small convoy a hundred miles west of the Bay of Biscay. He radioed that the convoy appeared to be only lightly escorted, and that he was getting ready to . . .

Then the U-boat's signals stopped abruptly. Something had seemingly destroyed the submarine so suddenly that it had not had time to send even a distress call.

Doenitz and his aides were puzzled by the event, but it was soon brushed off as one of those unexplained mysteries of war. However, a month later, in the same general region of the Atlantic, the *U-587* radioed that it was shadowing a small convoy. Then the submarine vanished.

Now Doenitz grew concerned that some strange situation was unfolding in the Atlantic. So, three weeks later, when a third boat, the *U-252*, flashed an identical message, the admiral went to the unusual action of personally radioing the skipper to be extremely careful. The *U-252* was never heard from again.

A worried Doenitz made it a point to personally interrogate all the skippers who returned from Atlantic patrols, in an effort to unravel the baffling riddle of the disappearing U-boats, but he could not uncover a clue.

Only much later would the admiral learn that British scientists had developed a startling new capability for finding U-boats on the surface, even in foul weather and at night. This defensive system consisted of a greatly improved radar mounted in aircraft, combined with the Leigh light, named for its inventor, Humphrey de Verde Leigh.

Previously, RAF pilots could not detect U-boats on the surface at night, and in the day, lookouts on the deck could usually spot a patrolling aircraft in plenty of time for the submarine to dive.

A British technician cleans the lens of a Leigh light fitted under the wing of an RAF bomber. (National Archives)

Later it would be learned that the first of the "vanishing" U-boats had been cruising on the surface at night when the deck watch heard an approaching airplane. No precautions were taken, because the skipper was convinced his submarine could not be detected.

Suddenly the comforting blackness was pierced by a strong beam from a searchlight (the Leigh light) mounted under a wing of a Royal Air Force bomber. Before the U-boat captain had time to react, his vessel was hit by bombs and soon sank, taking the crew with it.

When mounting evidence convinced Doenitz that the British were employing revolutionary defensive tactics against his U-boats, he urged German scientists to develop a countermeasure. They soon created Metox, a device that detected approaching aircraft through radar emanations and enabled the U-boats to dive and escape destruction.

Each U-boat was equipped with a receiver connected to a makeshift direction-finding antenna or wire wrapped around a wooden frame. This device, when installed on the conning tower of a surfaced submarine, picked up incoming radar signals from RAF planes and sent them to the receiver, warning the skipper to submerge immediately before the patrolling bomber arrived.[5]

The Germans' Four-Poster Beds

DURING THE LAST half of 1941 in Europe, the Royal Air Force Bomber Command was sending missions over the Third Reich almost nightly and in steadily increasing numbers. The British were paying a ghastly price. Some bombers were shot down by German antiaircraft fire, but two-thirds of the destroyed planes were the victims of Luftwaffe nightfighters.

British electronic engineers suspected that the Germans had radar: How else could their night fighters be so deadly unless they were being guided to RAF bombers by radar? Until now, the British had thought they had a monopoly on this invaluable system, which had played a key role in defeating the Luftwaffe in the bitter Battle of Britain the previous year.

However, if the Germans had developed radar, where were the huge towers, like the chain of them along England's southern and eastern coasts? Was the Reich using radar that did not require tall towers—or no towers?

In an effort to provide answers to these haunting questions, the British launched an all-out investigative campaign. The Royal Air Force Photographic Reconnaissance Unit (PRU) took thousands of low-level pictures of suspected radar facilities in sweeps over Germany and Nazi-occupied countries in western Europe.

British agents on the Continent contacted French, Belgian, and Dutch underground groups and urged them to watch for any curious-looking towers or other facilities the Germans might have built. In England, barracks holding Luftwaffe prisoners of war were bugged.

RAF bombers dropped homing pigeons during missions over the Continent. Tiny printed slips were clamped to the birds' legs, requesting finders to report any unusual German apparatus that could not be identified. If any were detected, the person was to write a brief description and location and send it to England via a pigeon.

Conjecture by British scientists and RAF air intelligence would prove to be well founded. With radar as the key component, the Germans had built a highly sophisticated air-defense line that extended 650 miles, from the northern tip of Denmark southward along the western borders of Germany, the Netherlands, and Belgium to the Swiss-Italian boundary.

Principal architect of this monumental technological achievement was Major General Josef Kammhuber, who had been ordered by Reichsmarschall Hermann Goering to accelerate the enormous project, designed to take a heavy toll on RAF bomber streams winging toward targets in the Third Reich.

Kammhuber had been given the highest priority in manpower, materials, Dezimeter Telegraphie (radar), searchlights, antiaircraft guns, and nightfighters. The air-defense barrier became known to the British as the Kammhuber Line.

The key to the Kammhuber Line's success was the Würzburger Reise (Giant Würzburg), one of the Reich's most closely guarded secrets. Beside each

Giant Würzburg was placed a cache of explosives, which was to be used to blow up the device in the event of a British raid to capture it. The new equipment replaced the standard Würzburg, which had been developed in the late 1930s under cover of the German post office to mask its existence. The Giant Würzburg could track a swiftly moving airplane with great precision, and its twenty-four-mile range was double that of an earlier model.

The Kammhuber Line consisted of a series of "radio boxes," with each box about eighteen miles long. Code-named Himmelbett (four-poster bed), each box had two Giant Würzburgs and one Freya, a radar that could reach farther than the Würzburg but that could not determine aircraft altitude. The three radar devices were arranged in a triangle, and in its center was a small building housing the Himmelbett's ground controller.

When early-warning systems along the Channel coast reported the approach of British bombers, one Me-110 or Me-109 nightfighter in each box took off and began circling its Himmelbett. The fighter was tracked by one of the Würzburgs, and its pilot was in contact by radiotelephone with his Himmelbett ground controller.

When hostile bombers neared the Himmelbett, the second Giant Würzburg took a fix on them, and they appeared on the controller's screen as a red blob. All the while, the first Würzburg continued to track the circling Messerschmitt fighter, which showed as a blue blob on the controller's screen. Then the controller, by radiotelephone, "talked" the fighter plane (the blue blob) into contact with the British bombers (the red blob).

The Germans had a name for a British bomber caught alone in one of the boxes: *helle Nachtjagd* (illuminated night fighting). Almost invariably, the trapped bomber was shot down.

Scientists at the Telecommunications Research Establishment (TRE) in England volunteered as observers for hazardous bomber flights into and around the Kammhuber Line, in an ongoing effort to uncover clues regarding possible German radar. They were given commissions in the RAF in the event they had to parachute or crash-land on missions over the Continent.

One of the TRE volunteers, Howard Cundall, was in an airplane that was flying over France on November 4, 1941, when an antiaircraft burst sent shrapnel through an engine. Everyone had to bail out, and they landed routinely.

Alone and in pairs, the Britons roamed around the region for two weeks and escaped capture. Cundall reached the coastline in Normandy and spotted a rowboat. He attached a makeshift sail to the craft in an effort to cross the often tricky English Channel, but he was detected by a German patrol and taken into custody.

Eventually, all who had parachuted from the damaged airplane were captured, except for the pilot, who finally made it to Spain and then back to England. German intelligence officers counted heads and decided that the entire bomber crew was in custody, which was fortunate for Howard Cundall. The captors did not suspect that he was a scientist and had been along on a special undercover mission.

Soon Cundall was ensconced in a POW camp, and he gave his job description on the airplane as gunner. In the months ahead he was able to continue to conceal the fact that he had special knowledge of British radar. Using components smuggled into the camp one or two at a time, the enterprising officer built a radio transmitter over which he was able to establish contact with an intelligence facility in England.

While careful not to confide in a "plant" (an English-speaking German put in the POW camp to eavesdrop), Cundall held numerous conferences with RAF inmates who had just been captured. He kept his contact in England informed about the newcomers' experiences with German air defenses and nightfighters before they themselves had been shot down. Therefore Cundall was able to aid the ongoing effort to pry out the secrets of the Kammhuber Line so that countermeasures could be developed.

In the meantime, members of Belgium's Armée Secrète had been risking their lives to collect information about the Kammhuber Line. These underground warriors had been asked to concentrate on searchlight positions. After a site had been identified and word reached England, RAF reconnaissance planes would swoop in to photograph it.

To transfer these secret reports to England, underground groups in western Europe established a chain of couriers that ran from Belgium southwestward to Lisbon, in neutral Portugal. One courier in France, a locomotive fireman, was especially innovative. He hid the priceless information under the coal in the bin. On one occasion, Germans halted the train to inspect it, so the fireman simply shoveled coal and the incriminating underground reports into the firebox as Gestapo agents climbed into the locomotive.

One day Reginald Jones, the intelligence chief of the Air Staff, was perusing the Belgian underground reports that had arrived by RAF plane from Lisbon. Unfolding a large sheet of paper, he held his breath in astonishment. It was a detailed map showing the deployment of hundreds of searchlights in the Kammhuber Line throughout southern Belgium. The map was an intelligence bonanza.

Jones and his colleagues would never learn for sure how the map (stamped Top Secret) got into the hands of the Armée Secrète. But applying the logic used in their technical work, they concluded that one or more Belgian resistants had burglarized a German headquarters and pilfered the map. They also deduced that the German commander failed to report the theft to his superiors for fear of a severe penalty—possibly execution.

Although the map had belonged to a German searchlight regimental headquarters, it also had plotted the positions of the Giant Würzburg and Freya radar stations.

A few weeks after the pilfered map had reached British hands, the Belgian Armée Secrète radioed London that all of the hundreds of searchlights in the Kammhuber Line had mysteriously vanished. RAF reconnaissance planes confirmed the curious act: photographs showed empty emplacements.

Only much later would the perplexing puzzle be solved. Adolf Hitler himself had ordered the powerful searchlights to be brought back to Germany and emplaced around major cities.

Early in the war, Reichsmarschall Hermann Goering had loudly boasted that no British bomb would ever fall on the Third Reich. Now, with the RAF stepping up its raids over Germany, Hitler wanted to show civilians that he was doing something tangible to defend them.

During the next few weeks, the Photographic Reconnaissance Unit pilots flew many low-level missions over Belgium to take pictures of the radar stations shown on the stolen map. After studying these photos, Reginald Jones and his team concluded that the Kammhuber Line's effectiveness had not been diminished by the withdrawal of the searchlights—a fact the führer no doubt had been told before he issued the order. The radar stations alone had the technological capability of directing nightfighters to intercept British bombers.

By late fall of 1941, British scientists had obtained air reconnaissance photos of Freya sites along the Channel coast in France, and they pored over them in the hope of finding evidence of a Würzburg, which could determine both the height and the position of an airplane. The Würzburg, the sleuths were convinced, could be the key to the Germans' system of nightfighting along the Kammhuber Line.

One photo showed two Freyas situated at the top of a four-hundred-foot cliff at Bruneval on the Channel coast, about fifteen miles north of the major port of Le Havre. A track ran southward from the Freyas for several hundred yards to a large villa. These clues seemed to imply that the structure was the headquarters of the radar station and the track had been worn by traffic going between the villa and the Freyas.

However, Charles Frank, who had known Reginald Jones since boyhood and had been involved with him in numerous Air Intelligence projects even before war erupted in Europe, pointed out that the track did not run all the way to the villa but ended in a loop a hundred yards from the house. Next to the loop was a tiny speck.

With the suspicion that the speck might be a clue in unmasking the presence of Würzburgs along the Channel coast, a photoreconnaissance sortie was requested. Within hours, RAF Squadron Leader Anthony E. "Tony" Hill climbed into his Spitfire and set a course for Bruneval.

Hill belonged to a unique and elite group: the pilots of the Photographic Reconnaissance Unit, Britain's spies in the skies. He was dashing, charismatic, courageous—a role model for every schoolboy. On occasion, his Spitfire's camera would fail. On landing at his base, he would insist on going back to get a photo the next day, even though the Germans would have been alerted about British interest in their site.

At this stage of the war, taking low, oblique photos from an airplane was a difficult task. The camera was pointed sideways, and its lens was looking slightly aft from the fuselage just behind the cockpit. So a pilot, who often was under heavy antiaircraft fire, had to fly at low level toward the object to be photographed. That object would disappear from sight under the wing, and the pilot had to guess when it would show up again behind the wing and snap the shutter.

Now, when twenty-four-year-old Squadron Leader Hill approached Bruneval, his Spit was targeted by heavy gunfire from the ground. Clearly the Germans did not want low-flying British planes snooping around the locale. Hill made two runs at the "speck" and snapped pictures, then hightailed it for home.

After Hill's film was developed, British leaders were elated. The "speck" was a Giant Würzburg, the backbone of Germany's air defenses.[6]

The Century's Most Audacious Heist

ONLY HOURS AFTER Squadron Leader Tony Hill's discovery, RAF planes took hundreds of photographs of the Bruneval locale. The Giant Würzburg stood near the edge of the towering cliff and in front of an isolated mansion (code-named Lone House by MI-6) that was thought to be living quarters for the radar technicians.

About a quarter mile north of the Würzburg, a compound named La Presbytère housed about one hundred Feldgrau (field gray, after the color of their uniforms; the average German soldier) whose mission was to protect the precious radar installation.

After minutely studying the air reconnaissance photos, British scientists were stunned: here was proof that the Germans not only had radar, but also were probably ahead of the British in its advancement. Could the Giant Würzburg at Bruneval be stolen, dismantled, and returned to England during a British commando-type raid?

Prime Minister Winston Churchill promptly put his stamp of approval on the bold venture, and Rear Admiral Francis A. V. Nicholas (and later his successor Lord Louis Mountbatten), the chief of Combined Operations, eagerly prepared for the mission.

Nicholas and his staff realized one stark factor: the Würzburg was protected by fifteen machine-gun posts along the clifftop, so a frontal assault from the sea would be suicidal. Therefore the site would have to be entered through the "back door," by paratroopers.

Twelve Whitley bombers, led by Wing Commander Charles Pickard, would drop a force of 119 men under thirty-year-old Major John D. Frost. The paratroopers were to seize and dismantle the Giant Würzburg and secure the beach below the cliff. A small naval flotilla, under Australian Commander F. N. Cook, would evacuate the paratroopers and, it was hoped, the dismantled Würzburg. A contingent of 32 officers and men of the South Wales Borderers and the Royal Fusiliers would be aboard Cook's vessels to cover with fire the withdrawal of Frost's men down the steep cliff to the beach.

Someone with technical radar knowledge had to go on the raid, because if the Würzburg could not be dismantled, he would study the device before the raiders withdrew. Reginald Jones, scientific intelligence director on the Air Staff, and an associate, Derek Garrard, volunteered, but were rejected. They knew too much about British scientific projects to risk their capture.

D. H. Priestly, a capable scientist but one not so deeply involved in secrets, was chosen to land with the naval force. Doing the actual dismantling of the Würzburg would be RAF Flight Sergeant C. W. H. Cox.

Sergeant Cox was an unlikely candidate for the job of perpetrating the century's most audacious heist. He was the son of a mailman and a former actress. Before joining the RAF in 1940, he had been a movie projectionist. The closest he had come to violence was when he had shown old Al Capone gangster movies. Prior to the war, Cox had never been on a ship or an airplane, so he had never parachuted until given a crash course for the Bruneval mission.

When Cox had been mysteriously whisked away from his post at a radar station in southern England (without being told he had been selected for one of the war's most perilous raids), he was ordered to report for "special duty" to an air commodore. The officer said to the bewildered Cox, "Congratulations for volunteering for this mission." To this the brash sergeant replied, "Blimey, sir, I didn't *volunteer* for anything!"

On the afternoon of February 27, 1942, after a series of postponements because of bad weather, the operation was launched. Under a brilliant blue sky, Commander Cook's flotilla slipped into the English Channel and set a course for Bruneval, eighty miles distant.

Two hours prior to midnight, Major Frost and his paratroopers boarded the Whitleys in high spirits, eager to strike a telling blow at the Germans. They were unaware that Frost earlier had confided to an aide: "If the enemy gets an inkling of this operation, we shall all be doomed!"

An hour later, the sky over Bruneval was awash with scores of billowing white parachutes. After crashing hard onto the frozen, unyielding turf, the

"Lone House," on cliffs at Bruneval, was quarters for technicians who operated supersecret Würzburg radar (circular object near bottom left). (Courtesy General John D. Frost)

troopers rapidly formed into groups and silently stole through the night to carry out their predesignated assignments.

Johnny Frost and his contingent rushed to the Würzburg and took up defensive positions around it. Off to the north could be heard a heavy firearms fight. Forty paratroopers under Lieutenant John Timothy were engaging the one hundred Germans at La Presbytère.

Without wasting a moment, the unflappable Flight Sergeant Cox plunged into the intricate task of dismantling the Würzburg. He had been allotted one hour and thirty minutes to complete the job. Working by the dim beam of a flashlight, he dismantled the radar with surprising ease, and in fewer than fifty minutes he said evenly, "Well, it's done, mates!"

Components of the radar were rapidly piled into a two-wheeled cart. Moments later, mortar shells were exploding around Lone House and the Würzburg site. Three trucks, presumably loaded with German soldiers assigned to the region, were discerned moving toward the scene.

Major Frost gave orders to head for the evacuation beach four hundred feet below. Several troopers began pulling the cart across the plateau and toward a path that led down the cliffside. Negotiating the steep, icy slope was difficult, and the heavily loaded cart thrashed about. Then Germans holding the beach raked the cliffside with machine-gun fire, pinning down the descending para-troopers. Three bullets tore into Sergeant Major G. Strachan's stomach, and, bleeding profusely, he was dragged to cover by Major Frost.

Two other paratroopers were cut down. One, Corporal Stewart, a Scotsman, was a heavy gambler, and his wallet was bulging with currency. Before leaving England, he had solemnly declared that if he was killed on the raid, he wanted his comrades to split up his money and go on a binge after they returned.

Hit in the head by a grenade fragment and bleeding, Stewart lay on the beach and called to the nearest man, Lance Corporal Alan Freeman, "I've had it. Here, take my wallet."

Freeman took the wallet and looked at Stewart's wound. "Oh, it's only a wee bit of a gash!" he told the other Scotsman.

"Then gie me back my bloody wallet!" Stewart exclaimed as he got to his feet.

All the while, Commander Cook had been waiting anxiously offshore for the signal to approach the beach. Two German destroyers and a pair of speedy E-boats (equivalent to a U.S. PT boat) had moved past, less than a mile from his flotilla. Just after 2:35 A.M. Cook spotted green signals coming from the beach and ordered six landing craft to head for shore. Major Frost had just finished deploying his men for a last-ditch stand when a shout rang out: "The boats are coming in! God bless the bloody navy!"

Aboard the approaching craft were the South Wales Borderers and the Royal Fusiliers, who, following orders, opened a murderous fire against the cliff and to both sides of the evacuation beach. The six craft scraped onto the sand, and the raiders scrambled aboard. Left behind were two dead and six missing (all of whom would be captured). By 3:30 A.M. Major Frost and his paratroopers were aboard Cook's flotilla, which was racing for Pompey (British Navy slang for Portsmouth).

In England the next morning, Reginald Jones had components of the Giant Würzburg, one of Germany's most closely guarded secrets, scattered around the floor of a large room and was piecing the device together. In all respects, the Bruneval raid had been a rousing success: the stolen radar provided the British with the know-how to develop countermeasures against the German night air defenses that had been taking a heavy toll of RAF bombers.[7]

A Secret Move to a Secret Site

THE SENSE OF TRIUMPH in high British circles following the Bruneval raid was tempered by concern. Would Adolf Hitler, in his fury, retaliate? If so, in what manner? A parachute or commando-type strike along England's southern coast seemed the most likely form. And located there was the Telecommunications Research Establishment (TRE) at Swanage in Dorset, where nearly all British radar was being developed.

TRE was as vulnerable as had been the Würzburg site at Bruneval: on the water's edge, isolated, fine beaches for attack and escape, and top-secret radar equipment that could be stolen in a raid. Swanage was minimally guarded and a choice plum waiting to be plucked by vengeful Germans. What a devastating stroke it would be if German raiders were to wipe out Britain's radar scientists.

Not long after Major John Frost and his men returned, TRE officials were handed an alarming intelligence report: seventeen trainloads of German paratroopers were converging on Cherbourg, France, across the Channel from Swanage, to assault TRE. As a result, a British regiment was rushed to Swanage, and Royal Engineers placed explosives in secret equipment.

TRE scientists, some in their late sixties and early seventies, held long, solemn discussions over what course they should take when the enemy paratroopers struck: flee, or stay and fight to the death.

The reports that the Germans might try to retaliate and pilfer British radar components and related materials spurred TRE officials into finding a new home inland. Chosen was a boys school nestled among the rolling hills of Worcestershire.

The scientists and their helpers would miss the beautiful English Channel seascape of Dorset, but they were eager to go, knowing that the new location would minimize the chance of awakening at night when German paratroopers were dropping on top of them.[8]

Poking Out Britain's "Eyes"

IN HIS LONDON OFFICE, French Major André Dewavrin (code-named Colonel Passy, after a famous Paris subway station) was reading an electrifying message that had just reached him from an agent in Brest, France. Passy was commander of the Bureau Central de Renseignement et d'Action (BCRA), the secret service of General Charles de Gaulle, who had escaped to England when France fell in the spring of 1940. Now it was January 28, 1942.

Three of the Germans' most powerful warships—*Prinz Eugen, Gneisenau,* and *Scharnhorst*—were preparing to bolt out of Brest (at the tip of the Britanny peninsula) and make a daring dash generally eastward on the English Channel to sanctuary in the Third Reich.

Adolf Hitler, furious that a glorious symbol of national pride, the mighty *Bismarck,* had been sunk by the British Navy ten months earlier, had ordered his navy commander, Grand Admiral Erich Raeder, to risk no more surface ships in the Atlantic. So the three warships had been holed up at Brest. Raeder, who always refused to give a Nazi salute, felt that these three potent vessels lurking in the French port could force the British to hold some of their own large warships in home waters.

The British Admiralty had considered that the three German ships might try to bolt for home, but the Royal Navy was heavily occupied elsewhere, so the task of keeping a watchful eye on Brest was turned over to the Coastal Command and to the chain of all-seeing radar along the southern coast of England.

At a tension-packed conference on January 12, Hitler himself had decided to risk destruction of the three prized warships. At the session held at the Führerhauptquartier (Hitler's battle command post) in East Prussia, Admiral Raeder had declared that any effort made by warships to bolt for home ports up the Channel "under the noses of the British" would be "sheer folly."

After the Luftwaffe's chief of staff, General Hans Jeschonneck, gave assurances that his aircraft would cover the breakout, Hitler overruled his navy chief. "You will see," the führer exclaimed. "This will be the greatest naval exploit of the whole war!"

Secrecy and surprise. Surprise and secrecy. Those were the ingredients on which Hitler was counting for the three ships to escape to the Third Reich. To achieve that secrecy until it would be too late for the British to halt the daring operation, German scientists would lull the English to sleep by jamming their radar. Britain's eyes along its Channel coast would be poked out.

As soon as Hitler had issued the order for the Channel dash, German planning was launched under the deepest secrecy. Until almost the last minute, only a small group of officers knew what was afoot. Five code names were created to cloak the true one, Operation Cerberus.

Soon the Luftwaffe was brought into the planning, and a force of 250 Focke-Wulf 190s and Messerschmitts under General of Fighters Adolf Galland was covertly assembled on airfields along the Channel coast in France.

This sizable force of swift fighter planes would form an umbrella over the five-hundred-mile route between Brest and Germany. Air controllers would be on the three warships to direct the fighters should the RAF attack. Sixteen German planes would be constantly overhead, and for twenty minutes of each hour as the relays changed, there would be thirty-two Luftwaffe aircraft hovering in the sky like mother hens over their broods.

In Brest, meanwhile, the French spy radioed Colonel Passy in London: "Sailing imminent. Keep close watch on period of the new moon [February 10 to 15]."

Actually, German planners had picked the night of the eleventh for the breakout, during the period of dark nights and favorable tides that would add to the ships' speed.

Although the French secret agent's reports had been remarkably accurate in the past, the British scoffed at his prediction that the enemy ships would depart from Brest at night. The Admiralty was convinced that the departure would be in daylight so the ships could reach the twenty-mile-wide bottleneck at the Strait of Dover, three hundred miles to the northeast, some twelve hours later, under the protective cover of night.

In the mental cat-and-mouse game between Adolf Hitler and the British Admiralty, the führer had chosen a night departure from Brest because, he reasoned, that was precisely opposite to how the British would expect the break-out to be timed. Hitler hoped that his three ships could reach the Strait of Dover before the enemy woke to the fact that they had broken out of Brest.

On the afternoon of breakout night, large sections of Brest were cordoned off by German security forces so no one could go into or out of the harbor area while the ships were getting up steam. That move kept Colonel Passy's spy from reaching his hidden radio set and sending a warning to London.

Across the English Channel that same day, Colonel Robert Wallace of British Signals was both frustrated and angry. For more than a week, the radar along the Channel coast had been jammed, and the electronic obstruction was getting more intense each day.

Colonel Wallace rushed to see Reginald Jones, the young Air Staff scientific intelligence chief, who had already scored a series of victories in confusing the Germans' radio communications and bomber guidance systems. "I am sure that the Germans are up to something," Wallace told Jones, "but no one will listen to me."

Jones promptly sent one of his scientists to investigate. Events would prove that the colonel had been the only one to detect the subtle "blinding" of British radar along the Channel coast. For the past two weeks, the Germans had slightly increased the intensity of the jamming. As planned, the acceleration had been so gradual that by the night of February 11, the British technicians did not realize that the jamming had rendered their radar virtually useless.

At 9:45 P.M. *Prinz Eugen, Scharnhorst,* and *Gneisenau,* escorted by a group of smaller ships, slipped out of Brest. Destination: Germany. Almost at once, the British encountered a series of incredible difficulties that indicated the gods of war were smiling on Operation Cerberus.

Just before the German flotilla emerged from the harbor, *Sealion,* the submarine assigned to keep watch on the exit, had withdrawn to recharge her batteries. Two Coastal Command planes patrolling outside the harbor had radar breakdowns (possibly due to German jamming). A third British patrol plane was summoned home shortly before the fleeing ships neared the aircraft's search area. None of these gaps in the patrolling system were reported to Coastal Command headquarters.

By this time, Vice Admiral Hans Ciliax, the *Flottenchef* (flotilla chief), was gaining confidence that the "impossible" feat might indeed be pulled off. His optimism soared when, at 7:32 A.M., the first squadrons of General Adolf Galland's fighter planes roared in overhead.

Admiral Ciliax could not believe his good fortune. His ships had traveled some 250 miles and not been discovered. The radar jamming had been so cleverly done that British operators along the Channel coast took it for atmospheric interference. A few blips coming through did not make much sense.

The first true warning came by accident. At 10:42 A.M. on breakout day, the pilots of a pair of British Spitfires chasing two Messerschmitts over the Channel saw below them the astonishing panorama of the German flotilla.

It was not until 11:23 A.M., more than twelve hours after the three ships had sneaked out of Brest Harbor, that Admiral Bertram H. Ramsay, commander of the port of Dover, was notified that the German vessels were nearing the twenty-mile-wide bottleneck between Dover and Calais, France.

Taken totally by surprise, the British reaction was piecemeal. Singly or a few at a time, RAF planes, motor torpedo boats, and destroyers attacked the escaping flotilla. None hit the *Prinz Eugen, Gneisenau,* or *Scharnhorst* with a bomb or a torpedo. Of the 398 RAF planes taking part in the effort to sink or badly damage the German ships, 71 were lost from the fire of the Luftwaffe air umbrella, guns of the fleeing vessels and their surface escorts, and the heavy ack-ack fire of batteries along the French coast at the Strait of Dover.

By 12:56 P.M. the beleaguered German flotilla had battled its way through the Dover bottleneck and sailed into the North Sea. *Scharnhorst* had survived two blasts from mines, and *Gneisenau* was limping from another mine explosion, but at dawn on February 13, all three warships had reached friendly ports in Germany and Nazi-occupied Denmark.

At his battle headquarters in East Prussia, Adolf Hitler was jubilant. He had overruled his top admiral and outfoxed the British Admiralty, a feat made possible by the Germans who had fine-tuned the jamming of radar to hoodwink the British.

In Great Britain, the public was stunned and furious over the escape of the big German ships, and the War Cabinet was soundly plastered by an outraged press. *The Times* of London bellowed: "Nothing more mortifying to the pride of sea-power has happened in home waters since the 17th Century."[9]

A Plan to Turn Hitler Feminine

CARL EIFLER, a bear of a man at six feet, six inches and close to three hundred pounds, strolled into the headquarters of the Office of Strategic Services (OSS) at Twenty-fifth and E Streets in Washington, D.C. So covert was the activity of America's first cloak-and-dagger agency that cocktail-party gossip in the capital held that the initials stood for Oh, So Secret. It was April 1942.

Eifler had graduated from the Los Angeles Police Academy, had worked as an undercover agent tracking down drug smugglers for the U.S. Customs Service, and had several shoot-outs with bandits in the mountains of Mexico. So it was only natural that the rough-and-tough giant would join an outfit that promised heavy action.

Eifler had come to Washington at the behest of William J. "Wild Bill" Donovan, the OSS director who had founded the espionage and sabotage operation the previous year. As colonel of New York's "Fighting 69th" Infantry Regiment in World War I, he had been awarded the Congressional Medal of Honor, the Distinguished Service Cross, three Purple Hearts, and other combat decorations.

Führer Adolf Hitler. (Signal *magazine*)

During the two decades of peace between the two world wars, Donovan earned a law degree, and he was an attorney on Wall Street in New York City when President Roosevelt asked him to form and direct a global undercover apparatus. Eager for adventure and a chance to serve his country, he promptly accepted the monumental challenge.

Now Donovan wasted no time in chitchat with Carl Eifler. Time was too precious. He informed Eifler that he was sending him and six other new agents for training in covert warfare to Camp X, a supersecret British-operated venture on the shore of Lake Ontario in Canada.

On completing the short but intense course on how to create mayhem, Eifler, along with the other six men, was assigned to the China-Burma-India (CBI) Theater by Bill Donovan. The big man would be commander of the first detachment to be sent into the field. Eifler and his team would travel to their new assignment in civilian clothes and pretend that they did not know one another.

When preparing to depart for extended overseas duty, Eifler called on Stanley P. Lovell, the fifty-two-year-old scientist who was head of the OSS Research and Development branch. Lovell turned over to Eifler forty pounds of a new explosive called Composition C. Because the blasting material resembled flour and could literally be baked into biscuits, Lovell called the new stuff Aunt Jemima, after a popular pancake mix.

For all of his rough-and-tumble background, Eifler, like most OSS operatives early in the war, was incredibly naive in some respects. He called on Colonel Preston Goodfellow, an aide to Donovan, and asked if the Treasury Department had issued the necessary papers for transporting explosives into foreign countries.

"Major, we didn't even ask for it," Goodfellow replied. "You used to be a border guard. Don't you know about smuggling?"

Eifler packed the forty pounds of Aunt Jemima into a suitcase, then filled an identical suitcase with his legitimate apparel. Through a glib tongue, a sharp wit, and sleight of hand, the OSS agent carried Aunt Jemima past customs officials in Rio de Janeiro, Brazil; Cairo, Egypt; and Calcutta, India.

Aunt Jemima had been developed by George Kistiakowsky, a scientist widely recognized as an expert on explosives. Born in Russia, he had fought with the White Army of the czar in the Russian Revolution in 1918. After the Communists triumphed, Kistiakowsky fled to Germany and earned a doctorate at the University of Berlin.

A friendly professor urged his young student to go to the United States. "You'll never get a job in Germany," he said. "Here you will always be a Russian."

Princeton University in New Jersey accepted the émigré on a fellowship, and he later moved to Harvard University in Massachusetts and became professor of chemistry in 1938.

Stanley Lovell was an internationally known chemist and holder of many patents when he had been recruited into the cloak-and-dagger outfit from a high-paying post with a large corporation by Bill Donovan. When Lovell had arrived in Washington for an interview in early 1942, Donovan left no doubt about the type of man he was looking for: a combination of Sherlock Holmes (brilliant deduction) and Professor Moriarty (the evil genius who was the sleuth's nemesis).

A few nights later, Lovell was a guest in Donovan's home. The candidate was reluctant. He was not sure if he wanted to model himself after a criminal genius.

Donovan snapped, "Don't be so goddamn naive, Lovell. You known damn well the Germans and the Japs won't hold anything back against us!"

Typically, Wild Bill's sales pitch had been right on target. Lovell had been given a choice of being branded as unpatriotic or shedding his lifelong scruples and becoming the Peck's Bad Boy of American scientists. He chose the latter type.

With typical alacrity, Lovell plunged into his task of developing gadgets and techniques for bedeviling and killing America's enemies. Being a chemist, he was especially fascinated by toxins and bacterial agents, and he created several of them. One was a botulinus toxin that was secretly sent to an OSS agent in Burma to poison Japanese Army officers with the help of the victims' native houseboys, who hated the occupying army.

Soon Lovell received word from the OSS operative that the botulinus toxin was ineffective, that he had tried it on a donkey and it did not faze the animal.

Lovell explained that donkeys, for whatever reason, are among the handful of creatures immune to botulinus toxin. In other animals—and humans— it quickly paralyzes the lungs. Because no chemical trace lingered after death, it was perfect for assassinations. Unless a physician were present at the time of death to notice the lung paralysis, it would be impossible to prove that a murder had even taken place: the victim presumably had died of natural causes.

Lovell repeatedly came up with schemes for killing, disabling, or maiming Adolf Hitler. When it was learned through Ultra, the British process that intercepted and decrypted German messages, that the führer and his Italian crony Benito Mussolini were going to meet, Lovell's fertile mind went into high gear.

"How would Professor Moriarty capitalize on this situation?" Wild Bill Donovan asked.

Lovell had a ready answer. The two leaders would meet on Hitler's private train parked on a rail siding in the Brenner Pass, which straddles the border between Austria and Italy. An OSS agent in that region would be furnished a small container of mustard gas.

When the dictators adjourned to eat in the dining car, the agent was to pour the mustard gas into a water-filled vase on their table. The reaction would release fumes that would paralyze the optic nerves of everyone in the car, permanently blinding them. Thus Germany and Italy would be left leaderless—or so went Lovell's theory.

Although this caper was too much for the OSS to pull off, Lovell never ceased trying to concoct a plot to neutralize Hitler. A psychological study by a scientist in the Washington headquarters concluded that the führer was susceptible to female hormones, so Lovell created a toxin filled with female hormones that, it was hoped, an undercover agent could spray on beets and carrots in Hitler's vegetable garden at Berchtesgaden, his mountain retreat in southern Germany.

It was known that Hitler was a vegetarian. Cooks at Berchtesgaden would pick the doctored beets and carrots, then feed them to him. Ingested with female hormones, the führer's voice would become high-pitched, his trademark mustache and much of his hair would fall out, and his breasts would expand. Such a grotesque appearance would certainly cause most of the German people and the armed forces to lose confidence in him.

That devious plot also failed: Berchtesgaden was heavily guarded by SS troops.

Stanley Lovell and his scientific team developed a wide array of technical gadgets designed to wreak mayhem on the Germans, Japanese, and Italians. These ingenious items included limpet mines that stuck to ships underwater; detonators with a time release attached; flashlight batteries with concealed message compartments; exploding pencils; suitcases with false bottoms; "sudden death" tablets to be dropped into drinks; and "The Mole," an explosive device that was fused to detonate after a train plunged into the sudden darkness of a tunnel, thereby creating an explosion that would block the cavity for days or even weeks.[10]

Geniuses in a Dungeon

EARLY IN THE MORNING of April 20, 1942, President Franklin Roosevelt, barely able to keep the glee out of his voice, announced over the radio that a force of U.S. bombers under Lieutenant Colonel James H. Doolittle had departed from Shangri-la and bombed Tokyo.

In fact, Doolittle's sixteen twin-engined B-25 bombers had taken off from the U.S. aircraft carrier *Hornet*, which had sneaked to within a few hundred miles of Japan. It had been a nuisance raid as far as property damage was concerned. But in Tokyo, the people nearly panicked. They had been assured that no U.S. bomb would ever strike the home islands.

In the United States, citizens were electrified by Doolittle's audacious raid. Since war had broken out at Pearl Harbor four and a half months earlier, Americans had been engulfed by an avalanche of bad news. General Hideki Tojo's stunning blitzkrieg had swallowed up huge areas in the Pacific. *Hakko-ichiu* (bring the eight corners of the world under one roof) had become the national slogan.

Leaders of the Imperial General Staff were bewildered by Roosevelt's Shangri-la disclosure, unaware that it was a mythical Himalayan retreat in James Hilton's novel *Lost Horizon*. So they scoured maps and concluded that tiny Midway Island, the nearest U.S. outpost, at twenty-one hundred miles east of Tokyo, had to be Shangri-la.

Seizure of Midway had long been part of the Japanese master plan for widespread conquest in the Pacific on the road to an invasion of the West Coast of the United States. So now Admiral Isoroku Yamamoto, commander of the Combined Fleet and who had been the architect of the Pearl Harbor sneak attack, began assembling a mighty force to launch Plan MI for the capture of Midway, code-named "AF." Yamamoto had not counted on the fact that American electronic eavesdroppers would be snooping over his shoulder.

For more than a year, the Americans had been trying diligently to crack the Japanese Navy's operational code, JN25. Collaborating on the project were the navy's Combat Intelligence Office (familiarly known as Hypo), set up in Hawaii under Commander Joseph J. Rochefort, and the army's Special Intelligence Service (SIS), led by William F. Friedman, in Washington.

A lean, intense man whose gentle manner belied a fierce tenacity toward solving complex problems, Joe Rochefort insisted on maximum security arrangements. Soon after reaching Honolulu in 1940, he had moved the Hypo to the basement of naval headquarters. An armed marine was put at the only door of what the cryptologists called the "dungeon."

In the U.S. Army and Navy, the cryptanalyst was a unique bird, belonging to the services but not fully accepted by them. No one knew where he or she fit into the overall scheme of national defense, perhaps somewhere between intelligence and communications.

Few could excel as a cryptanalyst: it required a peculiar type of mentality, combining a high IQ and a genius for mathematics with an infinite capacity for painstaking detail. He or she needed unbridled enthusiasm for the demanding task and had to hold on to a scholarly detachment so as not to go chasing down blind alleys.

Equally important to the successful cryptanalyst was a capacity to be almost without an ambition for promotion in rank and decorations, which rarely came his or her way. Chances of ever having a star pinned on a shoulder were about those of being elected president of the United States.

In Hypo, the cryptanalysts spent their days in the "dungeon," where sunlight was not allowed to penetrate, poring almost endlessly over letters and numbers in permutations. Sorting and interpreting a gargantuan number of call signals from the Japanese Navy's General Staff in Tokyo to Combined Fleet headquarters, and then to each of scores of subordinate commands and on down to destroyers and remote shore stations in the western Pacific, was a mind-numbing chore.

JN25 included some fifty thousand five-digit numbers representing words and phrases. An even larger group of meaningless numbers was available to the sender, which he could insert at random in the message to confound enemy cryptanalysts. A special group of numbers notified the recipient of the message where the smoke screen would begin.

These Japanese aircraft detectors failed to sound an alarm on approach of Doolittle's bombers. (Author's collection)

Despite the enormous challenges in cracking JN25, by April 1942, four months after Pearl Harbor, Hypo could read many groupings in each JN25 message. No one person had achieved the monumental breakthrough; rather, it was the result of teamwork and bulldog tenacity. As each new group was decoded, it made the next one slightly easier.

During the first week in May 1942, Admiral Yamamoto, who liked to boast that he was "a country boy who had made good as a sailor," gathered his top commanders in the wardroom of the superbattleship *Yamato*, which weighed more than sixty thousand tons (as compared to the average U.S. battleship of forty-five thousand tons). For nearly two hours he briefed his subordinates on his grand design, in which Plan MI (the capture of Midway) would be but the first step.

Yamamoto would deploy the most powerful naval armada ever assembled to that time. Hoping to lure elements of the U.S. Pacific Fleet from Hawaii, the Japanese would launch a diversionary operation against the Aleutian Islands, some two thousand miles northeast of Japan. Then Yamamoto's main force, heavy with battleships and aircraft carriers, would strike against Midway. Secrecy was crucial, the admiral stressed.

After the *Yamato* conference in a Japanese harbor broke up, Commander Joe Rochefort and his men in the Hawaiian "dungeon" began plucking from the air a blizzard of intercepts that left no doubt Yamamoto was preparing an all-out naval offensive. But where would it hit? Australia, far to the south of Japan? Or eastward, in the direction of Hawaii?

This was a perilous time for the United States in the Pacific. Unless Rochefort and his men could balance the odds by discovering details of Yamamoto's looming offensive, U.S. naval forces would be dangerously outnumbered and destroyed, leaving the gate open for the Japanese to seize Hawaii, only 1,150 miles southeast of Midway, and then to invade California.

In the days ahead, Rochefort and his associates studied hundreds of intercepts. Radio intelligence is not a precise science; rather it is the product of skilled cryptanalysts and linguists painstakingly piecing together countless clues, then reaching a decision about enemy intentions. There is never a certainty that their conclusions are accurate.

One day Rochefort made an electrifying discovery. An intercept mentioned *koryaku butai*, a term the Japanese had used in previous military operations for "invasion force." Another intercept used the geographic designator "AF" in relation to the words "forthcoming campaign."

Now Admiral Chester W. Nimitz, the astute, soft-spoken commander of the Pacific Fleet in Hawaii, felt confident that Yamamoto was preparing to invade "AF." But where was "AF"?

To find the crucial answer, Lieutenant Commander Jasper Holmes, one of Rochefort's assistants, came up with an ingenious hoax. He proposed that the U.S. garrison commander on Midway send out a wireless message about a fictitious water shortage. The idea was to see if the Japanese would swallow the bait.

Before the war, Holmes had studied Midway when he was an engineering student at the University of Hawaii, so he knew that the island's entire freshwater supply was obtained from an evaporator plant built by Pan American World Airways, whose flying boats had refueled at the atoll en route to the Far East.

Nimitz was delighted, and he authorized the machination. By underwater cable, a coded message was sent to the Midway commander to immediately radio an urgent request for fresh water. He was to explain that an explosion had wrecked the evaporator plant. The Midway dispatch was to be sent in a code Rochefort and Holmes knew had been captured by the Japanese at Wake Island.

As expected, the fake wireless message was picked up by a Japanese listening post on the small island of Kwajalein and flashed to the Special Duty Radio Group outside Tokyo for decoding and analysis.

Two days later, Rochefort's cryptanalysts in Hawaii intercepted a dispatch that disclosed that Yamamoto had swallowed the bait. Various commanders in

Commander Joseph J. Rochefort led the team that cracked the Japanese naval code, preventing an invasion of California. (U.S. Navy)

his invasion force were informed by radio that "AF" was short of water. Another intercept instructed the Japanese invasion force to take a two-week supply of fresh water onto "AF."

Although the identity of "AF" had been nailed down, that intelligence would be of minimal use to Admiral Nimitz unless his electronic snoopers could identify N-Day, the date on which the Japanese Navy would open fire on Midway.

On May 26, 1942, Rochefort's sleuths decoded an order for two groups of Japanese destroyers to leave Saipan in the Mariana Islands on the twenty-eighth and proceed in a northeasterly direction at ten knots for a June 1 rendezvous with eleven troop transports. The destroyers were to escort the transports to "AF," arriving on June 6.

The men in the "dungeon" were elated. If the invasion soldiers and marines were to reach Midway on June 6, that meant the naval sea and air bombardment to soften up the island's defenses would hit a day or two earlier. Therefore, by deduction, Rochefort and his men concluded that N-Day would be either June 4 or 5.

Chester Nimitz now crossed the Rubicon. Only a few ships were available, but he sent them all. Task Force 16, under Rear Admiral Raymond A.

Spruance, stole out of Pearl Harbor on May 28. With it were the carriers *Enterprise* and *Hornet*. A day later, Task Force 17, commanded by Rear Admiral Frank J. Fletcher, sailed from Pearl to rendezvous with Spruance on June 2 at "Point Luck," 325 miles northeast of Midway.

With Fletcher's battle group was the carrier *Yorktown*, which had been badly damaged in the Battle of the Coral Sea in the South Pacific early in May. It had limped back to Pearl Harbor and been patched up in time to join Fletcher's force.

Meanwhile, Commander Edwin T. Layton, Nimitz's intelligence chief, and Joe Rochefort's unit launched an intricate radio deception scheme to hoodwink Admiral Yamamoto into believing that he would strike at Midway virtually unopposed. The hoax was based on the assumption that the Japanese high command had concluded that the *Enterprise* and the *Hornet* were still in the Coral Sea, more than two thousand miles to the southwest of Midway. Actually, the two carriers had been ordered to return from the Coral Sea to Pearl Harbor under strict radio silence.

The deception machination was kicked off by the seaplane tender *Tangier* at an island in the New Hebrides east of Australia. The ship's radiomen, working furiously around the clock, sent out a steady flood of messages while assuming the role of a carrier flying combat missions in the region. This same technique was used by the heavy cruiser *Salt Lake City*, which was on patrol in the South Pacific.

Hopefully, the Japanese listening post on Kwajalein would pick up the signals from the *Tangier* and the *Salt Lake City* and send the contents on to Tokyo, where analysts at the Special Duty Radio Group would be convinced that Spruance's carriers *Enterprise* and *Hornet* were several days' sailing from Midway.

In the meantime, 145 ships, including eight carriers, in Admiral Yamamoto's potent armada were at sea. By comparison, the thirty-five surface ships that Admiral Nimitz had been able to muster were alarmingly few.

Knowing that the enormous ship movements from ports around the western Pacific would be detected by U.S. electronic snoopers, the Japanese launched a deception plan of their own to mask Midway as the target. Centerpiece of the scheme to convince the Americans that Yamamoto's armada was bound southward to invade Australia was the torpedoing of a ferryboat in Sydney Harbor.

At Pearl Harbor, Joe Rochefort and Ed Layton knew too much about Yamamoto's plan to be taken in by the Japanese hoax.

But Tokyo was completely fooled by the *Tangier* and *Salt Lake City* radio deceptions. Admiral Chuichi Nagumo, whose task force of four carriers and escort ships was steaming toward Midway some three hundred miles ahead of the main fleet, received several reassuring reports from Tokyo that the *Enter-*

prise and the *Hornet* were far away in the South Pacific, and that the *Yorktown* was laid up in dry dock at Pearl Harbor.

Shortly after dawn on June 3, Admiral Nimitz and several of his key assistants were gathered in his office to await developments. The climate was tense. What if Rochefort's and Layton's predictions about the target and N-Day were wrong and Yamamoto struck virtually undefended Australia?

Just past 7:00 A.M., an ensign rushed into the room and handed Nimitz a radio report: "Main body . . . bearing 262 [degrees from Midway], distance 700 miles, course 090, speed 19 knots."

Nimitz's eyes lit up like beacons. "Layton," he said to his intelligence officer, "the Japanese force has been sighted. It ought to make your heart warm."

Beaming broadly, the admiral waved the dispatch reporting the invasion force west of Midway precisely where Layton and Joe Rochefort had predicted it would be.

Nimitz flashed an upbeat message to his task force leaders, Raymond Spruance and Frank Fletcher: "The situation is developing as expected. Tomorrow may be the day you can give them the works."

Early on the morning of June 4, Admiral Nagumo, commander of the fast carrier force spearheading the operation, sent his bombers against Midway and discovered that there were unidentified ships not far to the northeast, where they had no business being. These ships were the carriers *Yorktown*, *Enterprise*, and *Hornet*.

For three days, a fierce clash raged in the skies and on the water around tiny Midway. Both sides fought with exceptional valor, and each paid a fearful price. When Admiral Yamamoto broke off the engagement, he had lost 4 carriers, 1 cruiser, 322 aircraft, and 2,500 men, including 220 of his elite carrier pilots. The United States had lost 1 carrier *(Yorktown)*, 1 destroyer, 147 planes, and 347 men.

It had been a stunning defeat for the Japanese Navy, the first one since 1592, when the Koreans under Yi Sunsin, in history's first engagement of ironclad ships, drove Hideyoushi's fleet from the scene of battle.

Few realized it at the time, but Midway had been one of history's decisive battles. It canceled Yamamoto's threat to Hawaii and California.

In the wake of the U.S. victory at Midway, an outcome made possible through the breaking of the Japanese codes, that precious secret was nearly destroyed. The *Chicago Tribune*, one of the nation's largest-circulation and most influential dailies, plastered across the front page an eight-column banner:

NAVY HAD WORD OF JAP PLAN TO STRIKE AT SEA

It was one of the most irresponsible disclosures in the history of American journalism. Washington was outraged. Congressman Elmer J. Holland made a bad situation worse by taking to the floor of the House and, in his fury, denouncing the *Tribune*.

Then muckraking syndicated columnist Walter Winchell, whose radio news program was tuned in by many millions of Americans, twice mentioned that the U.S. Navy had advance notice of Japanese fleet movements.

Incredibly, Japanese security forces somehow failed to give credence to these shocking public revelations, possibly believing that these lapses were components of some devious American trick to throw the Japanese armed forces off-guard. Whatever may have been the case, the codes were not abandoned.

Meanwhile, Admiral Chester Nimitz, realizing Hypo's enormous achievement of tricking the Japanese into confirming that AF signified Midway, urgently recommended to Admiral Ernest King, chief of naval operations in Washington, that Commander Joe Rochefort receive a high decoration for his crucial role, which, along with the valor of the fighting men, upset Yamamoto's scheme for invading California.

Known to President Roosevelt as the Big Bear because of his size and often grumpy demeanor, King curtly rejected the recommendation of his commander in the Pacific. No one person should be singled out for intelligence work, King declared. Presumably, in his eyes, cryptanalysts were good enough to win crucial battles, but not quite respectable.

Prior to Midway, many senior officers in the U.S. forces in the Pacific had regarded Joe Rochefort and his handful of cryptanalysts and linguists to be "a bunch of nuts, in a dungeon, dreaming up wild hallucinations." After the war, however, Admiral Nimitz would say "the fate of the nation had quite literally depended upon [these] dozen men . . . in radio intelligence."[11]

A Test Goes Up in Smoke

ON A BEAUTIFUL spring morning in 1942, a galaxy of top British leaders gathered at a Royal Air Force field in the Midlands to witness a presentation of a revolutionary scientific development: a rocket-assisted liftoff of a Stirling four-engined bomber. The guest notables included a member of Prime Minister Winston Churchill's cabinet, a top-ranking general, and a clutch of senior Royal Air Force officers.

The new technique consisted of a barrel containing some twenty-four rockets under each wing. As an airplane's throttles were opened, the rockets would be fired progressively by means of a rheostat, a device for regulating current.

Selected as the pilot for this historic demonstration of technological achievement was Squadron Leader Harold Huxtable. A few months earlier he had miraculously survived when a bomber crashed into the ground and blew up, hurling him far from the wreckage.

Now an aura of subdued excitement saturated the airdrome. The notables watched in fascination as Huxtable taxied the Stirling onto the runway, then turned it into the wind.

The big bomber advanced slowly, steadily. As it reached the rocket-firing stage, the guests were rocked by what an onlooker would describe as "the longest, loudest explosion ever heard in the Midlands."

Stationary on the runway, the Stirling was hidden by a large, thick cloud of black smoke. Angry flames licked at its fuselage, and spent pieces of rockets were scattered about. The brass and all the RAF personnel watching stood transfixed. Clearly, Squadron Leader Huxtable's luck finally had deserted him.

Moments later, when a stiff breeze cleared away the smoke, the Stirling become visible. An undercarriage had collapsed, the four engines were askew, and parts were pointing in all directions. Three propellers had vanished. Amazingly, Huxtable climbed out of the wreckage. The gods of airmen had been watching over him once again.

Later, investigation would disclose that the rockets, instead of firing progressively, had gone off at the same time, applying an enormous force and acceleration that the Stirling's designers had never contemplated.[12]

Goering an "Honorary Scientist"

THIRTY-SIX-YEAR-OLD Albert Speer, a virtual czar over the German economy as the minister for armaments and war production, was lunching in a private room of Horcher's, a popular Berlin restaurant, with Generaloberst Erich Fromm, commander of the Home Army and also chief of Army Equipment. The two men dined together almost weekly to discuss production problems and needs, but this time Fromm stunned Speer by declaring that Germany's only hope of winning the war was to develop an ultimate weapon. It was late April 1942.

Fromm's view about Germany's minimal chance of winning the war could have resulted in much trouble for him. Such talk could be construed as defeatism, for which numerous officers had already been executed. The general had been on Adolf Hitler's blacklist since the winter of 1941, when the Wehrmacht had been stalled in the bitter snows outside Moscow. At that time Fromm had said that peace should be made with the Soviets.

Fromm had learned from a prominent physicist, Carl Ramsauer, head of the German Physical Society and a researcher for the huge electrical firm Allgemeine Elektrizitatsgesellschaft, details of the German effort to build an atomic bomb. A single bomb might wipe out an entire city, the general told the astonished Speer. He urged the armaments chief to meet with the scientists spearheading the project.

At the same time, Albert Voegler, head of a large industrial firm, complained bitterly to Speer that the Reich Research Council was tightfisted with nuclear research funds and materials. Under Bernard Rust, the education minister, the council had been lethargic toward a program to develop an atomic bomb, Voegler told Speer.

Reacting to the suggestions and complaints of General Fromm and Voegler, Speer called on Adolf Hitler and made a seemingly bizarre recommendation: Appoint the grossly overweight and money-hungry Reichsmarschall Hermann Goering to take charge of the Research Council.

Goering, who it was whispered around Berlin had taken to rouging his cheeks and using narcotics, knew nothing about nuclear energy. But the tall, handsome Speer had good reason, as usual, for his recommendations. Goering, the number two man on the Nazi hierarchy pecking order, would give the Research Council enormous impact in its request for money and materials.

Goering's appointment triggered snide remarks from Germany's intellectuals. "He's our 'honorary scientist,'" was one barb.

An architect by trade, Albert Speer was Hitler's fair-haired boy, it was widely known throughout Nazi Germany. In the years prior to his appointment as armaments czar, the young architect had spent countless hours with the führer poring over drawings and models for the huge and ornate structures that Hitler one day planned to build in Berlin as a testament to his own exalted status.

Hitler's choice of Speer to be a sort of super field marshal in charge of war production back in February 1942 had seemed to the inner circle in Berlin to be a peculiar one. Speer had no experience in industry, no background in economics, and no standing with German financiers. Yet, in the months ahead, he would drive German industry to gargantuan feats of production despite steadily heavier Allied bombings and a shortage of materials.

Because of his standing with the führer and his own drive and intelligence, Albert Speer was the ideal German leader to marshal the full force of the economy behind building an atomic bomb, so the architect invited a large number of top German military officers and foremost nuclear physicists to a conference in Berlin on June 4.

Speer entered the meeting room with his top civilian advisers, including Ferdinand Porsche, the designer of the Volkswagen, and his own military confidants, General Erich Fromm ("Fritz" to his friends) and Field Marshal Erhard Milch, the deputy commander of the Luftwaffe. Among the scientists present were Werner Heisenberg, Carl von Weizsäcker, Otto Hahn, Kurt Diebner, Fritz Strassmann, and Erich Bagge. Presiding was Albert Voegler, who was also president of the Kaiser Wilhelm Institute for Physics, the nation's leading research operation.

As chief theoretician of the atomic bomb program, Heisenberg spoke angrily about drafting promising young scientists into the military and hustling them off to the front. He hammered (incorrectly) at the theme that American

Reichsmarschall Hermann Goering (left) and German armaments chief Albert Speer were bitter rivals. (National Archives)

scientists were making steady progress, while the German program was bogged down in apathy.

Once he had vented his anger, Heisenberg spoke mainly on the scientific aspect of nuclear research. But Albert Speer, General Fromm, and Field Marshal Milch were attracted to the conference because of the prospect of an ultimate weapon.

"How can nuclear physics be applied to the manufacture of atomic bombs?" the armaments chief asked Heisenberg.

"Well, yes, we could do it," Heisenberg replied. "But all the processes we know to produce these [atomic bombs] are so enormously expensive and it would perhaps take many years and expenses of billions [of marks] if we wanted to do it."

"How big must a bomb be in order to reduce a large city like London to ruins?" Field Marshal Milch inquired.

Heisenberg replied, "About as big as a pineapple."

A true Nazi general who had contempt for his immediate boss, Hermann Goering, but who never lost faith in Adolf Hitler, the portly Milch asked how long it would take the United States to build a reactor and a bomb. Heisenberg paused thoughtfully for long moments; then, based on gut instinct and perhaps the use of a crystal ball, he replied: "Even if the Americans were to launch an all-out program, they cannot build a working reactor before the end of the current year [1942], and a working bomb would take at least another two years. This means the Americans will not be able to build an atomic bomb until at least 1945."

Events would prove Walter Heisenberg's assessment of U.S. atomic-bomb capabilities to be incredibly accurate.

A few days later, Albert Speer entered the ornate Chancellery in Berlin to report to Adolf Hitler on the conclusions reached at the atomic-bomb conference. Speer was pessimistic, stating that something useful might develop from nuclear research, but any wonder weapon that would elevate Hitler to be the führer of the world was far down the line.

Like Winston Churchill, Franklin Roosevelt, and Josef Stalin, the German leader had only a vague layman's grasp of the intricacies of building an atomic bomb. Once, he jokingly told Speer that he expected the scientists to set the world on fire with their crazy experiments. Yet he continued to follow nuclear research and development throughout the year.[13]

A Nuclear Laboratory Explodes

WALTER HEISENBERG, Germany's leading nuclear physicist, and an aide were working in the laboratory at the University of Leipzig on June 7, 1942. They had been conducting a series of studies of atomic piles—an aluminum sphere containing powdered uranium metal and heavy water. The sphere was immersed in a large tank of water, which began steaming.

Heisenberg and his assistant were deeply alarmed. It was clear that the pile was heating up dangerously. Then they saw the pile start to quiver, and they bolted through an open door. Moments later, there was an enormous explosion. The blast set the building ablaze, but firefighting equipment rushed to the scene and doused the conflagration.

Heisenberg and the other man had been shaken badly but miraculously escaped with their lives.

Despite the secrecy that had cloaked the experiments, the chief of the fire brigade came up to Heisenberg and warmly congratulated him for his success in building such a huge bomb.[14]

A Gathering of "Luminaries"

IN THE LATE SPRING OF 1942, renowned scientist J. Robert Oppenheimer invited a coterie of America's foremost physicists to spend three weeks at the California Institute of Technology to delve into the mysteries of building an atomic bomb. Oppy, as he was known to friends, called his guests the "luminaries."

J. Robert Oppenheimer, as
eccentric as he was brilliant.
(National Archives)

Oppenheimer, the son of a wealthy Jewish businessman who had emigrated from Germany to New York when the boy was seventeen years of age, had built an exceptional reputation in theoretical physics throughout the 1930s. Frail and intense, he was a professor at Cal Tech.

In a series of seminars held in Oppenheimer's campus office suite, the galaxy of scientists put forward far-reaching theories that were promptly ripped apart. The discussions were intense, but often new solutions to technological problems emerged. A spirit of spontaneity and surprise prevailed during the three weeks.

At the conclusion of the event, the luminaries agreed that an atomic bomb could be built, but the project would require a gargantuan scientific and industrial effort.

Robert Oppenheimer had always marched to his own drummer during his life. He drank martinis, smoked cigarettes incessantly, and was unworldly in many respects. He seldom read newspapers or magazines, and he first heard about the great crash on Wall Street that plunged the nation into a long depression six months after the 1929 disaster.

Oppy paid virtually no attention to politics, and he had never voted until he cast his ballot for Franklin D. Roosevelt in 1936. After that election, the physicist began reading the Communist daily newspaper *People's World*, and he joined virtually every Communist-front organization, of which there was no shortage, on the West Coast.

Oppenheimer's pert, vivacious, and hard-drinking wife, Katherine, whom he had met in 1939 when he was a professor and she was a research fellow in biology at the University of California, had a background steeped in Communist activities. Her second husband, the son of a wealthy investment banker, had been a Communist union organizer and died fighting with the Abraham Lincoln Brigade, a Communist unit, during the Spanish Civil War of the late 1930s. Known to friends as Kitty, her IQ was a lofty 196.

A few days after the "luminaries" left for home, Oppenheimer sent a detailed summary of the group's findings to James Conant, the administrator of the S-1 program. (S-1 was for Section One of the Office of Scientific Research and Development.) Conant convened the S-1 executive committee to discuss what he called the "status of the bomb." After lengthy deliberations, the panel drew up a document stating that an atomic bomb project was far more crucial than had been previously estimated.

Over his signature, Conant sent the committee's report to President Franklin Roosevelt. "We have become convinced that success in this program before the enemy can succeed is necessary to victory," the scientist explained.[15]

Part Four

Turning of the Tide

A Spectacular Rocket Feat

ON A MORNING in mid-June 1942, a black-bodied Junkers flew into the airstrip at Peenemünde, on the island of Usedom, just off the German mainland on the Baltic Sea. When the plane taxied to a halt, out stepped Albert Speer, minister for armaments and war production.

Enthusiastically greeting Speer was the world's foremost authority on rockets, Wernher von Braun, along with Colonel Walter Dornberger, commander of the top secret site, the Heersversuchstelle (Army Experimental Station).

Von Braun and Dornberger knew that they had an ally in Speer, a powerful member of Adolf Hitler's inner circle and an energetic type bursting with ideas and innovations. Weeks earlier, Speer had expressed to von Braun a deep interest in remote-controlled missiles, and he had come to witness a test-firing of the huge A-4 (later to be dubbed the V-2).

Peenemünde had been a sleepy fishing village until late 1936, when Hitler began rapidly expanding his armed forces and developing new weaponry. An airfield was built, and a new north-south road split the northern section of Usedom into two parts.

The eastern side was taken over by the *Heer* (army) to develop long-range rockets, ones far more powerful than history had known. The Luftwaffe had control of the western side, where it was creating a pilotless aircraft, later to be designated V-1 by the Germans and known to the Allies as a buzz bomb or doodlebug.

The staff of scientists, physicists, mathematicians, engineers, and technicians at the two facilities would eventually number ten thousand persons. In addition, many prestigious scientific institutions in Germany were "invited" to contribute their expertise to the development of these two potentially devastating secret weapons: the V-1 and the V-2. These research facilities included the Hermann Goering Institut in Braunschweig, the Raketenflugtechnische Forschunginstitut (Institute of Technical Research on Rockets) in Trauen, and the Deutsche Institut für Luftfahrforschung (German Institute for Air Research) in Berlin.

Peenemünde was one of the most tightly guarded installations in the world. Abwehr agents and specially picked Gestapo men seemed to be everywhere. There was never any mention of Peenemünde or the experiments there in the German press, all firmly controlled by propaganda genius Josef Goebbels. Each person working at Peenemünde was sworn to secrecy under a threat of long imprisonment or even execution.

Both sides at Peenemünde—army and Luftwaffe—had been and were competing vigorously for manpower, materials, and the favorable attention of the bigwigs in Berlin. Jealousy was rampant between the two competitors. There was no contact between the engineers and designers involved with the flying bomb and those working on the missile, even though their experiments were closely related. Both sides spied on one another, rejoicing in failures by the competing camp.

During the first years of the war, the rocket experiments were more advanced, and the designers of the flying bomb worked themselves into lathers as they peered across Usedom to watch the fiery tails of rockets streak into the Baltic sky. The Luftwaffe people had not yet been able to launch pilotless aircraft, so they had to content themselves with registering repeated protests with Berlin that the army was illegally hogging the sky.

Technical director on the army side of Peenemünde was Wernher von Braun, who was only thirty years of age. Tall and sturdily built, he had become obsessed with rocketry in his boyhood, and adults had thought the lad was "slightly touched in the head" because he often excitedly talked of a manned flight to the moon one day.

Colonel Walter Dornberger was himself a scientist, and he had obtained a degree from Berlin Technical University. The Versailles Treaty, imposed on Germany by the victorious Allies at the conclusion of World War I, had limited the amount of artillery in the one-hundred-thousand-man peacetime army but said nothing about barring rockets. So in the mid-1930s, then Captain Dornberger was appointed chief of the German Board of Ordnance, and he focused on rockets.

Now, after his arrival at Peenemünde to view the test-firing of the A-4 missile, Speer, who had been Hitler's favorite architect prior to the outbreak of war, was escorted to a clearing among the pines. Aimed skyward to his front was a missile five stories high.

Von Braun labored to conceal the anxiety he felt. If this test were to fail, it was quite possible Hitler might give a priority to the Luftwaffe flying-bomb project.

There was silence as Speer and the others watched. Wisps of smoke revealed that fuel tanks were being filled. Then, at the predetermined second, at first with a faltering motion and then with a roar seemingly of a supernatural unleashed giant, the rocket surged upward and vanished into the low clouds.

Speer's face reflected incredulity. He was thunderstruck by this technological feat, at the way it seemed to abolish the laws of gravity, so that thirteen tons could be hurled high in the sky. Few humans had ever witnessed such a near-miracle.

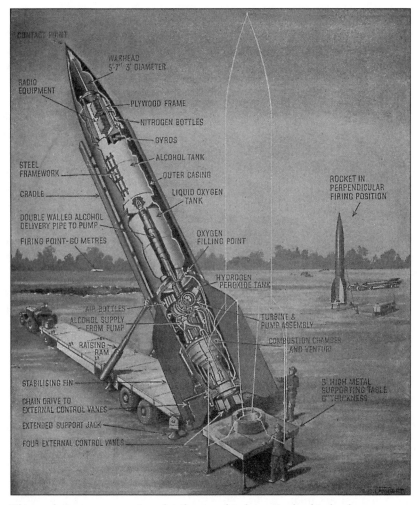

This revolutionary supersonic rocket threatened to bring England to her knees.
(Author's collection)

All those present then began jumping around and congratulating one another. Suddenly they froze where they stood. Ninety seconds after liftoff, a rapidly swelling howl indicated that the rocket was falling in the immediate vicinity. Speer, von Braun, and Dornberger remained standing; others flopped to the ground. The A-4 smashed into the earth less than a half mile away, its guidance system having gone haywire.

Curiously, von Braun and his rocket team were not downhearted. The young man grinned and told Speer: "Well, that proves we've solved the liftoff problem!"

Time was running out on the rocketeers. Their "spies" told them that the Luftwaffe scientists and engineers next door had nearly perfected the flying bomb, which could be built far cheaper (only the equivalent of six hundred dollars each) and much faster. However, other "spies" in Berlin informed von Braun and Colonel Dornberger that Hitler had not yet decided on which of his V-weapons (V for Vengeance) to give a production priority.

Then on October 13, four months after Speer had witnessed the A-4 rocket fizzle, another test-firing was in progress. Hopefully, von Braun and his team had worked out the kinks. A warning flare was sent up to alert those on Usedom. An engineer threw a switch, and a brilliant red-yellow flame shot from the rear of the rocket. Cables and wires fell away.

With what sounded like an enormous clap of rolling thunder, the metal monster slowly lifted; then, with a strident screech that could be heard for miles, it leaped into the cloudless sky. Thousands of eyes all over the island were glued on the swiftly ascending missile. One minute ticked past. Two minutes. Four minutes. The A-4 continued on course, out into the Baltic Sea.

Von Braun stood as though mesmerized: for the first time, a man-made object had broken through the sound barrier. Shouts of joy rang across the test area.

On the western side of Usedom, the Luftwaffe's flying-bomb camp was shrouded in gloom. The army's missile, after a previous failure, had attained a speed of 3,500 miles per hour, soared 35 miles high, and traveled some 120 miles.

In the wake of the spectacular A-4 success, von Braun, Dornberger, and others on the rocket team felt convinced that the führer would now give the green light for vastly accelerated research, development, and production. Their exuberance soon vanished. Hitler remained skeptical, filled with distrust of any technological innovation that went beyond his World War I experience as a corporal in the kaiser's infantry.[1]

Stealing German Weather Forecasts

A GLITTERING ARRAY of British and American generals and admirals was gathered around a long conference table in the War Office in London. They were to decide where the Western Allies would establish a second front to aid the hard-pressed Soviet army. It was July 20, 1942.

Almost at once, a heated argument erupted. Led by General Alan Brooke, chief of the Imperial General Staff and a highly decorated war hero, the British demanded an invasion of Algeria and Morocco, French colonies in northwestern Africa governed by Adolf Hitler's puppet regime in Vichy, France.

General George C. Marshall, the U.S. Army chief of staff, deeply resented what he considered Brooke's patronizing attitude toward American generals—

"newcomers to war from the Colonies." After one especially rowdy session, Brooke penned in his diary: "[The Allies] everywhere are holding on by our eyelids. . . . In light of that existing situation [Marshall's] plan for a cross-Channel assault [from England] against [Normandy] France for September 1942 is just fantastic."

After four days of intense argument, the British carried the ramparts: the second front would be established, not in Normandy, but in French northwestern Africa in an operation code-named Torch.

Two weeks later, U.S. General Dwight D. Eisenhower, who had been appointed supreme commander for Torch, and his sizable American and British staff moved into old, sprawling Norfolk House in St. James Square in London. With the arrival of the Americans, Royal Air Force Squadron Leader Frederick Winterbotham, whose crucial function was to protect the security of Ultra, was confronted by an entirely new ball game. Who among the Americans would receive regular distribution of Ultra decrypts?

It was decided that top U.S. commanders and their chief intelligence officers would be made privy to Ultra, the creation of the scientists at Bletchley Park (also known as Station X), north of London.

One afternoon in early August, Winterbotham and Stewart Menzies, chief of MI-6 (British intelligence), were escorted into the great room on the first floor of Norfolk House, which would be the planning center for Torch. Menzies had come along to add weight to the Ultra presentation. Minutes later, in strolled General Eisenhower and U.S. Lieutenant General Mark W. Clark, the chief planner for the invasion.

Eisenhower, known since boyhood as Ike, introduced the forty-seven-year-old Clark and his chief intelligence officers. Then he excused himself, explaining that he had already been told about Ultra by Prime Minister Winston Churchill.

Mark Clark, tall and lanky, was restless from the start. He shifted his weight in his chair, and glanced at his wristwatch every few moments. Clearly, he felt that all this was nonsense, a waste of his valuable time.

Trying to attract Clark's interest, Winterbotham gave several pertinent examples of what Ultra could do for Allied commanders. By Clark's facial expression, the RAF officer knew that the American did not believe him. After only fifteen minutes Clark rose, said that he had something important to do, and left the room.

Stewart Menzies was upset and angry. However, he calmed down when Winterbotham expressed the view that Eisenhower would make certain that Clark would properly use the Ultra information.

Winterbotham encountered a quite different reception from Major General Carl A. "Tooey" Spaatz, commander of the U.S. Eighth Air Force, which had steadily been building up in England. Astute, soft-spoken, but with a delightful sense of humor, Spaatz was immediately enthusiastic about the potential Ultra would provide, and he soon began making maximum use of it.

Ultra played a crucial role in briefings by Spaatz's meteorological officer for bombing missions over German-occupied western Europe. The Nazis kept the atmospheric conditions each day a closely guarded secret—except that Ultra picked up the German weather forecasts and flashed them to Spaatz's headquarters.

On occasion, Spaatz invited Frederick Winterbotham to attend briefings by his meteorologist for bombing raids over Europe. In great detail, the officer would tell of the weather all the way to the target and back. On occasion a doubtful flight commander asked about the source, at which time Tooey Spaatz would glance at Winterbotham with a twinkle in his eyes behind his gold-rimmed glasses and say quietly, "I think you can rely on that."[2]

"I Fear We Are in the Soup!"

AFTER A WOEFULLY unprepared United States had been bombed into global war on December 7, 1941, President Franklin Roosevelt was confronted for many months with colossal decisions that no chief executive in history had known. Most of his burdensome verdicts involved priorities in the production of the accoutrements of war.

In an address to Congress in January 1942, Roosevelt pledged that the United States would rapidly tool up and produce 125,000 airplanes, 75,000 tanks, and 8 million tons of shipping. Despite this enormous commitment of the nation's resources and manpower, Roosevelt, in June 1942, heeded the urgent recommendation of America's foremost scientists and secretly gave the green light to a program to develop an atomic bomb.

It was clear that the enterprise would be on such a massive scale that it could not be handled exclusively by a group of scientists, so control of the program was handed over to the Army Corps of Engineers. Colonel James C. Marshall, a West Point graduate with a background of building air bases, was selected to direct the program.

Marshall set up an office in New York City, and the covert operation gained a code name: Manhattan Engineer District (later Manhattan Project).

For weeks, the urgent atomic bomb enterprise lingered. Colonel Marshall had been unable to drive the project ahead of the countless other national priorities.

Each day, Vannevar Bush, head of the Office of Scientific Research and Development, stewed over the lack of progress. Like many other American scientists, he was gripped by an underlying fear that the Germans would develop the ultimate weapon first.

Bush discussed his deep concerns with Lieutenant General Brehon B. Somervell, the hard-nosed logistics genius who headed the global Army Service

Forces. What was critically needed, Bush stressed, was a strong military officer who would crack some heads and get things done.

Somervell agreed: "I have just the right man—Colonel Leslie Groves."

Lieutenant Colonel Kenneth D. Nichols, a Ph.D. in hydraulic engineering who had served under Groves, described his boss as "the biggest son of a bitch I've ever known—and one of the most capable. He has absolute confidence in his decisions, and he is absolutely ruthless in how he approaches a problem to get the job done."

When Nichols' analysis of Groves was passed along to seventy-five-year-old Secretary of War Henry Stimson, he exclaimed: "Great! Those are the precise qualities we are looking for!"

Unaware that his name was being bandied around in the highest councils of the armed forces, forty-six-year-old Colonel Leslie R. Groves received exhilarating news on the telephone. It was 10:35 A.M. on September 17, 1942. Twenty-four years after graduating fourth in his class at West Point and never having heard a bullet fired in anger, the three-hundred-pound engineer officer was being offered the command of a regiment that was going overseas. Now, after overseeing construction of the massive five-sided Pentagon, he would have the chance to prove what he could do on a battlefield. He was eager to get out from behind a desk—and out of Washington.

Later that same day, Groves bumped into General Somervell in a corridor of the House of Representatives Office Building where the engineer officer had just finished testifying before the Military Affairs Committee.

"About that duty overseas," Somervell said evenly, "you can tell them no."

Shocked, Groves replied: "Why?"

"Secretary of War Stimson has selected you for a very important assignment."

"Where?"

"Washington."

At that moment, Leslie Groves was the "angriest officer in the United States Army." The general's stars he sought so eagerly seemed to have vanished. Somervell's assurance that he would be promoted to brigadier general was only a slight comfort. This meant the end of his dream to lead troops in battle.

Brigadier General Groves—his promotion had been rushed through the bureaucracy in only six days—launched his crucial mission with all the delicacy of a blockbuster-bomb explosion. One of his first acts was to travel across Washington to confront Vannevar Bush, the Office of Scientific Research and Development director. Groves was unaware that Bush's ego had been bruised because the engineer officer's appointment to head the Manhattan Project had not been cleared with him.

Within moments after General Groves walked into Bush's office, sparks began to fly. Bush was brusque, evading Groves's questions. Then the general got angry. One word led to a thousand.

General Leslie Groves (second from left) discussing the Manhattan Project with a few scientists. From the left: James Chadwick of Great Britain, Richard C. Tolman, and H. D. Smyth. (U.S. Army)

Soon after Groves departed, Bush hurried to call on Brigadier General Wilhelm D. Styer, Somervell's chief of staff. Bush was still angry. He told Styer that he doubted if Groves had the tact needed to get the job done. Styer agreed that Groves was "sometimes blunt," but that he had other sterling qualities to overbalance.

That afternoon, Bush scrawled in his diary with regard to the Groves appointment: "I fear we are in the soup!" Translation: The atomic bomb program is in big trouble.

Next, Groves took it upon himself to draft a letter on the stationery of the War Production Board for the signature of Donald Nelson, a no-nonsense former Sears, Roebuck executive whom President Roosevelt had personally selected to be chairman of the agency. Nelson was virtually a czar. Groves's draft for Nelson's signature assigned an AAA rating—the first priority—to the Manhattan Project.

Groves himself carried the letter to Nelson, who, like the general, was no shrinking violet. Nelson rejected the proposal. There were too many important projects in the works to be giving an AAA rating to some vague program whose goal might be unattainable.

A heated debate ensued. Finally, Groves said that unless Nelson reversed himself, the general would have to call on President Roosevelt and tell him that the Manhattan Project would have to be scuttled because the chairman of the War Production Board refused to cooperate with Groves's needs.

Recognizing blackmail when he heard it, Nelson had a sudden change of heart. The first-priority rating was granted.

That afternoon, Groves was back in his office and approved a directive that had been lying on his predecessor's desk all summer. It called for the government to purchase fifty-two thousand acres of land in eastern Tennessee near the small town of Oak Ridge. On this site, a huge laboratory would be built in record time.

Almost at once, the brusque Groves clashed with the scientists on the project. As a military officer throughout his adult life, he instinctively regarded most scientists as totally undisciplined and impractical. For their part, most of the intellectuals distrusted a military officer, and deeply resented being told what to do by a gruff man who was ignorant of nuclear physics.

Groves was tough on the scientists in the Manhattan Project, and he treated them as though they were a wayward crowd. The general played no favorites. On one occasion he told Arthur Compton, the head of the University of Chicago laboratory that was working to establish a nuclear chain reaction: "Dr. Compton, you scientists don't have any discipline. You don't know how to take orders or to give orders."

Speaking to a group of physicists later, the new general was conceivably bent on proving to them that he was no scientific idiot.

"You may know that I have no Ph.D.," he said. "But let me tell you that I had ten years in which I just studied. I didn't have to make a living or give time to make a living, I just studied. That would be the equivalent of about two Ph.D.'s, wouldn't it?"

Groves had pulled a monumental boner. He appeared to be telling these intellectuals, some of whom had received Nobel Prizes in physics, that he was twice as smart as they were.

Only a week after taking charge, Groves learned that Secretary of War Stimson was going to appoint a nine-member atomic bomb oversight committee of military officers and civilians. Groves told Stimson, who was the number two man behind President Roosevelt in the military pecking order, that nine persons would be too unwieldy. Three would be just right. Stimson agreed, and appointed Vannevar Bush to be chairman of the Military Policy Committee.

Few, if any, generals ever *told* Stimson what he should do.

Groves's most serious clash with a scientist erupted in October 1942, about a month after the general had taken on his new job. The general's opponent was Leo Szilard, a Hungarian émigré, who was known for not only his scientific skills but also to a few as a troublemaker. Szilard, in fact, frequently indulged himself in what he had described as "my favorite hobby"—baiting the brass hats.

Szilard bent Groves's rule that forbade the scientists to openly discuss their own work among themselves in the name of security. The general tried to coerce Szilard into resigning. He refused.

Groves decided drastic action was required, and he drafted a letter to the U.S. attorney general labeling Szilard as "an enemy alien" and requested that the Hungarian be locked up for the remainder of the war.

Arthur Compton, the head of the nuclear laboratory in Chicago, got word of the letter and pleaded with Groves not to send it because an arrest of Szilard by the Federal Bureau of Investigation would create great unrest, even resentment, among fellow scientists.

Reluctantly, Groves scrapped the letter, but he put Szilard under surveillance. He had become convinced that the scientist was a German spy who had infiltrated the Manhattan Project, ignoring the fact that three years earlier, Szilard had been one of the three émigré scientists who had urged President Roosevelt to launch an atomic bomb program before the Nazis developed the ultimate weapon.

The surveillance of the innocent but tactless and eccentric scientist continued for several months. Although the sleuths involved reported no evidence of any subversive contacts, Groves insisted that the shadowing continue. Anyone who caused Groves such a pain in the neck as did Szilard *must* be a Nazi secret agent.

Early on, General Groves decided that what the Manhattan Project urgently needed was militarylike discipline throughout the entire organization. So he considered asking the War Department to induct all of his scientists into the army. Officer commissions would be awarded to the most important ones.

The scheme to run the Manhattan Project along the lines of a military chain of command died within a few weeks when a handful of scientists impressed on Groves that many of their colleagues would not continue their work if inducted into the army.

Whatever may have been General Groves's own idiosyncrasies, he would prove himself to be an organizational and administrative genius. The Manhattan Project, already the largest scientific research endeavor that history had known, would expand to gargantuan proportions during the next three and a half years. It would involve scores of often huge industrial efforts and the employment of hundreds of scientists, chemists, engineers, and technicians.

All of this Groves achieved while operating from a few rooms in the old War Department building in Washington, D.C. Many generals considered it a status symbol to have a huge personal staff, but Groves worked with only thirty people, including a secretary, two army officers to handle security matters, and a group of what the general called "my expediters." Their job was to prod lethargic entities, on behalf of Groves, by personal visits and telephone calls.

Groves, the scientists, and others in the Manhattan Project were acting on faith alone—no one knew if an atomic bomb could even be built.[3]

Fiasco in Chesapeake Bay

IN THE SPRING OF 1942, Army Chief of Staff George C. Marshall and the Chief of Naval Operations, Admiral Harold R. "Betty" Stark, recognized that eventual victory would require scores of amphibious landings. The two leaders were also aware that this type of operation, especially at night, was the most difficult of military maneuvers, requiring intricate coordination of army and navy.

Moreover, there was good reason to believe that Murphy's Law would take hold during an amphibious landing: If anything could go wrong, it would.

Consequently, General Marshall and Admiral Stark (who had received his quaint nickname when he was a plebe at the U.S. Naval Academy) asked the National Defense Research Committee to appoint a group of scientists to tackle the daunting problems inherent in night amphibious landings.

Working with army and navy officers, the scientists set about developing devices and techniques whereby assault troops, hopefully, would hit the right beach at the right time—without the enemy being alerted that a landing was in progress. Achieving that goal would require pinpoint navigation of troop transports to assembly areas some ten miles offshore. Then accurate guidance and split-second timing would be crucial if the landing craft were to find a beach within two hundred yards of a target and within one minute of H-Hour—all in the blackness of night.

In top-secret tests conducted at Woods Hole Oceanographic Institution, which operated major laboratories for the study of underwater sound and underwater explosives, the scientists concluded that radar could furnish tangents and ranges for ship navigators. But other devices to facilitate amphibious landings were developed, such as radio sonobuoys, fathometers, odographs, and gyrocompasses.

In a desperate attempt to make up for time lost in research and development in the previous two decades, a decision was made in the early fall of 1942 to conduct a test of the new devices and doctrine under battlelike conditions, even though these developments had not been perfected.

On a black night in early October, a small flotilla of ships dropped anchor in Chesapeake Bay, a long arm of the Atlantic Ocean that splits the state of Maryland, on the East Coast. On board one transport was Major General Ernest N. Harmon, a scrappy, salty-tongued warrior who was leader of the U.S. 2nd Armored Division.

With dawn about to break, hundreds of Harmon's foot soldiers slithered down rope ladders and scrambled into assault boats that, helter-skelter, headed for the beach. The beam of a lighthouse onshore would help the novice coxswains steering the landing craft to locate their targets.

The dry run (as such operations were known to American soldiers) was a fiasco. Only one boat, the one carrying General Harmon, reached its designated beach. The remainder of the craft were scattered for miles up and down the shore. It took Harmon until noon the next day to round up all the stray lambs.

"Old Gravel Voice," as Harmon was called, was shaken by the disastrous dress rehearsal. "If they can't find their beaches in peaceful Chesapeake Bay, with a lighthouse beacon to help," he barked to an aide, "how are they going to find an objective in the darkness on a foreign shore under conditions of war?"

Clearly the new devices and equipment created by the scientific committee still needed to be "debugged." It was equally obvious that the green soldiers and the young sailors navigating the assault boats had much to learn about the operation of these developments.[4]

The Soviets' Secret Nuclear Laboratory

IN THE SPRING OF 1942, Soviet scientists, whose preliminary research into developing an atomic bomb had been disrupted a year earlier when the German Wehrmacht invaded Russia, were now back in the business of trying to unlock the secrets of nuclear energy. Large numbers of scientists, including noted physicist Igor Kurchatov, who had told Josef Stalin two years earlier about the possibility of building an atomic bomb, had fled to Kazan, a city four hundred miles east of Moscow.

With the aid of a brutal winter, the seemingly invincible German war juggernaut had been stalled at the gates to Moscow in late 1941, then driven back by one hundred fresh Red Army divisions. Consequently, most of the scientists returned to Moscow.

Now that the front had been stabilized, the Soviet government resumed its interest in developing an atomic bomb, and it appointed a study committee that included Igor Kurchatov, who was named chairman. At its first meeting, the panel endorsed expanded research.

Scientists, physicists, mathematicians, and chemists were recalled from the battlefront and from institutes that had been evacuated far to the rear. They were ordered to assemble at Kurchatov's new laboratory at an abandoned farm on the Moscow River outside the capital. A nearby artillery-impact range provided a place for testing explosives. The supersecret institute was called simply

Laboratory Number 2, and it would be the center of atomic bomb research in the Soviet Union.[5]

Prediction: Hitler Will Have A-Bomb

ENERGIZED BY the Japanese attack on Pearl Harbor in December 1941, scores of scientists, physicists, mathematicians, and engineers were working on nuclear research projects scattered about the United States: Columbia University in New York City, Princeton University in New Jersey, the University of Chicago, the California Institute of Technology, and other locales. Nobel laureate Arthur Holly Compton, as coordinator of the nation's nuclear program, knew that there was duplication of effort and skirmishing among sites for funding, equipment, and manpower, as though the "enemy" were another research facility.

Otto Frisch, an émigré from Nazi Germany, was typical of those who ran experiments all day, then thought about physics far into the night. Frisch once explained to a friend that he came home from work, ate dinner, took a fifteen-minute nap, then sat down with a pencil and sheet of paper under a bright lamp.

"I usually worked until one or two o'clock in the morning, until I started having hallucinations," Frisch said. "When I began seeing queer-looking animals walking around the room I knew it was time to go to bed."

A scientist in the U.S. atomic energy program often carped that he would have no voice in deciding what military or political uses would be made of the ultimate weapon he and his colleagues were toiling to build. But he had only one choice: Pour his heart and know-how into the program or get out.

Most chose to remain, partly due to a sense of patriotism, but they harbored a far more intense motivation—fear that Adolf Hitler and the Nazi war machine would build an atomic bomb and thereby rule the world. So the specialists were engaged in a race against time.

Convinced that it was crucial for the scattered projects to be brought under one roof, Arthur Compton called the leaders at various research sites to a showdown meeting at his Chicago home on January 24, 1942, seven weeks after the United States had been bombed into global war.

Even before the session got under way, the air was thick with tension. Each scientist passionately presented the reason why his site should be selected. Most arguments had merit. Then Compton made a plea for Chicago.

Work would be done on the campus of the University of Chicago, whose vice president had already pledged to "turn the place inside out if necessary to win the war," Compton stressed. Moreover, the Windy City, as it was called, was centrally located, making travel easier and faster to facilities around the nation.

Compton's sales pitch convinced no one. Raucous arguments erupted and continued for nearly two hours. Finally Compton, who was bearing the brunt of the criticisms, reached the point of near exhaustion, and he declared that Chicago would be the central location of the research project.

Ernest Lawrence, the Nobel laureate from Cal Tech, refused to accept the decision. "You'll never get a chain reaction going in Chicago," he snorted. "The whole tempo of the University of Chicago is too slow."

Compton glared at his friend for several moments, then snapped, "We'll have a chain reaction going by the end of the year [1942]."

"I'll bet you a thousand dollars you won't," Lawrence fired back.

"I'll take you up on that," Compton retorted.

Lawrence hedged, "Well, let's make the stakes a five-cent cigar."

"Agreed!"

Within hours, Arthur Compton took over the large number of unused rooms under the west spectator stands of Stagg Field, named after a legendary football coach, on the University of Chicago campus. Several years earlier, the learning institution had dropped its football program in favor of scholarship.

The new research center was given a bland name, Metallurgical Laboratory (Met Lab, for short), a ploy designed to confuse Nazi spies, if any, and to minimize speculation among the university students concerning the sudden burst of activity in abandoned Stagg Field.

Despite widespread grumbling, nearly all of America's top physicists—mainly the group of émigrés from Europe such as Enrico Fermi, Edward Teller, and Leo Szilard—moved with their families to the Illinois metropolis on the banks of Lake Michigan.

Within weeks after Szilard arrived, he became angry and anxious over what he considered to be official U.S. government indifference toward the possibility that Nazi Germany was developing an atomic bomb. In a memo to Arthur Compton, he made a unique proposal: Establish a "friendly" physicist in Switzerland (adjoining the Third Reich) to contact scientists for news about atomic bomb development in Germany.

Szilard closed his confidential memo with a gloom-ridden observation: "Of course . . . there is not much point in our trying to find out what the Germans are doing since there is no possibility of any defense anyway."

Although Szilard was the most outspoken of the American nuclear energy scientists, his views reflected the fears of all throughout the war. "I often had a hard time going to sleep at night wondering if the Germans had mastered an atomic bomb," Vannevar Bush would later state.

Only days after Szilard had proposed sending an undercover physicist to spy on the Germans, the Hungarian émigré Eugene Wigner sent a frightening memo to Compton, listing a probable German schedule for the production of plutonium, an ingredient in the makeup of an atomic bomb. Wigner stated he

Physicist Leo Szilard. General Leslie Groves thought he was a Nazi spy. (Argonne National Laboratory)

was convinced that Adolf Hitler would have the ultimate weapon by Christmastime 1942—only six months away.

In the wake of Wigner's analysis, Compton appointed a physicist, J. C. Stearns, to develop defenses against German bombs carrying poisonous fission by-products from a working reactor. Word of Stearns's secret assignment leaked out, and the Met Lab was soon rife with outlandish rumors—the Germans had developed radiological weapons, scientists in Chicago were moving their families far out into the countryside, army officials were ringing sprawling Chicago with radiation detectors.

One day, physicist Hans Bethe, a German émigré, was passing through Chicago and paid a call on his old friend Leo Szilard. Bethe had been a professor at the University of Tübingen in the early 1930s. But his mother was Jewish, and when Hitler had issued his anti-Semitic decrees, Bethe was dismissed.

Bethe was not alone in his predicament. More than a thousand Jews on the teaching staffs of German universities had been curtly cut off from their livelihoods. Most of them hoped to find teaching jobs abroad, but the majority were young and without reputations. Bethe, however, had been widely known in the international academic community, and he sailed for the United States with his family in 1935 to teach at Cornell University.

Now in Chicago, Bethe found Szilard to be as irascible and quick-tempered as always. The Hungarian still was upset because, he said, American leaders showed no urgency in building an atomic bomb. Most alarming was the fact that the Germans were far ahead of the Americans in development of an ultimate weapon, he declared.

"I am going to write down all that is going on these days in the [nuclear research] project. I am just going to write down the facts—not for anyone to read, just for God."

"Don't you think God knows the facts?" Bethe chided.

"Maybe he does," Szilard admitted. "But not *my* version of the facts!"[6]

Eavesdropping on
Roosevelt and Churchill

IT WAS PAST MIDNIGHT on March 6, 1942, and Adolf Hitler was poring over reports that had reached his command post, code-named Wolfsschanze (Wolf's Lair), in the gloomy woods behind the Eastern Front. When he came to a top-secret document from fifty-eight-year-old Wilhelm Ohnesorge, minister of the postal organization Deutsche Reichspost, the führer's interest intensified.

Ohnesorge's report concerned the result of a telephone experiment that had been carried out during the past year under such clandestine conditions that even Hitler knew little about the project. The report stated that Reich scientists had developed a technique whereby they could eavesdrop on "scrambled" transatlantic telephone conversations between Allied leaders in London and those in Washington.

The führer stomped his foot in glee over the prospect of learning the word-by-word discussions between Prime Minister Winston Churchill and President Franklin Roosevelt.

A complex monitoring station was built near Eindhoven in the Netherlands. Technicians tapping the transatlantic radiotelephone conversations were all trusted men of the Sicherheitsdienst (SD), the security and intelligence service of Reichsführer Heinrich Himmler's elite SS. Only Hitler, Himmler, and Foreign Minister Joachim von Ribbentrop received translated intercepts. Even Admiral Wilhelm Canaris, chief of the Abwehr, was kept in the dark about the Nazi intelligence triumph.

Churchill in particular was addicted to the telephone. At any moment he might grab the instrument at his underground bunker in London and call his good friend Roosevelt. Both men used code names when discussing persons or military operations. But German intelligence, based on transcripts of the talks, could deduce the terminology of the two men and gain valuable, even highly secret, information.

Churchill and Roosevelt were not concerned about tipping off the Germans because there had been elaborate security precautions built into the com-

German intelligence eavesdropped on transatlantic telephone calls between President Roosevelt (left) and Prime Minister Churchill. (National Archives)

munications system between London and Washington. The lengthy conversations between the two Allied leaders were routed through the American Telephone & Telegraph Company's main switchboard at 47 Walker Street, New York City. There, in a guarded and tightly locked room, the words were mangled by what was called the Bell A-3 device and rendered incomprehensible to anyone tapping into the radiotelephone link—or so it was thought. As a further safeguard, the operators handling the calls often, at random, switched the link from one frequency to another.

Wilhelm Ohnesorge had learned of the existence of the A-3 device, and developed a means to unscramble most of the talks and also keep abreast of the frequency changes.

Ohnesorge's intricate creation was so ingenious and efficient that from interception at Eindhoven to the delivery of translated copies in Berlin, only a few hours would elapse. It was probably the fastest procurement of significant intelligence in the history of secret service operations.[7]

A Burglar Alarm at Gibraltar

THERE WERE tension-filled days and nights at the large Victorian mansion at Station X, the secret home of Ultra at Bletchley Park north of London. The British were especially alert to detect any sign among the hundreds of decrypts in the fall of 1942 that the German high command had even an inkling that the Anglo-Americans were preparing to invade French Northwest Africa (code-named Torch) in November.

So far, the decrypts had disclosed that German intelligence was assuring Adolf Hitler that the Western Allies were incapable of major offensive action. Then Ultra unbuttoned a frightening message: The Germans were mounting some kind of covert activity along the Strait of Gibraltar, the narrow body of water leading into the Mediterranean and through which hundreds of Allied ships would have to pass to reach Torch landing beaches in Morocco.

Had the vigilant Abwehr, which had scores of spies planted in Spain, many of them focusing on the Strait of Gibraltar, learned that the Allies were about to strike in North Africa?

More Ultra decrypts disclosed that the Germans had given the activity the code name Bodden. (Bodden is the name of a narrow strip of water separating the German island of Rügen from the mainland.)

Station X passed this ominous information to thirty-year-old Harold A. "Kim" Philby, a top official at MI-6, the British Secret Service. Brilliant and arrogant, he was the son of Harry St. John Bridger Philby, a noted explorer who had been an aide to Winston Churchill in the Admiralty during World War I.

In 1940 Harry Philby had been jailed for his outspoken criticism of Great Britain going to war against Nazi Germany, which, at that time, had a friendship pact with the Soviet Union. Son Kim himself had Communist ties going back to his days at elite Trinity College at Cambridge, where antipatriotism had not just been tolerated, it also had been fashionable.

Despite his Communist-tinged background and his father's public harangues against the British establishment, Kim had been appointed to his high-level post by Stewart Menzies, the MI-6 chief. Menzies felt that young Philby had a nose for vital military intelligence.

Philby's "nose" now told him that the Germans were indeed engaged in some covert project at the Strait of Gibraltar. So he took the Ultra decrypts and the evidence he himself collected to the young Air Intelligence scientist Reginald Jones.

After studying the information, Jones and his team were convinced that the Germans were in the process of setting up a huge "burglar alarm" to detect Allied ships passing through the bottleneck.

It became clear that the Germans were mounting three infrared search-lights in Spanish Morocco, on the southern coast of the strait. These beams were

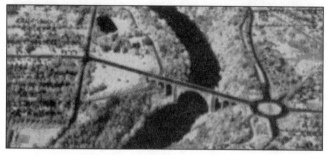

Secret German infrared-film posts were set up to monitor British convoys passing through narrow Strait of Gibraltar. In this random scene, the photo taken with infrared film (bottom) brings out landscape features not evident in photo (top) taken with regular film. (Author's collection)

aimed northward to an infrared detector on the Spanish shore, even though Spain was officially neutral.

Infrared rays pass through matters that block ordinary light rays, so they can "see" objects at night or through fog by reflecting on hot objects, such as the funnels on ships.

Royal Air Force reconnaissance planes were dispatched to the two sites of German activity at the strait, and their photos confirmed the conclusions reached by Jones and his team.

Now, with Operation Torch fast approaching, the knotty problem confronting the British was how to counter this unexpected threat to the invasion armada. One option was to assign a large number of ships to steam back and forth in the strait at night to confuse the German infrared scientists so they could not focus on the Torch convoys as they passed through the bottleneck.

That scheme was rejected by the Admiralty because the decoy ships might collide with the Torch vessels, tipping off the Germans that an Allied invasion was in progress.

Another option was to have the RAF bomb the two sites. That idea was also rejected because the British would be bombing officially neutral countries north and south of the strait. Even if the bombs were launched and hit the targets, the Germans could replace the equipment and set it up at a nearby site. Moreover, a bombing might alert the Abwehr that the Allies had something big brewing in the western Mediterranean.

Finally, Reginald Jones and MI-6 officers decided to use a diplomatic approach to get the Spanish government to oust the Nazi infrared facilities from its soil. That overture in itself would be fraught with thorny obstacles. For one, Generalissimo Francisco Franco, the Spanish dictator who called himself El Caudillo (the leader), was a crony of Adolf Hitler. So how would he react to a British demand that he, in essence, take issue with Nazi Germany?

The key player in the diplomatic-approach scenario would be the British ambassador to Spain, Samuel Hoare, who had been appointed to that post by Winston Churchill in May 1940. Colleagues considered Hoare to be intelligent, but lacking in worldly sophistication despite having held many top government posts for twenty-five years.

Hoare was devoid of technical knowledge, yet he would be expected to present a convincing case to Spanish leaders. But if British scientists were to fly into Madrid to "coach" him on infrared technology, the suspicions of Nazi spies might be aroused. So Reginald Jones would have the highly complicated task of briefing Hoare by a series of telegrams. These communications, moreover, could conceivably be intercepted by German agents, thereby disclosing a sudden British interest in the Strait of Gibraltar.

When Ambassador Hoare met with Spanish officials, he had to be scrupulously careful not to drop clues about the true source of British enlightenment—Ultra—concerning the German burglar alarm. His sales pitch was a mixture of appealing to the Spaniards to reinforce their neutral posture by evicting the German facilities while hinting that the Allies might retaliate against Spain should Franco turn a blind eye toward the infrared stations. Ambassador Hoare, Winston Churchill, Reginald Jones, and other British scientists involved in the diplomatic approach were unaware that Franco now believed that the Nazis were going to lose the war, so he did not want to alienate the Allies.

Franco's conviction resulted from a secret episode that had occurred on October 23, 1940. At that time, Adolf Hitler, who had conquered most of western Europe and whose Wehrmacht appeared to be invincible, traveled by train all the way to the border town of Hendaye to meet with Generalissimo Franco. The führer had not made that long trip for social purposes; rather he asked the leader of neutral Spain if a division of German soldiers (traveling in disguise) could be given free passage through Spain to link up with an airborne assault to seize the Rock of Gibraltar from the British.

Franco had been hesitant, but he promised to give Hitler a reply to the request in a few days. In the meantime, Admiral Wilhelm Canaris, the wily Abwehr chief who knew of Hitler's scheme to capture the British crown colony, a massive rock towering fourteen hundred feet, paid a secret visit to the Spanish dictator. Canaris was deeply involved in a conspiracy inside the Third Reich to get rid of Hitler and the Nazi regime.

Canaris, seeking to undermine the führer, had astounded Franco by predicting that Germany would lose the war. Consequently, the incredulous El Caudillo had his foreign minister advise Hitler that it would be "too dangerous" for Spain to allow armed "foreign troops" on her soil.

Now, two years after the Canaris machination, Generalissimo Franco advised Ambassador Hoare that his government would formally request Germany to remove the infrared units.

A few days later, Royal Air Force reconnaissance planes were sent over the two German sites at the strait. Their photos, together with Ultra decrypts, disclosed that the Nazis had indeed left.

There was neither time nor inclination for the British scientists to celebrate their most recent behind-the-scenes victory. Along with Allied headquarters in London, they were gripped by a haunting specter: Had the timing of the infrared scheme been a happenstance, or had German intelligence discovered the secret of Torch? If the Luftwaffe and U-boats were to be concentrated near the strait bottleneck when the Torch invasion convoys were passing through, a monstrous debacle could be inflicted on the Anglo-Americans.

On the night of November 3—D-Day minus five—Covering Force H, commanded by British Vice Admiral Neville Syfret on his flagship *Duke of York*, began stealing through the Strait of Gibraltar. Syfret's force included two other battleships, two aircraft carriers, three cruisers, and seventeen destroyers. By dawn the formidable force had cleared the strait, and more ships carrying assault troops would follow that night.

Far from Gibraltar at two o'clock in the morning of November 8, 1942, Adolf Hitler was asleep in his private train parked in Munich. The führer had traveled all the way from his battle headquarters behind the Eastern Front to speak at the nineteenth anniversary of the Beer Hall Putsch of 1923, his first attempt at revolution, which had collapsed after a gunfight with police.

At this early hour, Hitler was awakened by Generaloberst (four-star general) Alfred Jodl, his trusted operations chief, and told that the Americans and the British were landing troops at several points in French Morocco and Algeria.

Hitler had been taken totally by surprise, thanks in a large measure to the Gibraltar burglar alarm having been dismantled.

A few weeks after the Western Allies had landed in North Africa, Reginald Jones uncovered clues that the Germans were still highly active in Spain. They had erected a radio facility, a type known as Elektra Sonne, along the coast in a remote region of northwestern Spain. This powerful station began to transmit radio beams westward over the Atlantic Ocean and northward across the Bay of Biscay, permitting Luftwaffe planes and U-boats to determine their positions.

Jones winced at the thought of having to go through the same Gibraltar scenario again, reflecting on how difficult and frustrating it had been to brief

The Strait of Gibraltar and the Bay of Biscay.

Ambassador Hoare by telegrams on technological aspects. So the young scientist hatched a machination.

The Royal Air Force was flying more missions over the Bay of Biscay in search of U-boats going and coming from their bases in France than were Luftwaffe planes flying escort above the U-boats. Therefore, Jones contacted the chief navigation officer at Coastal Command and posed a curious question: If the British scientists could provide Coastal Command with a fan of beams above the Bay of Biscay, could Royal Air Force planes make better use of them to orient themselves than could the Germans?

Two days later, the Coastal Command officer called back. The reply was "indeed we can," and he expressed deep appreciation to Jones and "to

Adolf Hitler" for the unexpected radio-beam service in the relentless search for U-boats.

Now all Jones had to do was to send reconnaissance planes to photograph the station. From the position of the station's aerials and the direction of their alignment, the necessary instructions were created, requiring only charts, a simple receiver, and a stopwatch in each Coastal Command aircraft. The code name Consol was given to this pirated system by the British.

It was one of the most bizarre situations of the war. German scientists had provided much technical expertise to the project, the Nazi treasury had poured money into building and maintaining the secret station, and German manpower kept the facility operating around the clock. But throughout the war, the British would be taking advantage of the German radio beams to hunt down U-boats in the Bay of Biscay with considerable success.[8]

Feuds among Nazi Bigwigs

BY LATE 1942, both the Germans and the Western Allies were relying heavily on the growing technology of communications intelligence developed by brilliant scientists in both camps. From embryonic beginnings in World War I, the new instruments for eavesdropping on an enemy had become one of the most effective and dramatic weapons of the hidden war.

Like the Anglo-Americans, German operatives tapped telephones, intercepted telegraphic messages, and tuned in on enemy radio traffic. But these interceptions were of no value unless their codes could be deciphered, and the Germans had much success in this difficult science.

Almost a dozen separate agencies in the Third Reich were involved in electronic snooping. Special needs of various branches of the German armed forces accounted for part of this proliferation. But mainly these rival agencies had sprung up and been nourished in recent years because of a lust for power. Many Nazi bigwigs had set up their own eavesdropping organizations even though they all tended to produce similar intelligence that was jealously guarded.

Although this intramural rivalry in the highest Nazi councils of power proved to be a plus factor for the Allies on numerous occasions, Adolf Hitler secretly approved of the duplication. No single would-be führer could collect all of the enormous stream of decoded intelligence and use it for his own plan to topple Hitler and seize total power in the Reich.

Reichsmarschall Hermann Goering, the number two man in the Nazi pecking order, had built up his personal snooping bureau, the Forschungsamt (Communications Intelligence Service), which had an astonishing six thousand employees. They listened round-the-clock to telephone conversations and intercepted radio and telegraphic messages.

Goering's personal telephone-tapping operation alone was prodigious in scope. His web linked more than a thousand taps within the Reich and Nazi-occupied countries as well as Allied radio and telephone conversations. When a call passed through a tapped line, a bulb lit up in a local listening post. A monitor known as a Z-man either recorded the message or took notes of the conversation, which was forwarded to Berlin for decoding and evaluation.

Foreign Minister Joachim von Ribbentrop, one of the most intense Nazi schemers among a group of experts in that field, had his technicians monitoring on a twenty-four-hour basis the radio traffic of foreign missions. Ribbentrop had gathered an exceptional group of codebreakers, and they managed to crack the diplomatic ciphers of thirty-four nations—including those of Germany's war partners Italy and Japan.

Von Ribbentrop became frustrated at his inability to seize control of Goering's Research Office and was envious over its meddling into diplomatic snooping. So he sometimes had Research Office intelligence reports retyped on his own Foreign Ministry letterheads and stamped to infer to Adolf Hitler that the information had been obtained by his own ministry.

Top German leaders devoted much of their time and energy not to the war effort, but to taking over their rivals' eavesdropping operations. Goering was eager to incorporate into his already huge Research Office the ace codebreakers in Chi, the ciphers branch of the Oberkommando der Wehrmacht (high command).

The number three Nazi, Reichsführer Heinrich Himmler, chief of the dreaded Gestapo and commander of the elite Schutzstaffel (SS), connived relentlessly to get Goering's Research Office folded into his own security apparatus, the Sicherheitsdienst (SD). Himmler was aided and abetted in his quest by his protégé, thirty-seven-year-old Reinhard Heydrich, head of the SD.

Brilliant and with the instincts of a barracuda, the ambitious Heydrich paid mainly lip service to Himmler's plot to take over Goering's Research Office. Heydrich dreamed of immense power in which he himself would absorb all of the Reich intelligence services and become chief of the single organization.

Although Chi cryptanalysts had scored a monumental achievement in breaking the Black Code (which was used by U.S. embassies around the world to radio Washington reports from military attachés), it was the German Navy's codebreakers who outshined all others in the Reich. This branch, commonly called B-Dienst, short for Beobachtungs-Dienst (Observation Service), featured Wilhelm Tranow, a civilian of colossal talent as a cryptographer.

Tranow had broken his first code as a teenage radioman aboard a German battleship in World War I. Because of his talent, he had been accepted into what became known as the B-Dienst. His assignment had been to crack the British Navy's ciphers, and by the time war broke out in Europe in 1939 he could read the Admiralty's main codes.

After 1939 and in the years that followed, Tranow continued to excel at his specialized craft. The British kept changing their codes, and B-Dienst, led by Tranow, kept solving them.

By mid-1943, B-Dienst had established forty-four intercept stations, stretching for some two thousand miles, from the northern tip of Norway to southern France. These posts conducted an incredible amount of business, logging a total of about eighty-five hundred intercepts daily, then shuttling them on to B-Dienst headquarters in Berlin. There, in the British section alone, some one thousand codebreakers, analysts, and clerks transformed the raw information into intelligence reports for distribution to armed forces headquarters.

As the war progressed, however, the Western Allies created increasingly complex codes. Even the gifted Wilhelm Tranow and B-Dienst were hard put to keep up with the secret Allied electronic traffic.[9]

A Chess Game in the Atlantic

TWO WEEKS AFTER New Year 1943 burst forth over a world engulfed by bloody conflict, President Franklin Roosevelt and Prime Minister Winston Churchill, with their entourages, arrived in Casablanca for Symbol, code name for a high-level strategy conference. An invitation had been cabled to Soviet dictator Josef Stalin, but he rejected it.

Convening at the Hotel Anfa, a resort overlooking the sparkling blue Atlantic Ocean, the conferees immediately got into a dispute. General George Marshall, the U.S. Army chief of staff, argued for launching a cross-Channel attack from England against northern France in the fall of 1943. General Alan Brooke, chief of the imperial General Staff, insisted that such a venture would be foolhardy until 1944.

It soon become evident that the British had an enormous advantage in the heated verbal skirmishing. In matters relating to Europe and the Mediterranean, they had a monopoly on intelligence about the Germans and the Italians, information gained mostly by Ultra, the secret process that intercepted and decoded enemy radio messages.

Ultra had stormed the American ramparts at Casablanca and carried the day for Winston Churchill. General Brooke's proposals were adopted. All of North Africa would soon be in the hands of the Western Allies, so an invasion of Sicily, a large island at the toe of Italy, was set for mid-1943. The first charge of the Anglo-Americans, however, would be the defeat of the U-boat menace in the North Atlantic to enable the Allies to build up a mighty army in England for an eventual invasion of France.

In 1942 the Allies had suffered a maritime catastrophe, losing 1,665 ships, mostly in the North Atlantic. It was on this vast ocean battleground that Adolf

Hitler hoped to win the war against the Anglo-Americans or gain a negotiated peace.

Winston Churchill would later declare that the dominant elements in the fight against the U-boats were "groping and drowning, ambuscade and stratagem, science and seamanship." He could have added cryptanalysis.

Although the Western Allies—mainly the British—had taken a heavy toll of U-boats in the first forty-five months of the war, Admiral Karl Doenitz, commander of the submarine service, began the year 1943 with more undersea craft than ever before. Affectionately called der Löwe (the Lion) by his officers, Doenitz had about four hundred U-boats available, compared to fifty-seven he had had at the outbreak of the war.

All along, Doenitz had one amazing advantage in the death struggle in the Atlantic: American insurance firms continued to wire detailed cargo and sailing-date information to neutral countries in Europe. One recipient of this crucial intelligence was an insurance agent in Zurich, Switzerland, who routinely passed it along to a colleague in Munich. He, in turn, slipped the information to German naval intelligence.

It was not until February 1943, more than a year after the United States had gone to war, that Congress passed an act to force insurance companies to cease the procedure.

At his new headquarters in Berlin's Hotel-am-Steinplatz, Admiral Doenitz was being consistently informed about the makeup and movements of Allied convoys. B-Dienst, the highly efficient German radio monitoring and decoding organization, had broken the British naval codes. German cryptanalysts, therefore, were able to pinpoint convoy routes, the type of cargo, and the number of warship escorts.

A few hundred miles from Berlin, Royal Navy Captain Rodger Winn was steadily reading Ultra decrypts in the Submarine Tracking Room at The Citadel, an old fortress not far from Buckingham Palace, home of the Royal Family, in London. It was Winn's job to issue orders to the convoys in the Atlantic based on the intelligence collected by Ultra.

Winn had another distinct advantage, a British scientific marvel the sailors had labeled Huff-Duff, a high-frequency direction finder. Installed at stations on the coasts of Newfoundland, Iceland, and Greenland, the network blanketed the North Atlantic. Huff-Duff was also installed in the escort ships for convoys. The electronic detection device could tune in on radio messages that a U-boat at sea sent to Admiral Doenitz's headquarters in Berlin. After a submarine had broadcast only a few digits, Huff-Duff could zero in on its location.

Curiously, the astute Doenitz never grasped the fact that Huff-Duff was in use, even though German air reconnaissance photographs showed Huff-Duff antennas aboard escort ships and B-Dienst intercepts disclosed indiscreet comments about the revolutionary new apparatus in Allied ship-to-ship radio conversations.

A German U-boat skipper scans an enemy convoy through a periscope. (Author's collection)

Doenitz presumed that each radio message being broadcast at sea was being picked up by the British, thereby giving away a submarine's location. But radio communication was crucial to collecting a wolf pack to attack Allied convoys detected by B-Dienst. So U-boat skippers were instructed to keep their radio broadcasts terse and to frequently change wavelengths to make it more difficult for British radio monitors to find them.

At the Hotel-am-Steinplatz in Berlin and The Citadel in London, Admiral Doenitz and Captain Winn were engaged in a high-stakes game of chess for supremacy in the North Atlantic. Each man focused on a large table some ten feet square, upon which were tiny flags, symbols, and pins representing the locations of Allied convoys and the German wolf packs. As intelligence flowed into these two key centers from B-Dienst and from Ultra and Huff-Duff, Doenitz and Winn shuffled around the tiny "pawns" to bring the battle situation up to the moment.

During the first three weeks of March 1943, B-Dienst cryptanalysts decoded 175 Allied radio signals, among which were ones indicating that two England-bound convoys, SC122 and HX229, had sailed from New York. Decrypts disclosed that these convoys were heavily loaded with tanks, airplanes, guns, and ammunition.

These B-Dienst decrypts triggered the largest battle of the war in the Atlantic: forty-two U-boats against more than one hundred cargo ships and escorts. In Berlin, Admiral Doenitz was determined to bag every ship, thereby striking a gargantuan blow at Great Britain.

B-Dienst information provided der Löwe with knowledge of the two convoys' speed, their course, and the weather. Subsequently, tactics were communicated to the U-boat skippers through Goliath, the huge U-boat transmitter at Frankfurt an der Oder.

Far out in the Atlantic near Greenland, the U-boats of the Stürmer (Daredevils) wolf pack were ordered by Doenitz to slip in front of oncoming convoy HX229. At the same time, Captain Winn was reading Doenitz's signals through Ultra, so he promptly gave orders for HX229 to alter its course.

In the meantime, Doenitz obtained information on the second convoy, SC122, a group of about sixty-five heavily escorted ships, so the U-boat chief instructed the Dränger (Harrier) wolf pack to get across the path of SC122.

Ultra then decrypted Doenitz's signal, and Winn warned SC122 to change its direction.

It was a bizarre situation. The two convoys maneuvered over the sea, sometimes under a bright moon, at other times in fog, even among icebergs—both inching steadily toward England at ten knots (a knot is the equivalent of 1.1516 miles per hour). Steadily, SC122 and HX229 merged, resulting in a huge amount of shipping in a relatively small space of ocean.

Dränger and Stürmer steered toward this mass of cargo vessels and warships. A torpedo could hardly miss. Captain Winn at The Citadel warned the two convoys, but it was too late. At one minute past two o'clock in the morning of March 17, the U-boats struck. In one minute, four ships—*Fort Cedar Lake, Aldermine, King Gruffyd,* and *Kingsbury*—were hit by torpedoes. Gigantic explosions and bursts of orange fire from fuel and ammunition lit the sky.

A few of the U-boats were armed with FAT (short for *Federapparat,* or coiled-spring) torpedoes, a recent creation of German scientists. These metal fish could be preset to steer in a straight line for a specified distance, then weave back and forth in a series of shallow loops. A FAT would cut back and forth across the path of a convoy until either it hit a ship or the power in its electric motor fizzled. Before firing, a submarine's radio operator always warned other U-boats in the vicinity so they could get out of the way before the zigzagging torpedo blasted a friendly hull.

The battle over a huge region of the North Atlantic had been an Allied debacle. One of every five ships that had sailed with the two convoys from New York had been sunk. In all, the Allies lost a staggering ninety-seven vessels in the first three weeks of March.

Admiral Doenitz was euphoric. He radioed the U-boat skippers that they had achieved "the greatest success ever in a single convoy battle."

In mid-April, Ultra disclosed frightening news to Captain Rodger Winn at The Citadel. Ninety-eight U-boats—the most Doenitz had ever sent out at one time—were streaming into the North Atlantic. Because of this dire threat to

Preparing to fire a Hedgehog at a submerged German U-boat. (Author's collection)

Great Britain's lifeline, Prime Minister Winston Churchill, in desperation, cautiously reduced the use of Ultra to gain tactical advantage. It may have been the only time in the war that such a drastic step had been taken by the British.

Although U-boats were continuing to rack up kills, Doenitz lost forty-one submarines in the first three weeks of May, so he ordered his wolf packs to withdraw from the North Atlantic until he had established what new devices the Allies had been using for this sudden reversal of German fortunes at sea.

As Doenitz suspected, Allied scientists had created a number of revolutionary and highly effective means for waging war against the U-boats. One of these developments was the Hedgehog, which was installed at the bow of escort warships. A mortarlike weapon that could hurl twenty-four projectiles 250 yards ahead of the ship, the Hedgehog was unlike conventional depth charges. Its thirty-two-pound bombs exploded only on contact with a U-boat lying silently on the bottom of the ocean. This feature eliminated the need to estimate the submarine's depth, a chancy procedure at best.

British scientists, meanwhile, also had developed a system whereby U-boats could be pinpointed, even at night and in foggy weather. Code-named H2S, it was the first ten-centimeter radar that employed a revolutionary valve called the magnetron. Fitted inside British search planes, H2S had exceptional range and accuracy. Moreover, it neutralized Metox, a secret device developed by German scientists that detected approaching aircraft through radar emanations and enabled the U-boats to dive and escape attack.

With Ultra unleashed from the shackles that had bound it since war had broken out, Captain Winn in The Citadel was able to tell search airplane commanders where surfaced U-boats were located by radio. Then the aircraft, through H2S, would pounce on the unsuspecting submarines.

In the meantime, German scientists, under Admiral Doenitz's urgent prodding, developed several countermeasures, including "foxing devices" designed to fool detectors and cause British patrol planes to rush into wild-goose chases. One of these ingenious new creations was code-named Aphrodite.

Aphrodite was relatively simple in scope. It consisted of a small balloon anchored to a floating device. A U-boat would deploy the apparatus, which hovered on the water. When draped with aluminum foil, the contraption gave off echoes like those in a genuine wolf pack of U-boats.

Detecting the echoes on their H2S devices, British planes would rush to the site, where they would find only Aphrodite. The U-boat that had placed the contraption had long since fled.

German electronic engineers had been able to unlock the secret of H2S after retrieving the apparatus from a Royal Air Force bomber that had been shot down near Rotterdam, in the Netherlands.

In September 1943 Admiral Doenitz sent his U-boat wolf packs back into the North Atlantic. They were armed with these new devices and high hopes. But the inexorable pendulum of battle had swung in favor of the Western Allies. During the next three months, seventy-two German submarines were destroyed.

The decisive Battle of the Atlantic was over. Karl Doenitz had lost much more than a lethal conflict. His two sons had been killed during the death struggle on the boundless ocean.[10]

History's First Nuclear Spy

NEVER IN AMERICAN HISTORY had security been as tight as it was around the Manhattan Project, the atomic bomb development program. Everybody and everything had code names. General Leslie Groves, who was in charge of the project, was called "Relief." Arthur Compton, director of the Metallurgical Laboratory at the University of Chicago, was "A. H. Comas" or "A. Holly." Enrico Fermi, who had split the atom for the first time in history in December 1942, became "Henry Farmer."

The huge gaseous diffusion plant at Oak Ridge, Tennessee, was "K-25"; a facility at Los Alamos, New Mexico, was "Site X"; and the scientist in charge of an atom-splitting operation at Stagg Field, the abandoned football stadium in Chicago, had the title "coordinator of rapid rupture."

American leaders were hoping that the tight security net would keep the Manhattan Project a secret from Nazi Germany, so they were jolted early in 1943 when the Federal Bureau of Investigation (FBI) uncovered a chilling *Mikropunkt* (microdot) message being sent at Hamburg, Germany, from Ast X, the branch of the Abwehr (secret service) directly responsible for espionage in North America and England.

German scientists had created a masterpiece of espionage communication, an ingenious technological breakthrough with the microdot. Developed at the Institute of Technology in Dresden, the process permitted the Germans to photograph a large sheet of paper and reduce it to the size of a postage stamp. Then, using a new type of microscope, it would be photographed again and shrunk to the size of a dot. Hiding places for these dots were infinite—in any kind of letter or document, or even on the outside of an envelope.

The microdot message from Ast X detected by the FBI said in part:

> There is reason to believe that the scientific works for the utilization of atomic energy are being driven forward into a certain direction in the United States. Continuous information about the tests made on this subject are required and particularly the [answers to these questions]:
>
> What tests are being made with uranium? What other raw materials are being used in these tests? What process is used for transporting uranium?

The names and addresses of several prominent scientists who were Americans or émigrés and involved in atomic research were listed.

German-born Alfred Hohlhaus, the recipient of the microdot message and a longtime resident of the United States, held a high-paying job as an industrial chemist. He reported to Ast X that a number of American helium plants were expanding rapidly to increase production of the gas. He had used his professional connections to be taken on escorted tours of helium plants across the nation.

"Since helium production had been ample to meet normal needs in the United States, the expansion must be related to some other important purpose, such as the harnessing of atomic energy for military purposes," Hohlhaus wrote in the invisible ink he had been provided.

Meanwhile, in the Third Reich in mid-1943, top Nazi leaders were putting heavy pressure on Admiral Wilhelm Canaris, the Abwehr chief in Berlin, to ferret out the secrets of America's atomic experiments. A search was launched for a qualified spy, preferably a physicist. Chosen for the crucial mission was fifty-one-year-old Walther Koehler, a native of Gouda, the Netherlands, who had been a spy for the German kaiser in World War I.

Koehler had lived in New York City for several years in the late 1930s as a "sleeper" (an agent who was deep undercover until called on for a specific mission). He had been ordered back to Germany in June 1941 to await an assignment. Now Ast X promised him substantial amounts of money to spy out atomic secrets in the United States.

Koehler could never resist the lure of money, so he accepted the offer. He was given a crash course in nuclear physics and provided a new "cover" and phony American credentials expertly crafted. One plus factor was evident: his harmless appearance—he was a chubby, shy man who squinted through thick-lensed glasses. No one would suspect that he was a German secret agent.

Walther Koehler, history's first nuclear spy, and his wife left Hamburg for Madrid on the first leg of the trip back to the United States. The couple would be posing as anti-Nazi, devoutly Catholic refugees on the run from the Gestapo. Crammed into Koehler's pockets and sewn into the linings of his luggage were the valuables he had been given by the Abwehr as the initial payment for his services: $16,230 in cash, traveler's checks, and gold coins (the collective equivalent of some $170,000 in 1999).

Within hours of arriving in Madrid, the Koehlers took evasive action to shake off any tails and headed for the U.S. consulate. While the Dutchman poured out his fantastic story of being a German spy whose mission was to dig out nuclear secrets in the United States, the vice consul eyed him suspiciously.

Koehler explained that he had been given orders to establish a covert radio station in the United States and send back reports to Ast X.

The vice consul sat silently, clearly unimpressed. So Koehler dug into a suitcase and pulled out the espionage accoutrements he had been given in Hamburg—a special Leica camera, call signs, security checks, chemicals for making invisible ink, a personal cipher, and a Dutch prayer book on which his code would be based. Finally, he revealed the $16,230 in cash he had been given.

Part of the vice consul's skepticism resulted from the fact that he had never heard of nuclear energy. But Koehler continued to bore in. He said that he had accepted the espionage job only because he feared that he and his wife would never have gotten out of Germany alive on any other basis. He knew, too, many Abwehr secrets and techniques. If permitted to enter the United States, the Dutchman stressed, he would eagerly work as a double agent—pretending to work for Ast X, yet taking his instructions from Americans.

A cable was sent to the headquarters of the Federal Bureau of Investigation in Washington. Did the agency know anything about a Walther Koehler? Back came the reply: indeed it did. His record showed that he had been a German spy in both world wars.

J. Edgar Hoover, the square-jawed, dynamic director of the FBI, distrusted double agents. But this one might pay big dividends. "Send him along," Hoover cabled.

Koehler and his wife sailed for the United States aboard a creaking old Portuguese ship, and they were met in New York City by a "welcoming committee" of FBI agents. The couple was taken to a comfortable Manhattan hotel and registered under a phony name. The FBI promptly confiscated the money and valuables furnished by Ast X, and the Koehlers were told that they would be furnished with a generous weekly allowance.

However, Koehler's wife was not concerned about the confiscation. She had smuggled in ten thousand U.S. dollars that had been sewn into her girdle.

Hoover's G-men—as they were popularly called—promptly set up a clandestine shortwave radio station for Koehler some thirty miles from Manhattan, in a large old house on a secluded estate on Long Island. Police dogs guarded the premises. This would be an especially tricky operation: even a minor blunder could destroy the entire undercover scenario. Koehler would never be allowed near the secret station.

At 8:00 A.M. on the cold, bleak morning of February 7, 1943, two G-men manning the station flashed Koehler's call sign, his cipher, and his first message to Ast X: "Am now ready to operate. Necessary to be careful, but I feel safe. Will listen for you at nineteen hundred [7:00 P.M.] tonight."

Five days passed. No reply. No doubt Ast X experts were studying Koehler's style for telltale flaws. Had he become a double agent? Then the Long Island radio crackled and a message came in from Hamburg: "Uncle is highly pleased. He declares his appreciation and well wishes." Uncle was the Abwehr's big chief, Admiral Canaris.

The FBI men manning the station on an around-the-clock basis grinned broadly: The German secret service had been taken in—hook, line, and swastika.

In the months ahead, "Koehler"—that is, the FBI agents—engaged in a complicated *Funkspiel* (radio talk game) with the Dutchman's handlers at Ast X. A special team of G-men carefully concocted messages with doctored information on America's nuclear research. The script team had to be careful not to give the impression that Koehler knew too much: one man could not collect complex scientific information based on only a four-hour crash course in nuclear energy.

On occasion, the scriptwriters would create some scientific nonsense to be sent to Hamburg. One message from "Koehler" stated that "they are producing a powder that contains 'heavy water.' The strength of this powder is five hundred to a thousand times greater than usual."

When Ast X followed the routine of passing along "Koehler's" message to Henry Albers, a chemist who handled scientific intelligence for the Reich Research Council, the gibberish generated guffaws. Curiously, however, childish reports of this type strengthened Koehler's credibility with Ast X.

At other times, the FBI script team would consult with genuine American scientists, and from the interviews, the group would create a message that contained true, but harmless, facts about nuclear research in the United States.

Within weeks it became clear that Henry Albers trusted "Koehler" completely. At Easter, Albers had Ast X send his warmest greetings. So the G-men at the shortwave radio station responded in kind, concluding their message with "Heil Hitler!"

In Koehler's name, the FBI would send a total of 121 messages to Ast X, many of them dealing with matters other than his primary target, atomic bomb development.

After the war, U.S. intelligence officers inspected Koehler's file in Hamburg and discovered that Ast X had received a total of 231 messages, not the 121 sent by his FBI stand-ins.

Delving into this mysterious discrepancy, the Americans uncovered evidence indicating that Koehler had been furtively contacting another Nazi agent in New York City. This unknown spy had radioed 110 of Koehler's messages without the knowledge of the FBI.

Shy, soft-spoken, introspective Walther Koehler, who loved the color of money, had succeeded in double-crossing both sides and raking in heavy payments from the Americans and the Nazis alike. He had not been just a double agent, but a triple agent.[11]

A Rain of Metallic Foil

THROUGHOUT THE early months of 1943, the relentless cat-and-mouse game between Allied and German radar/radio scientists continued to rage behind the scenes. Meanwhile, the steadily growing Royal Air Force Bomber Command had been joined by hundreds of U.S. four-engine Flying Fortresses and Liberators to make a greater wreck of the Greater Reich.

British Air Marshal Arthur T. Harris, the often irascible, usually brilliant chief of Bomber Command, had received from the Anglo-American Joint Chiefs of Staff a dramatic directive. It called for a new approach to the air war: the "progressive destruction and dislocation of the German military, industrial, and economic system, and the undermining of the morale of the German people."

Translation: Forget about precision bombing; instigate area bombing that could raze entire major cities.

On May 27, 1943, Air Marshal Harris issued Most Secret Operation Order 173. It called for wiping out Hamburg, Germany's second-largest city, a North Sea port some 180 miles northwest of Berlin.

Harris's order stated that the "Battle of Hamburg" could not be "won in a single night. It is estimated that at least ten thousand tons of bombs will have to be dropped to complete the process of elimination."

Hamburg should be "subjected to sustained attacks," the order concluded. "It is hoped that the night attacks will be preceded and/or followed by heavy daylight attacks by the United States VIIIth Bomber Command [Eighth Air Force]."

The razing of Hamburg was code-named Operation Gomorrah. Pathfinder bombers equipped with a new electronic guidance system developed by British scientists and code-named Oboe would mark the target with flares and incendiary bombs for the main bomber stream to follow.

Oboe had replaced the navigational aid, code-named Gee, that Bomber Command had been using with modest success for the past year. German electronics technicians had succeeded in jamming Gee.

Oboe utilized two radar stations on the ground, one in southern England and the other two hundred miles to the north. Both radar sites sent beams toward Germany, and the rays intersected at the target. When a bomber reached a prearranged distance from the intersecting beams, the navigator was told that he was over the objective and to drop his explosives or incendiaries.

In one of Oboe's first test missions, a factory some two hundred miles from England had been demolished by a direct hit.

Meanwhile, behind the scenes and in the strictest secrecy, British scientists, led by Joan Curran and Robert Cockburn, had developed a radar-jamming device code-named Window (Chaff to the Americans). It consisted of strips of aluminum foil packed in bales to be pitched out of bombers en route to the target. The strips would disperse in the wind, creating the impression on German radar screens much like that seen by the human eye in a snow blizzard. It was impossible to distinguish objects.

This ingenious invention, designed to minimize Bomber Command losses, became the topic of heated debate among scientists and top government leaders. There were those who argued that the metallic strips might get into the air intakes of subsequent aircraft, clog their engines, and cause them to crash.

Home Secretary Herbert Morrison, whose main job was the security of the British people, heard about the stunning new creation. Typically, he vehemently protested the use of Window over Germany, alarmed by the possibility of civilian casualties in the United Kingdom if the Nazis in turn used a Window-like substance.

There was a basis for Morrison's deep concern, although there was no evidence that a shower of metallic foil would cause harm to humans. About a year earlier, German scientists had discovered the principle of Window. They had made trials at the Düppel Estate near Berlin and later over the Baltic Sea.

Grasping a technological principle and developing a working product are two separate factors. The German trials had been embarrassing fizzles. So Reichsmarschall Hermann Goering, the Luftwaffe chief, had ordered all relevant data to be burned, and he forbade those involved in the experiments to even mention them for fear that the British might copy the idea.

On July 15, 1943, Prime Minister Winston Churchill presided at a meeting of cabinet ministers and foremost scientists to make a decision on the use or nonuse of Window. Home Secretary Morrison again raised strident objections, and threatened to take up the matter with the War Cabinet. Puffing on a long black cigar, Churchill replied evenly that the matter was far too technical for the War Cabinet and that he would take personal responsibility for the use of Window.

On the night of July 24, a mighty armada of 791 British bombers was winging toward Hamburg. At a designated point, bales of Window were pitched out. German radar defenses were thrown into chaos. Frantic radar operators reported that more than 12,000 British planes were approaching.

Radar-controlled searchlights leaped wildly about the black sky, and anti-aircraft guns directed by radar filled the night with bursting shells aimed at false echoes, not genuine bombers. Luftwaffe night fighters, which relied on radar to steer them to the intruding bombers, chased about the sky in confusion.

Twelve British bombers were lost in the heavy attack—a percentage far below normal losses in similar missions.

Heavy daylight raids by the U.S. Eighth Air Force hit the tortured, burning city on July 25 and 26. Then, just past midnight on July 28, a stream of 787 British bombers, pitching out Window en route, dropped explosives and incendiary devices.

Set in the blackness of Hamburg was a turbulent dome of bright red fire like the glowing heart of a vast brazier. Above the city hovered a misty red haze. A rain of large sparks blew down the dark streets. Asphalt roads melted.

Perhaps as many as forty-five thousand men, women, and children, many of them flaming torches, died in ancient Hamburg that night.

In Berlin, Josef Goebbels, the Nazi regime's propaganda genius, tried to put the best face possible on the Hamburg holocaust. Over the German radio and in newspapers and magazines—all of which he controlled—Goebbels charged that the Anglo-Americans had launched a terror campaign of chemical weapons. The peg for his story was a cow somewhere near Hamburg that had eaten one of the metallic strips and died.

Window, the technological marvel of British scientists that would save the lives of thousands of Anglo-American airmen, was begrudgingly hailed by Reichsmarschall Goering. In his personal daily diary, he scrawled:

> In the field of radar the [British and Americans] have the world's greatest geniuses and we have the nincompoops. I hate the British rogues like the plague, but in one respect I am obliged to doff my cap to them. After this war's over, I'm going to buy myself a British radio set. Then I'll at least have the luxury of owning something that has always worked.

In the turmoil in the high circles of government and the military in Berlin, the Hamburg disaster called for the mandatory isolation of a scapegoat. To wear the horns, Adolf Hitler selected Major General Josef Kammhuber, who had done a brilliant job in thwarting British bomber raids on the Third Reich from exacting a heavy toll since the war began.[12]

Smuggling a Renowned Scientist

LATE IN FEBRUARY 1943, the Danish underground in Copenhagen received a covert message from Ronald Turnbill (code-named Jarlen), a top British operative in Stockholm, Sweden. It stated that a group of keys containing a highly important communication was being sent by the British government to Niels Bohr, a noted Danish physicist.

Within hours, Captain Volmar Gyth, a leader in the highly effective Danish underground, picked up the keys. With them were instructions and a diagram explaining how to extract the message. Blind holes had been drilled in the bows of two of the keys, identical microdots implanted, and the holes sealed. The diagram pointed to the holes.

Niels Bohr had been a national hero since being awarded the Nobel Prize in physics in 1922. At that time the Danish Academy of Science had granted him free lifetime occupancy of the House of Honor, a palatial estate that was the most prestigious address in Denmark after King Christian's.

When Adolf Hitler's war machine had occupied Denmark in the spring of 1940, the Nazis had permitted Bohr to continue his research into nuclear energy, no doubt planning to capitalize on the Dane's discoveries.

For nearly a year, Royal Navy Lieutenant Commander Eric Welsh, who was with British secret intelligence in London, had been trying to create a scheme to spirit Bohr out of Denmark and to England. Welsh was in charge of secret communications between undercover agents in German-occupied Denmark and neutral Sweden.

British scientists had concluded that Bohr, long a leading light in the international scientific community, could provide a wealth of information on Nazi atomic bomb progress. Bohr had been a close friend of Werner Heisenberg, regarded in the West as the foremost German scientist in the nuclear energy field. Heisenberg had been a student of Bohr in 1922 at the Institut fur Teoretisk Fysik (Institute for Theoretical Physics), founded by the great Dane in Copenhagen a year earlier.

Even after the Germans had occupied Denmark in 1940, Heisenberg had made numerous trips to call on his friend Bohr and exchange nuclear theories.

Now, a day after Captain Gyth picked up the set of keys, he called on Bohr at the House of Honor. While the two men were having tea, Gyth offered to extract the microdots and have them enlarged. With all of his scientific brilliance, the physicist knew nothing about such a procedure. Quipping that he was not a secret agent, he told Gyth to proceed with the task.

Physicist Niels Bohr was smuggled out of Nazi-held Denmark. (National Archives)

Following the instructions, Gyth gently filed the keys at the points indicated until the holes appeared. Then he floated the microdots onto a microslide.

The message was from an old friend of Bohr's, British physicist James Chadwick, director of a research laboratory at the University of Liverpool, where he was engaged in nuclear experiments. The letter invited Bohr to come to England, where "you will receive a very warm welcome. You will be able to work freely on scientific matters."

Chadwick added: "There also are special problems in which your cooperation would be of considerable help."

Bohr instinctively grasped his friend Chadwick's point: the Dane might have knowledge that would accelerate the efforts of British scientists in the development of an atomic bomb.

Bohr promptly rejected the invitation. In a letter to Chadwick, he stated that he felt an obligation to remain to defend the scientists in exile who had sought refuge in Denmark.

There the matter stood until the spring of 1943, when two German physicists, Hans Suess and Hans Jensen, called on Bohr at his institute. For whatever his reason, one of the visitors let drop that German scientists were producing the uranium metal required for a nuclear reactor.

The delicate facade of an independent Denmark—the Germans had allowed the country to keep its constitutional monarchy and govern itself—was shattered in late August when the Danish underground called a nationwide strike. At the same time in Berlin, a decision was made to round up and deport the eight thousand Jews who had been allowed to remain in Denmark in return for the "cooperation" of Danish leaders.

Then, in early September, Niels Bohr learned that the Nazis were preparing to arrest his émigré scientists. Acting with typical alacrity, the Danish underground collected the émigrés, loaded them into rowboats, and took them across the stormy Øresund, the body of water between Denmark and Sweden, to safety.

On September 28, Gustav von Dardell, a Swedish diplomat, took tea with Bohr at the House of Honor and tipped off the physicist that the Gestapo was going to arrest him within a week. A day later, Bohr received word from the underground that an anti-Nazi clerk employed at the Gestapo headquarters in Copenhagen had seen an order from Berlin calling for the arrest and deportation of Niels Bohr and his young brother, Harald, also a scientist.

There was no time to lose. Bohr and his wife, Margrethe, slipped out of their ornate home that afternoon to avoid the German-ordered night curfew. Their two sons had to be left behind, to join them later. For nearly two hours, the Bohrs, trying to project a nonchalant appearance, walked through Copenhagen to a seaside garden. Waiting for darkness, they hid in a small shed. At a predesignated time, the couple stole out of the dilapidated shack and walked two hundred yards to the shore of the Øresund.

Members of the underground met them in a tiny boat and rowed them out to a fishing vessel that took the Bohrs to landfall near Malmö, Sweden. There Margrethe waited for the Bohr sons to arrive, and the physicist took a train for Stockholm. Seated alongside him during the trip was Captain Volmar Gyth, the Danish underground leader.

Stockholm was saturated with Nazi spies and Gestapo agents under cover, so Bohr was carefully guarded by Gyth and Swedish intelligence officers in civilian clothes. Bohr never went out alone. He stayed in the home of an old friend, a Danish diplomat, Emil Trop-Pedersen. Gyth and the Swedes impressed on the physicist the need for strict secrecy. Yet every time the phone rang, he answered, "This is Bohr."

Soon Bohr received a communication from Lord Cherwell, the scientific adviser to Prime Minister Winston Churchill. Again the Dane was urged to come to England and be warmly received. Captain Gyth assured Bohr that the Gestapo had orders to kill him, and urged him to go. This time Bohr accepted the British offer, asking only that his twenty-one-year-old son Aage be taken along. He understood that his wife and other son would have to remain in Sweden.

When Bohr left Stockholm on October 6, he faced a journey loaded with peril. At a remote airfield outside the city, Bohr put on a flight suit and a parachute. The pilot of the unarmed two-engine Mosquito bomber that would carry him to England handed him a helmet with built-in earphones for conversation with the cockpit and pointed out the location of his oxygen mask.

Almost since war had erupted in Europe, the British had flown a diplomatic pouch between Stockholm and Scotland in a Mosquito, a light, swift aircraft that could fly high enough to thwart German antiaircraft batteries when it crossed Norway. The bomb bay had been fitted for a single passenger, and it was into this crevice that Bohr squeezed.

Before the Mosquito lifted off, the pilot handed the scientist a batch of flares. He explained that if the airplane were attacked by Luftwaffe fighters while over the North Sea, the pilot would open the bomb bay and Bohr could parachute into the icy water. The flares would aid his rescue, the pilot explained — "if you survive."

When the Mosquito soared to more than twenty thousand feet to get above German ack-ack fire, the pilot gave the word over the intercom for the physicist to put on his oxygen mask. Bohr did not hear the order, and he soon fainted as the air grew thin.

The lack of response worried the pilot. He knew his passenger was a VIP (very important person). As soon as he could, the pilot took the plane much lower and went back to check. He was shocked to see his charge unconscious — and presumably dead.

Soon Bohr began to stir, and by the time the Mosquito landed at its regular airport in Scotland, he had revived. On the ground, he told those who had come to greet him that he had had a nice sleep during the trip.

Among those in the welcoming party was James Chadwick, who had commenced the operation to lure Bohr to England a few months earlier. Chadwick and Bohr, old friends, flew to London together, and the Dane was put up at the fashionable Westminster Hotel under a *nom de guerre* (war name).

After spending several weeks in England, Bohr was approached by Chadwick and other British scientists, who recommended that he and his son Aage (who had arrived from Stockholm by another plane) go to the United States to join the atomic bomb program, which was far ahead of research in Britain.

The Bohrs sailed from England on the British ship *Aquitania*, and on the night of December 6, 1943, they were on a dock in New York City. There followed a cloak-and-dagger scenario in Hollywood-like fashion. A flood of British security officers, who had been guarding the Bohrs, handed them over to American security agents. Before surrendering their charges, the Britons required that the Americans sign a formal receipt, as though the Danes were precious merchandise.

Forty-eight hours later, the American bodyguards slipped the Bohrs onto a train at midnight, and they headed for Washington, D.C. There the security men received a signed formal receipt from the undercover agents, who took charge of the émigrés.

A day later, an intelligence agent who had been assigned to shadow Bohr during the train trek reported to General Leslie Groves, director of the Manhattan Project, which was trying to develop an atomic bomb. The gumshoe said that Bohr "wanders everywhere without rhyme or reason, and talks to strangers or anyone else."

Obsessed with security, Groves planned to send Bohr, a "loose-tongued foreigner who had consorted with the Germans," into exile for the duration at supersecret Site X—Los Alamos, in remote northern New Mexico. The sprawling facility had been built earlier in 1943 as a place in which to carry on atomic bomb research away from prying hostile eyes and ears.

On December 27, 1943, the Danish physicist and his son Aage arrived by train in Chicago. There they were joined by General Groves, who said that he would go along on the two-day rail trip to New Mexico. Before boarding, the general, never inhibited by tact, explained to the Bohrs the need to keep their mouths shut, and that they were to remain in their adjoining compartments at all times. Their meals would be brought to them.

Recalling the report about Bohr's penchant to wander around and strike up conversations with strangers, Groves and his personal scientific adviser, Richard Tolman, agreed that they would take turns keeping Bohr company in his compartment to discourage any temptation of his to roam the train.

Tolman took the first shift. After an hour, he came out of Bohr's compartment, complaining that the physicist had jabbered incessantly. "I can't take any more," he told Groves. "You are in the army, you'll have to do it."

Consequently, for two days Groves sat in Bohr's compartment. When the train arrived at the station near Los Alamos, the general howled to aides that he had had to listen to the Dane for "three hours each morning, four hours each afternoon, and two more hours at night."[13]

A Plan to Poison the German Food Supply

WORLD-RENOWNED SCIENTIST Enrico Fermi, an émigré from Italy and a key figure in developing an atomic bomb, came up with an innovative scheme in April 1943. He suggested to a fellow scientist, J. Robert Oppenheimer, that radioactive fission products bred in a nuclear reactor could be utilized to poison the German food supply.

Two weeks later, Oppenheimer traveled to Washington, D.C., and called on Leslie Groves, director of the Manhattan Project and now a major general. Oppenheimer outlined Fermi's idea for poisoning the German food supply. Groves was not surprised. He disclosed that a committee of leading scientists already had been working on countermeasures if the Germans attacked U.S. cities or food supplies with radioactive fission products.

Oppenheimer then met with James Conant, president of Harvard University and chairman of the countermeasure committee, and discussed Fermi's scheme with him. Later, Oppenheimer told Fermi that Conant seemed to feel that the idea of poisoning the German food supply was "promising."

Oppenheimer also discussed Fermi's plan with Edward Teller, an émigré scientist from Hungary who was a key figure in the Manhattan Project. Teller indicated that the idea "appears to offer the highest promise."

Citing the need for total secrecy about the scheme, Oppenheimer told Fermi to delay work until the "latest possible date" because "we should not attempt a plan unless we can poison food sufficient to kill a half a million men."

Because of insurmountable problems, including an inability to kill only German men and not women and children, the scientists' food-poisoning plot finally died because of lack of nourishment.[14]

Bouncing Bombs and Dambusters

ADOLF HITLER'S ARSENAL was the Ruhr, a vast region in northwestern Germany that held the huge Krupp armaments works and steel, iron, and chemical industries. The Royal Air Force Bomber Command and later the U.S. Eighth Air Force had been pounding the Ruhr for nearly three years, but ingenious German production barons even accelerated the creation of the accoutrements of war.

In early 1943, the British Air Staff developed a unique plan to cripple the Reich's war production by knocking out three huge dams—Möhne, Eder, and Sorpe. These man-made monsters constituted the flood-control system for rivers in the Ruhr. Rupturing the dams would inundate huge areas, the Air Staff was confident.

The three great water barriers were indestructible by ordinary bombs, so the Air Staff decided to employ one of the strangest inventions of the war, a powerful explosive developed by Barnes Wallis, a renowned British scientist and aeronautical engineer. Code-named Upkeep, the five-ton bomb was distinctive for reasons other than its colossal size.

Upkeep did not have the contours of most bombs. Rather it was a cylinder like an oil drum, five feet long and almost that size in diameter. Upkeep would be fitted crossways in the bomb bay of a four-engine Lancaster. The aircraft would have to approach its dam target by skimming over the water at an altitude of only sixty feet. Ten minutes before the bomb was to be dropped, it would be given a backspin of about five hundred revolutions per minute by an auxiliary motor inside the bay.

When the gargantuan explosive device hit the water, it would skim like a flat stone being pitched along a farmer's pond, bouncing over defense nets in shorter and shorter bumps. Then, when the object hit the dam, the backspin would force the bomb to cling to the wall and cause it to crawl downward until it exploded on the command of a hydrostatic fuse set for forty feet below the surface.

By detonating with an enormous blast far underwater, Upkeep's destructive power would be magnified by the hammer effect of the shock waves moving though the incompressible fluid.

Air Chief Marshal Arthur "Bert" Harris, the hard-nosed and highly capable leader of Bomber Command, beset by "all sorts of enthusiasts and panacea-mongers," labeled Barnes Wallis's unique creation as "just about the maddest proposition as a weapon I have yet come across." However, in March 1943, Harris was overruled by Air Chief Marshal Charles Portal, head of the Air Staff. So Harris formed a new unit of four-engine Lancasters to drop Wallis's superbombs and labeled it 617 Squadron. Experienced crewmen were assigned to the unit, commanded by Wing Commander Guy Penrose Gibson, a natural-born leader.

Gibson had begun flying combat missions on the first day of the war, and in about a year he had completed a RAF bomber pilot's normal tour of thirty missions. Assigned to a training unit, he connived his way out of the tame duty and flew ninety-nine sorties as a night-fighter pilot.

Having survived the equivalent of four tours of combat duty, Gibson was assigned to a flight-training school, but he launched such vocal protests that he did yet another tour in bombers. If ever there was a fugitive from the law of averages, it was Guy Penrose Gibson.

The 617 Squadron had only six weeks to prepare for the mission: the dams had to be struck in the middle of May, when the water levels would be at their highest and the moon at its brightest.

When Gibson and his crews had been fully trained in their special bombing technique, a full-scale dress rehearsal, viewed by senior Royal Air Force officers, was held. It was a disaster. Airplanes went astray, a few nearly collided, and some even got lost.

Back at the squadron's airfield, Guy Gibson minced no words in telling top officers the reason for the fiasco: the radiotelephone sets that had been used for communication between aircraft were totally inadequate. A day later, a group of technicians arrived, and within hours 617 Squadron was equipped with the most advanced and efficient radios in the Royal Air Force.

On the next night, another dress rehearsal was held. It went off like clockwork, a total success.

A veil of darkness gripped the British Isles on the night of May 16, 1943, when eighteen Lancasters, each carrying a superbomb, lifted off and set a course for the first target, Möhne Dam. About an hour and a half later, down below, Möhne Lake was silent and black and deep. Gibson said to his crew, "Well, boys, I suppose we'd better start the ball rolling!"

Winging through a gauntlet of antiaircraft fire from towers at each end of the crucial dam, Gibson zoomed in at the required sixty-foot altitude. A stray thought flashed through his mind: "At this height, if I even hiccough I'll be in the drink!"

*Barnes Wallis (left) invented huge,
unorthodox "bouncing bombs" used
to smash dams in the German
Ruhr. An RAF plane (below) drops
one of his powerful bombs.
(National Archives)*

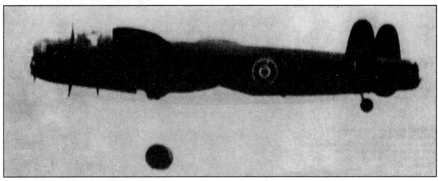

The squadron leader dropped his bomb perfectly, sending it bouncing across the surface and sinking out of sight at the dam. But when the lake calmed after the tremendous explosion, he could see that sturdy Möhne remained intact.

Rapidly gaining altitude, Gibson circled over the target and radioed his other planes as they made their attacks. German flak set the second plane afire, and its bomb overshot the dam. But the next three Lancasters all bounced their bombs precisely into the target, and the explosions ripped a breach in the dam nearly a hundred yards wide.

A tremendous gush of water twenty-five feet high surged down the valley, flooding or sweeping aside everything in its path—houses, railroad tracks, bridges, automobiles.

It took two more of Barnes Wallis's superbombs to destroy Eder Dam, but the Sorpe survived the one explosive that hit it.

Later, research would indicate that the bold dambusters had wreaked havoc on the Ruhr's industrial capacity, but Hitler's sprawling arsenal complex had not been totally crippled.

Of the eighteen Lancasters that had departed from England on the mission, two failed to reach the dam and eight were shot down. Guy Gibson received the Victoria Cross, Britain's highest award for valor, and twenty-nine other members of 617 Squadron were decorated.

So secret was the creation of Barnes Wallis's superbomb that its existence would not be known to the general public for more than twenty years after the war.

Grounded yet again after the dambusting mission, Guy Gibson's urgent plea to fly "one final mission" was finally granted. In September 1944 he led a night raid over Germany. After marking the target with flares and watching the bombs fall, he radioed his crews, "Nice work, chaps. Now let's beat it for home!"

It was Gibson's last message. During the return flight to England, his bomber was shot down.[15]

Part Five

Beginning of the End

Protecting a Sacred Secret

AT DAWN, men of the untested but eager U.S. 82nd Airborne Division were given electrifying news at their hot and dusty camp in the desert near the Muslim holy city of Kairouan, Tunisia, in North Africa. Within forty-eight hours, large numbers of paratroopers would spearhead Operation Huskey, the Allied invasion of Sicily, a large, mountainous island off the toe of the Italian mainland. D-Day would be July 10, 1943.

The All-Americans, as members of the division were called, were buoyed by the knowledge that they had been given the task of cracking open Adolf Hitler's Festung Europa (Fortress Europe). Moreover, this would be history's first major combat jump at night by paratroopers of any nation. Because of a shortage of C-47 transport planes, not all parachute elements could be dropped during the initial attack.

Jumping into Sicily just before midnight on July 9—D-Day minus one—would be a combat team of 3,403 paratroopers led by thirty-six-year-old Colonel James M. Gavin, known to his men as Slim Jim.

Gavin's combat team, built around his own 505th Parachute Infantry Regiment, was to drop a few miles inland on the heights known as Piano Lupo, north and northeast of the coastal town of Gela, where seaborne elements under U.S. Lieutenant General George S. Patton, Jr., were to storm ashore. The mission of Gavin's parachutists was to block enemy efforts to rush troops to Patton's landing beach and smash the invasion at the water's edge.

U.S. intelligence had informed Supreme Commander Dwight D. Eisenhower that the invading Anglo-American armies would meet only demoralized, ill-equipped, and poorly officered Italian units in Sicily. But only hours before Jim Gavin and his men were to bail out into the blackness of Sicily, a German radio message decrypted by the British intelligence apparatus Ultra landed like a blockbuster bomb on Eisenhower's desk in Algiers, in North Africa.

Instead of the invaders being confronted by only low-grade Italian troops, they would be up against two first-rate German panzer divisions that had been sneaked across the two-mile-wide Strait of Messina from Italy. One of these outfits, the veteran Hermann Goering Panzer division, was bivouacked only a short distance from where Gavin's lightly armed paratroopers would drop.

Eisenhower was faced with one of his most gut-wrenching dilemmas of the war. Gavin's paratroopers would have nothing with which to defend themselves against the Hermann Goering panzers but 2.36-inch bazooka rocket launchers, weapons that had been shockingly ineffective in earlier fighting in North Africa. If the panzers smashed through Gavin's men, they could reach Patton's beaches and rake the seaborne soldiers at point-blank range as they waded ashore.

Another agonizing concern that gripped Eisenhower was the crucial necessity to protect the secret of Ultra. Gavin's paratroopers would be better prepared to deal with the Goering Division if they knew in advance of its presence. But parachutists isolated behind enemy positions were likely candidates for capture, and German interrogators would soon learn that the Americans had known about the elite armored outfit.

This knowledge could cause Berlin to suspect that the Allies had broken the German Enigma code, and it would be abandoned and a new one established. That switch would deprive the Anglo-Americans of the enormous military advantage of knowing German plans in advance during the monumental battles that loomed on the European Continent before Adolf Hitler could be brought to his knees.

After painstaking deliberation, General Eisenhower decided that Ultra must be shielded at all costs. So even if Gavin's paratroopers were wiped out, even if the entire invasion were smashed, none of the sky soldiers would be told in advance about the Goering division.

An hour prior to midnight on D-Day minus one, Colonel Gavin and his paratroopers leaped out of their transport planes, unaware that swarms of German tanks lurked in the vicinity. Forty-eight hours later, Gavin had collected a force of paratroopers and clashed with a much larger Kampfgruppe (Battle Group) on a bleak piece of Sicilian real estate known as Biazza Ridge. The German panzers were trying desperately to break through to Patton's landing beaches, but at the end of the day, remnants of the Kampfgruppe pulled back.

A heavy price had been paid by the All-Americans. Scores of paratroopers were sprawled in death around the bloody battlefield.

Could the American losses have been fewer had the paratroopers known in advance of the presence of the Goering division? That question could never be answered. But known for certain was the fact that the sacred secret of the Ultra decrypting operation remained intact, and it would save tens of thousands of Allied lives in the months ahead and play a crucial role in defeating Nazi Germany.[1]

A Triumph for German Cryptanalysts

TWENTY-TWO-YEAR-OLD U.S. Air Corps Lieutenant Jesse D. Franks Jr. returned to his Quonset hut at an air base in Benghazi, Libya, in North Africa. He and

An American bomber flies through thick smoke over Ploesti oil fields. German codebreakers turned the bold mission into a disaster. (U.S. Air Force)

some eighteen hundred other airmen had been briefed on what appeared to many of them to be a suicide mission. A force of 178 four-engine bombers would go on a fifteen-hundred-mile flight across the Mediterranean Sea to blast the Ploesti oil fields in Romania. It was July 31, 1943.

To the general public, an American airman was a dashing, romantic fig-ure. Staff bands were removed from caps so the crown flopped down in a devil-may-care fashion. The young men sang loudly about going off into the wild blue yonder, and they had a strong *esprit de corps.*

There was scant glamor, however, for the men who had to wing into the teeth of swarms of German fighter planes and slither through bursts of deadly antiaircraft shells. That night, Lieutenant Jesse Franks wrote to his father, "One never knows what tomorrow may bring."

The daunting bombing mission against the Ploesti oil fields, the most important single source of natural fuel for Adolf Hitler's thirsty war machine, had been created not by combat commanders in the field, but by a special group of staff officers in Washington.

Calling for a single surprise attack, the plan had been developed on an academic basis. Because of heavy German defenses, the bombers would swoop in at treetop height, with each aircrew briefed to hit a different facility at the huge complex of oil fields. Mathematical probabilities had been worked out in great detail, including doubling the number of bombers deemed necessary to wipe out the installation.

At dawn on August 1, the force of B-24 Liberators lifted off at Benghazi and set a course for Ploesti. Soon after the bombers were airborne, a Luftwaffe electronic monitoring post in Greece intercepted a coded radio message about the mission. In a few minutes, German codebreakers cracked the cipher, and Luftwaffe bases all along the route from Benghazi to Romania were notified.

Soon the American sky armada was battling for its existence against a series of attacks by German fighters. Nevertheless, most of the bombers reached Ploesti. Scores of antiaircraft guns—most of them rushed to the target after the Germans had broken the U.S. code—threw up a thick curtain of flak. But many oil tanks became engulfed with brilliant orange flames and billowing plumes of black smoke.

Losses were enormous. Almost a third of the bomber stream was shot down during the operation. Only 13 of the original 178 planes came through to fly again. A total of 446 of the 1,733 airmen were killed. Lieutenant Jesse Franks was one of the first Americans to die.

It was small solace to the survivors to know that five Congressional Medals of Honor would be awarded—mostly posthumously—to participants in the Ploesti mission.

Although the daring raid had been partly successful, it was one of the foremost U.S. Air Corps disasters of the war. And it had been one of the greatest triumphs for German codebreakers.[2]

"You Scare Hell Out of Me!"

SCORES OF underground agents in northern France began sending London scraps of information about curious diggings being engaged in by the Germans. The excavations were scattered along the English Channel coast for 150 miles, from Cherbourg in the west to Calais in the east. It was July 1943.

These installations were apparently for firing something at London. But firing what? Alarmed British scientists requested Royal Air Force reconnaissance planes to swoop low along the Channel coast, and thousands of photographs were taken. The prints confirmed the widespread digging.

Now there was a need to know precisely what these scores of excavations were intended to accomplish.

At the same time, forty-five-year-old Michel Hollard, chief of the French underground's Réseau Agir (Network for Action), was roaming through northern France. When the Germans occupied Paris in 1940, Hollard had quit his job as an industrial designer and obtained a position as a salesman of charcoal-burning gas generators. These contraptions were used in automobiles in lieu of petroleum fuel for the civilian population.

While sipping wine in a café in the Seine River port of Rouen, Hollard overheard two construction contractors discussing mysterious digging by the Germans. Learning from other sources that a beehive of activity was taking place in a forest outside Auffay, twenty miles from Rouen, he donned workman's clothes and inspected the site.

Hollard was puzzled: Why were the Germans engaged in a major construction project in the middle of a forest far from any major city?

Pretending to be one of the laborers (most of them were foreigners), Hollard's eye was attracted to a fifty-yard strip of concrete that looked like the ski jumps he had seen in Switzerland in peacetime. Furtively taking out his compass, he found that the ramp was aimed in the direction of London.

Seeking more information, the underground chief managed to get one of his key agents (code-named André) assigned to a desk job as a clerk in the office of the German project manager. André soon noticed that the German kept a master plan in an inside pocket of his overcoat—and he wore the garment at all times, even when in his office. The only time the German removed the coat was at about nine o'clock in the morning, when he left briefly to heed a call of nature.

For a week, André timed the absences. They lasted three to five minutes. On the eighth day, the German shed his coat and went to perform his morning ritual. Like a jungle cat, André sneaked into the German's office, removed the master plan, and made a rapid tracing. Just as the Frenchman had replaced the blueprint in the overcoat, the German returned—unaware that he had just become the victim of a monumental intelligence coup.

Two days later, Michel Hollard, evading German patrols, walked toward the Swiss border. One false move would mean his death. He was dressed like a woodcutter, carried an ax in one hand, and had a sack of potatoes slung over his shoulder. Hidden among the potatoes was the master plan blueprint of the German mystery site.

Within seventy-two hours, André's handiwork reached London. British scientists and military leaders were shaken. Here was a blueprint of one of the scores of launching bases for Adolf Hitler's secret weapon the flying bomb, with which he planned to wipe London off the map.

Meanwhile, at Peenemünde, the isolated facility in northern Germany where scientists had been conducting experiments, a Heinkel bomber carrying a flying bomb on a test run lifted off and at a designated point released the secret weapon to fly on alone.

This photograph, taken on the coast of northern France, was the first to reveal the puzzling construction of concrete buildings shaped like skis. (U.S. Air Force)

Built by Volkswagen, the V-1 (as it was called) was a pilotless aircraft packed with explosives equivalent to a four-thousand-pound bomb. It traveled at 440 miles per hour, slightly faster than most Allied fighter planes. Its engine would be timed to cut off over a target, after which it would plummet to earth and explode with enormous impact.

Soon after the Heinkel released the flying bomb, its steering mechanism went haywire. The bomb flew much farther than planned and landed in a tulip field on the island of Bornholm, off the coast of Denmark, and failed to explode.

By happenstance, Police Inspector John Hansen, who was a leader in the Danish underground, was nearby when the flying bomb landed. He did not know what the strange-looking object was, but he noticed the German markings. Along with another underground operative, sea captain Hasager Christiansen, Hansen quickly snapped some photographs, then dismantled and hid smaller pieces of the secret weapon. With paper and pencil, he drew detailed sketches of the object.

Minutes later, a German security force rushed up, took charge of what remained of the V-1, and hauled it away.

Copies of Hansen's drawing, the photographs, and a descriptive report were carried to London by Captain Volmar Gyth of the Danish underground intelligence.

This had been the first flying bomb (later called a doodlebug or buzz bomb by the British and the Americans) to fall outside Germany. Most British scientists were elated to get such a wealth of eyewitness information. From this material they could construct a prototype with a view toward designing a defense against the V-1.

Lord Cherwell, the irascible scientific adviser to Prime Minister Winston Churchill, held the opinion that the flying bomb, based on the information received from the Danish underground, would be of no real danger to England. It could not fly far enough to reach London. Besides, he declared, this V-1 had been but a test model, and the weapons were not yet being mass-produced. Cherwell would be proven wrong on all counts.

Many British scientists spent sleepless nights haunted by a frightening specter: Would the flying bombs, if and when they began to hit England, carry nuclear warheads? The status of the German atomic bomb program had been a deep concern of many Allied scientists for many months.

Reginald Jones, the official in charge of scientific intelligence for the British Air Staff, was not too worried about atomic bombs in the pilotless craft, however. There were far too many ski ramps, he pointed out to his colleagues. German scientists conceivably may have created an atomic bomb or two. But scores of them?

When word of the ski ramps reached Washington, D.C., a young physicist whose job it was to monitor the German nuclear program was worried that the flying bombs would carry atomic weapons. Therefore he insisted that President Roosevelt should never meet with Prime Minister Winston Churchill in London for fear that both leaders might be killed when an atomic bomb attack hit the sprawling metropolis.

In the months ahead, British and American scientists on both sides of the Atlantic continued debating over the flying bomb threat. Then in mid-April 1944, when a mighty Allied force in England was preparing to launch a cross-Channel assault against Normandy, Supreme Commander Dwight Eisenhower received a visit from Vannevar Bush, head of the U.S. Office of Scientific Research and Development.

Bush had flown the Atlantic because he was deeply apprehensive. He felt that the Germans might arm flying bombs with poisonous fission by-products from working nuclear reactors. He stressed to Eisenhower that flying bombs containing these by-products might rain down on the staging areas of the invasion troops, causing a colossal number of casualties and even disrupting the looming attack.

When Bush fell silent, Eisenhower declared, "You scare hell out of me!" After a few moments the general asked, "What do we do?"

Bush replied that the best countermeasure to the danger would be to "bomb hell" out of the launching sites.

Pounding the ski ramps was not the best antidote to the flying bomb threat—it was the only one.

The Combined Chiefs of Staff in Washington agreed with Vannevar Bush's antidote, and Allied bombers began hitting the ski ramps and their storage depots. So when the first flying bomb exploded on Target 42—the German cipher for London—on June 13, 1944, only ten rounds had been ready to be

The historic Tower Bridge was the aiming point for the German robot-bomb onslaught.
(Author's collection)

launched. Only four bombs got anywhere near the aiming point—Tower Bridge in central London.

Sam Goutsmit, an American scientist who had arrived in England only a few days earlier, and a British colleague, Guy Stever, hurried to a buzz bomb impact site and checked the crater with a Geiger counter for any trace of radioactivity. They breathed sighs of relief: none was detected.

At about the same time that Goutsmit and Stever were poking into the bomb crater, across the Atlantic, Vannevar Bush and Secretary of War Henry Stimson were passengers in a limousine headed for the U.S. Capitol for a conference. A news bulletin from London flashed over the radio: a mysterious new bomb had exploded in the city.

The radio reporters had no way of knowing the fact at the time, so they missed the major part of the news story: the flying bomb carried nothing more frightening than conventional explosives, not a nuclear device.

Stimson turned to Bush. "Well, Van, how do you feel?" he asked. There was no need for him to explain the question.

"Very much relieved," Bush replied.

Euphoria in Britain and the United States over the seeming fizzle of Adolf Hitler's vaunted secret weapon was short-lived. Two days later, on June 15, a total of 244 buzz bombs flew off the ski ramps in France, and 145 of them exploded in England.

Despite continued massive bombing by the British and the Americans, more than 2,000 of the lethal robots hit England during the next ten days. By early July, tens of thousands of civilians were killed or injured, and perhaps 300,000 houses and other structures had been demolished or badly damaged.

Hoping to relieve the carnage, Reginald Jones, the scientific intelligence chief on the Air Staff, proposed an ingenious hoax. Through Ultra, the British apparatus that intercepted and decoded German radio messages, Jones knew that Colonel Max Wachtel, who was in charge of the buzz bomb onslaught, kept a record of the precise second that each robot was fired. While Wachtel could not be certain where the explosion would occur, he knew the time of impact within about one minute.

Jones arranged with authorities to have German double agents (spies who had been captured in England and "turned" against their former handlers) to radio to Berlin the site of the robots that landed north of London, using the impact times of the flying bombs that actually had hit south of the city. Jones hoped that Colonel Wachtel and his staff would conclude that the buzz bombs were landing "long" and shorten the range by adjusting the engine cut-off devices to decrease the flight times. Hopefully, Jones's ruse would result in the robots exploding in open fields south of London.

Jones's plan went up the pecking order to the War Cabinet, which approved it. The double agents began radioing back the phony reports concocted by Jones and his colleagues.

The intricate scheme was not an unbridled success. The Germans did shorten the buzz bombs range, but not all of the robots burst in open fields. Some hit blue-collar residential areas in southern London. Home Secretary Herbert Morrison protested vigorously, but Jones's ploy remained in force.[3]

Snooping on a Japanese Ambassador

DURING THE DRAB, melancholy days of January 1944, Field Marshal Karl Rudolf Gerd von Rundstedt, the sixty-nine-year-old Oberbefehlshaber Westen (Wehrmacht commander in the West), was enjoying the courtly life of a country gentleman in Saint-Germain-en-Laye, a suburb of once-glamorous Paris, which had been under the Nazi heel since mid-1940. His headquarters, at 20 Boulevard Victor Hugo, was a gigantic, three-story blockhouse, one hundred yards long and sixty feet deep, and imbedded in the side of a slope.

Known as "the last of the Prussian knights," the aristocratic von Rundstedt had grown increasingly dispirited over Adolf Hitler's vague and often meaningless orders from far-off Wolfsschanze (Wolf's Lair), the führer's command post near Rastenburg (now Ketrzyn), behind the Eastern Front. The ramrod-straight, dignified field marshal did little to conceal his low regard for the man he contemptuously called the "Bohemian corporal" from Hitler's World War I service as an infantry lance corporal in France.

Now von Rundstedt was reading Directive 51, in which Hitler laid down his plan for repulsing a looming invasion of "the Western Front of Europe." The führer had stated that the Pas de Calais, across the English Channel from Dover, was the logical site for the invasion because it was the shortest route. However, he warned von Rundstedt to expect diversionary attacks at other locales, such as in Normandy.

Although Directive 51 was issued in only twenty-seven copies, the total text reached the desks of Allied leaders within three weeks. The decrypt came from the U.S. Signals Intelligence Service, a secret wireless monitoring and codebreaking post at the illogical place of Asmara, Ethiopia, a primitive nation in East Africa. Few in the Pentagon even knew of the eavesdropping facility's existence.

When Hitler had declared war on the United States in early December 1941, three days after Pearl Harbor, German and Japanese intelligence agencies began a full exchange of information. In Berlin, General Hiroshi Oshima, a gifted soldier and skilled diplomat who was the Japanese ambassador, became a vast clearinghouse of intelligence on Nazi-occupied Europe.

Oshima transmitted the most important intelligence to imperial headquarters in Tokyo over a high-speed radioteleprinter link in a code that the Japanese considered to be unbreakable. When U.S. intelligence learned of Oshima's flow of information, it built an intercept station at Asmara and staffed it with more than three hundred technicians.

Ethiopia was a violently anti-Nazi and pro-Western democracy. In 1935, Italian dictator Benito Mussolini had invaded the economically poor nation, whose soldiers were often armed only with spears. Soon the Italians triumphed. The emperor, Haile Selassie, fled the country, but after the British drove the Italian Army out of Ethiopia in 1941, Selassie returned to the throne.

When the secret SIS post at Asmara acquired the raw intercepts from General Oshima's radioteleprinter in Berlin, hundreds of miles to the north, the messages were enciphered on an on-line radioteleprinter to Colonel W. Preston Corderman's two SIS operations in the United States. One station was at Arlington Hall, a mansion on the fringe of Washington, D.C., and the other at Vint Hill Farms, an estate in Virginia some fifty miles outside the capital.

After the intercepts from Asmara had been decoded at the two Washington area stations, they were shuttled on by radio across the Atlantic to the American signals center one hundred feet belowground near the British Museum in London. Then these intelligence reports were circulated to fewer than twenty top officials, in keeping with a strict technique to ensure security. These were the only persons in London who knew how the intelligence had been obtained.

A secret U.S. wireless monitoring post in Ethiopia snooped on messages sent from Berlin.

Most of the twenty recipients of the SIS intelligence were connected with Operation Overlord, the invasion of Normandy set for the spring of 1944. From these decrypts, and other intelligence sources, a small group of U.S. and British intelligence officers at London's Norfolk House, the main planning center for Overlord, produced a daily intelligence bulletin titled *Neptune Monitor Report*. (Neptune was the code name for the assault phase of the invasion.) These secret documents were circulated to those directly involved in the planning.

Twice a week, General Oshima reported to Tokyo in radiograms of one thousand to two thousand words the state of Adolf Hitler's Atlantic Wall, a formidable line of coastal fortifications that stretched for more than two thousand miles, from Norway to the Spanish border in southern France. It was from behind the Atlantic Wall that German soldiers would smash an Allied invasion, Hitler hoped.

Oshima most certainly was an expert on the Atlantic Wall. In late 1943, German officers had conducted him on a tour of the fortification along its entire length. Then he was given a detailed briefing on the coastal defense system by Field Marshal von Rundstedt.

American intelligence officers would quip that after the war, the Allies should pin a high decoration on General Oshima. His intercepted and decoded messages to Tokyo would save thousands of Allied lives on D-Day in Normandy.

At about the same time that Oshima's copious messages arrived in Tokyo, they had been decrypted at Asmara and reached Washington, D.C. When General Eisenhower was ready to launch his mighty force in England against Normandy, he and his commanders would have more detailed knowledge about the Atlantic Wall than would the German leaders in Berlin, based on information provided by the SIS, the French underground, and Ultra.[4]

A Rocket Genius Charged with Treason

REICHSFÜHRER Heinrich Himmler wielded gargantuan clout as head of the Gestapo and all German police forces, commander of the elite SS military unit, chief of the Reserve Army, and minister of the interior. The onetime chicken farmer was the second most feared man in Germany, and he had compiled thick dossiers (much of it rumor and gossip) on hundreds of Nazi leaders.

When the time was ripe, he would use these damaging materials to frame anyone who displeased him. One of those Himmler had targeted was Wernher von Braun, the world's foremost authority on rockets, who was putting the final touches on a huge missile code-named V-2.

On the cold night of February 21, 1944, von Braun, who piloted his own airplane on trips around the Third Reich, had just landed at his base at Peenemünde, the rocket development facility on the Baltic Sea. He was handed a telephone message that had arrived two hours earlier: report immediately to Reichsführer Himmler.

Von Braun was puzzled. He had had no dealings with Himmler, and the Nazi bigwig most certainly knew nothing about rocket development.

Soon after dawn, the thirty-two-year-old scientific genius wearily climbed back into his Messerschmitt-108 Typhoon and flew alone to Hockwald, East Prussia, where Himmler's field headquarters was located in his personal luxury train.

When von Braun entered Himmler's office, he was greeted with an icy stare. The Reichsführer, von Braun reflected, was as mild-mannered a villain as had ever slit a throat. Himmler, his steely eyes peering through a thick pince-nez, which gave him an owlish appearance, wasted no time on idle talk.

"The whole German people are eagerly awaiting the mystery weapon," Himmler said. He wanted to know why the V-2 rocket was not ready for mass production and deployment.

Taken aback, von Braun replied, "Herr Reichsführer, such delays as we're still experiencing are due to technical difficulties. You know, the V-2 is rather like a little flower. In order to flourish, it needs sunshine and a gentle gardener. What I fear you're thinking is a big jet of liquid manure. You know, that might kill the little flower."

Translation: Keep your nose out of our rocket development program because you know nothing about the topic.

Himmler's face flushed and he smiled a bit. It was a facial expression that many high Nazi officials had learned to fear.

A month later, on a Sunday in early March, von Braun felt a need for a brief respite from his grind of sixteen-hour workdays, so he attended a cocktail party at a private residence. Also present were several scientists, army officers, and civilian guests.

Von Braun, a witty and jovial man, soon joined two fellow rocket scientists in a corner of the room. In high spirits, they indulged in their dreams and talked excitedly about how the V-2 could be developed eventually for space travel, perhaps even reaching the moon, after the war. Von Braun suggested that a rocket might be developed to carry mail between Europe and the United States.

Friendly discussions about space travel were not unusual among Peenemünde rocketeers. These conjectures had gone on for years, even though friends had cautioned von Braun numerous times to soft-pedal such talk.

It was just past midnight on March 15, 1944, a few days after the convivial party, when von Braun was jolted awake in his Peenemünde bachelor quarters by heavy and persistent banging. Sleepily opening the door, he was confronted by three stern-faced men in civilian clothes and immediately sensed their identity—the Gestapo.

"*Anziehen Sie sich und kommen Sie mit uns!*" (You will dress and come with us!) one man exclaimed. The scientist was stunned. "But why?" he asked. "I am needed here at my work." "We have our orders," one Gestapo agent replied. "You will come with us to the *Polizei Prasidium* [police station] in Stettin."

Accompanied by the three Gestapo men, von Braun was driven to Stettin, about seventy miles to the south. At the police station he received another shock: his two fellow rocket scientists Klaus Riedel and Helmut Grötrupp, with whom he had discussed eventual space travel at the party a few nights earlier, had already been brought in by the Gestapo. The three rocketeers were put in separate cells without even a hint about why they had been arrested.

Two weeks after being locked up in the Stettin police station, guards hauled von Braun from his frigid cell and took him to a room where five SS officers, minions of Reichsführer Himmler, were seated stone-faced behind a wooden table. For the first time, the accused learned why he had been arrested: for sabotaging the war effort by declaring that he had never intended to develop the V-2 as a weapon but to use it for space travel.

As von Braun now realized, Himmler or his agents had planted among the guests at the cocktail party an informer who had purposely eavesdropped on the casual conversation among him, Klaus Riedel, and Helmut Grötrupp. It would later be learned that the snooper had been a female dentist, the girlfriend of an SS officer.

A second charge lodged against von Braun was treason. The "court" claimed that he kept an airplane in readiness at all times in order to flee to England and hand over top-secret materials on the German rocket program to British intelligence. How could von Braun prove that he had no traitorous intentions? It would have been a simple matter to fly to England in the Messerschmitt he used around Germany on business matters.

Wernher von Braun felt that he was doomed. Heinrich Himmler had made the charges against him, and Himmler's officers were going to sit in judgment. However, unbeknownst to the rocket genius, his guardian angel was watching over him.

Armaments Minister Albert Speer, Adolf Hitler's fair-haired boy and an admirer of von Braun and his work, learned of the arrests while confined to a hospital in Kressheim with a serious pulmonary ailment. He could not believe his ears. Von Braun had toiled indefatigably, night and day, for ten years to develop a revolutionary missile, and now Himmler was charging him with sabotaging the program and treason.

By happenstance, the führer took time from his backbreaking schedule to pay an unexpected visit to Speer's bedside. Speer seized the golden opportunity to plead for the release of von Braun and his two fellow scientists, reminding Hitler that von Braun was the genius behind the V-2 and that the missile program would likely flounder without the young scientist being available to smooth out the final kinks of the weapon. That would be a serious blow to the Third Reich's war effort, Speer stressed.

In Stettin, meanwhile, the three defendants, pale and racked with tension, sat before the five-man SS court. Each wondered if he would be shot or hanged. Then, in dramatic fashion, General Walter Dornberger, the army commander at Peenemünde and longtime friend of and coworker with von Braun, burst through the door of the "courtroom." He strode briskly to the presiding SS officer and handed him an official document. The SS man swallowed hard when he read the signature: "A. Hitler."

All charges were immediately dropped. Albert Speer's intervention from his hospital sickbed had saved the day—and the three scientists' necks—just in the nick of time.[5]

German Codebreakers Pinpoint Normandy

IN THE FIRST WEEK of May 1944, as the Allies' cross-Channel invasion from England neared, a rash of nervous tics erupted among top commanders in SHAEF (Supreme Headquarters, Allied Expeditionary Force). Ultra had just picked up an alarming directive in which Adolf Hitler ordered his military leaders to "watch Normandy."

In obedience to that order, elderly Field Marshal Gerd von Rundstedt, the commander in the West, began making the kinds of changes in troop dispositions that might be expected if the German high command knew that Normandy was to be the site of the Allied landings.

From his headquarters in suburban Paris, von Rundstedt began to almost double the antitank and antiaircraft defenses in Normandy. Most frightening of all to SHAEF was von Rundstedt's order that rushed Major General Wilhelm Falley's first-rate 91st Luftlande [Air Landing] Division into the same area in which the 82nd Airborne and 101st Airborne Divisions were to drop in the early-morning darkness of D-Day. Falley's outfit had been specially trained to fight enemy paratroopers and glidermen.

Why had Hitler suddenly focused his attention on Normandy? Had his highly efficient intelligence agencies unraveled the secrets of Neptune, the assault phase of the invasion? Or had German scientists developed some amazing apparatus, similar to the British Ultra, whereby the führer and his high command had a pipeline directly into SHAEF?

Actually, it had been the radio-monitoring and cryptanalytical service—the Funkabwehr—that had triggered the flurry of German movements in Normandy only a few weeks before the June 6, 1944, D-Day.

The Funkabwehr had been responsible for breaking an amazing series of enemy codes and ciphers during the war. It had totally penetrated the French system, and it had broken every Soviet cryptosystem, from the high command in Moscow down through battalions on the front line. The Funkabwehr would claim that its codebreakers had easily penetrated American radio traffic because of poor security.

British radio communications were the most closely guarded, and the Funkabwehr never was able to penetrate high-echelon cryptosystems. However, the German sleuths had enjoyed great success in analyzing the characteristic patterns, especially the radio traffic, of the Royal Air Force signals system. Funkabwehr officials would later state that codebreakers had been able to deduce carefully guarded British Army plans from lax security measures by the RAF.

While a buildup for the invasion of Normandy was unfolding in England in the spring of 1944, a security lid was clamped tightly on U.S. and British radio units. This action resulted in near-panic in the Funkabwehr, whose mission was to discover Allied plans. Relying only on an analysis of the Anglo-American radio messages and an occasional leak, the German electronics sleuths were able to piece together just a hazy portrait of the mighty force being assembled by Allied Supreme Commander Dwight D. Eisenhower.

Then, in late April, only six weeks before the Normandy assault, the Funkabwehr made a remarkable discovery. After intensive study of the radio-message stations of the scores of U.S. and British divisions in England, the German codebreakers realized that air liaison officers had been assigned to certain divisions. Their task was to coordinate air-support operations with ground troops.

From this startling revelation, the German cryptanalysts concluded that these were assault divisions to which the air liaison officers were being assigned, and that these units were preparing for a cross-Channel operation.

Although the Anglo-American deception artists filled the air with fake radio messages, the Funkabwehr was able to tune in on all of the divisions in southwestern and southern England broadcasting air-liaison messages. Consequently the German codebreakers were able to comprehend, with an amazing degree of accuracy, that *der Grossinvasion* was imminent and that the Allies would strike along the Bay of the Seine, between the major ports of Cherbourg and Le Havre—the true landing beaches.

Now the daunting problem was for the Funkabwehr to convince Adolf Hitler, who largely distrusted radio intelligence, that the information was accurate. To the astonishment of the German codebreakers, the führer on this occasion paid some attention. Now he realized that Normandy was vulnerable to an invasion, so he had ordered the reinforcements that had been giving General Eisenhower and other Allied commanders sleepless nights.

However, because Hitler had been hoodwinked by an ingenious Allied deception plan code-named Bodyguard, he remained convinced that the main enemy landings would take place at the Pas de Calais, the narrowest part of the English Channel, some two hundred miles northeast of the invasion beaches. So the führer had been merely covering all bets by strengthening Normandy defenses on virtually the eve of D-Day.[6]

"Hiding" a Mighty Invasion

IN THE SPRING OF 1944, the Western Allies were preparing feverishly to embark on the most complex, dangerous military operation that history has known—the invasion of Normandy, code-named Overlord. The printed plan for Neptune, the assault phase, was five inches thick. Even the single-spaced typelist of American units—1,400 of them—required 31 pages.

On D-Day alone, the equivalent of 500 trainloads of troops—57,506 American, 72,215 British and Canadian—along with their weapons, vehicles, ammunition, and supplies, would have to cross the English Channel in a mighty fleet of more than 4,000 vessels.

Preparations for Overlord already had taken two and a half years and involved the combined industrial, military, and intellectual power of the United States and the British Empire. Yet not even that enormous might was sufficient to assure the Western Allies of a successful invasion. Although Adolf Hitler's armies had suffered enormous bloodletting in the Soviet Union, North Africa, and Italy, a million Germans were entrenched along the intricate Atlantic Wall fortification.

If the Germans knew the site of the Allied landings and were ready and waiting, they could pour a hail of devastating fire into the assault forces that would destroy the invasion at the water's edge.

If Overlord failed, Great Britain probably would have to seek a negotiated peace with Hitler, for she would commit everything in her arsenal to the invasion. America's home front, appalled by the gargantuan bloodshed and the magnitude of the disaster, possibly would demand that Japan be defeated—a task that the Pentagon estimated might take ten years—before deciding on whether to take another crack at invading Nazi-held territory.

General Dwight Eisenhower, supreme commander for Overlord, wrote to a friend in Washington, D.C.: "In this particular venture, we are not just risking a tactical defeat; we are putting the whole works on one number."

Eisenhower set D-Day for the first week in June 1944, but in April he and his staff remained deeply worried about a monumental problem: how to "hide" the invasion fleet as it plowed for ten hours through the English Channel.

On the Channel coast in France and Belgium were ninety-two sites equipped with a wide array of sophisticated ground radar—Würzburgs, Freyas, Mammuts, Wassermans, and Seetakts. The task of these electronic devices was to keep watch around the clock for any movement by an Allied invasion fleet.

Thirty-three-year-old Reginald Jones, director of scientific intelligence for the British Air Staff, had been handed the daunting assignment of blinding these Cyclops-like "eyes" that would be "staring" at the approaching Overlord armada. His first step was to set up along the Channel coast of England three Ping-Pongs, intricate electronic direction-finders. These devices detected and provided "fixes" on the German radar sites on the Far Shore, as the French coast was known to Allied planners.

After the German stations had been pinpointed electronically, their existence was confirmed by low-level Royal Air Force reconnaissance flights. These crucial radar sites were heavily defended, and the loss of pilots was great. But these sacrifices permitted Jones and his colleagues to compile comprehensive dossiers on every German radar station on the Far Shore.

In the meantime, a bustle of activity was raging in a nondescript building below the ramparts of historic Tantallon Castle, perched on a height overlooking the Firth of Forth in Scotland. Two British scientists, Robert Cockburn and Joan Curran, were developing two "ghost fleets," a machination upon which the success or failure of the Normandy invasion might rest.

The fleets would be key components in an intricate deception plan, code-named Bodyguard, that had been implemented to hoodwink Adolf Hitler into deducing that *der Grossinvasion* would hit at the Pas de Calais region, at the narrowest point in the English Channel. Actually, the true landing beaches would be in the Bay of the Seine, some two hundred miles to the southwest. This *ruse de guerre* was intended to keep the German high command from rushing units along the Pas de Calais to the true Allied landing beaches.

Centerpieces of the intricate fake flotillas were Moonshine and Window. Created by Joan Curran two years earlier, Moonshine would be installed in airplanes. It received the pulse sent out by enemy radar and flashed it back to the same site in greatly magnified form, producing "echoes" similar to that of many ships. Moonshine had never been used, so the Germans would be unfamiliar with it.

Window, also developed by Curran, consisted of aluminum foils treated with a certain chemical and dropped by aircraft in large numbers at specified intervals of flight, thereby confusing enemy radar technicians by giving them the impression that hundreds of planes were approaching.

Each ghost fleet would have a line of launches spread across a front fourteen miles wide. Their task would be to jam the German coastal radar stations—but just enough to confuse their pictures. Another line of launches would be abreast some ten miles to the rear of the jammers. Each of these launches would tow a Filbert, a twenty-nine-foot-long balloon with a Moonshine built inside it, and tow another float with a Filbert.

High above the launches would be Royal Air Force bombers (eight to each fleet), which would fly oblong patterns parallel to the shore. To make the dummy fleet appear to be advancing at eight miles per hour on German radar screens, every seven minutes the bombers' oblong patterns would move forward a mile.

To inject realism into the electronic spoof, other RAF bombers, equipped with electronic jammers, would be circling nearby. These aircraft would be strategically positioned so that German radar could barely "see" through the cracks in the jamming blanket and "detect" the phantom fleets.

Such a large concentration of ships certainly would not be a silent one. So Robert Cockburn and his colleagues created another elaborate ruse. Once the ghost fleets halted ten miles from shore, real, smaller boats armed with powerful amplifiers would begin blaring out prerecorded sounds of a landing force debarking: the shrill noises of bosuns' pipes; warships' bugle calls; commands being shouted; and the rattles of chains lowering landing craft, and their incessant banging against the sides of the transports after reaching the water.

These noises had been recorded during the actual Anglo-American invasion at Salerno, Italy, in September 1943. It was hoped that the Germans on the French shore would hear the sounds and report that a major amphibious assault was about to be launched.

In the three weeks prior to D-Day, British and American bombers and fighter-bombers, using the voluminous data compiled by Reginald Jones and his colleagues, flew thousands of sorties to knock out most of the German radar on the Far Shore. A few of the sites at the Pas de Calais were deliberately spared. Hopefully, these surviving "eyes" would report to higher headquarters the approach of the two ghost fleets, before Moonshine turned their screens into snowlike blizzards.

On the evening of June 5, 1944, the mighty genuine invasion fleet—and the two ghost fleets—began leaving Great Britain. An hour after midnight on D-Day, the fraudulent flotillas were approaching the Pas de Calais. Three Moonshine sea-air rescue launches and six other small boats were bound for Cap d'Antifer (Operation Taxable), while fifty miles to the east, one Moonshine launch and eight other boats were steering toward Boulogne (Operation Glimmer).

As anticipated, German radar sites deliberately spared from bombing for this illusion discovered the Glimmer and Taxable "fleets," which were approaching at eight miles per hour, the same rate of speed at which a genuine naval force would advance.

Operators in the launches observed German radar signals on their cathode ray tubes, switched on their transmitters, and "Moonshined" the enemy sites. The electronic cat-and-mouse game was on. During the next three hours, scores of German radar signals were received by the launches, and the enemy transmissions were bounced back in highly amplified form.

Each launch also carried radio transmitters, which exchanged prerecorded orders simulating the preparations for a rocket barrage on the Pas de Calais shoreline. This radio traffic was not coded, so the German electronic ears along the coast could easily pick it up and understand it. Over these collections of tiny boats flew the Stirlings and the Lancasters, weaving their complex patterns and strewing Window.

When the twin phantom flotillas reached their stop lines ten miles off the Pas de Calais, RAF planes swooped in and blanketed the region with thick smoke, a standard technique in genuine amphibious assaults. Then, with the first hint of dawn, loudspeakers bellowed the prerecorded sounds of an invasion fleet debarking.

A critical factor the Allied deception artists had counted on—the fog of war—may have contributed to at least partial success for Glimmer and Taxable. A single young German draftee huddled before his radar screen would "see" through the jamming what appeared to be a large fleet, and he and other excited operators along the Pas de Calais would pass along their sightings to superiors. These hazy preliminary reports would climb up the chain of command in the West and eventually evolve into "confirmed facts" and become broad arrows signifying invasion forces on situation maps at many German headquarters.

At the same time, in the early-morning darkness, another electronic spoof was in progress. A flight of 31 British Lancasters and American Flying Fortresses was winging eastward above Amiens, France. Crewmen were pitching out thousands of pounds of Window that would make it appear to German radar that a large bomber stream was headed for the Third Reich. This was a decoy force whose mission was to draw German focus away from the 1,058 lumbering transport planes carrying paratroopers to Normandy, far to the west.

In Britain, the Kingsdown electronic monitoring station intercepted orders from a German air controller for all night fighters in the region to scramble and vector on the decoy bomber flight. A few fighters attacked the deception force, and one Lancaster was shot down while its crew was tossing out a bundle of Window.

While Luftwaffe night fighters in northern France were off chasing the small decoy flight of bombers toward Germany, thousands of American and British paratroopers were bailing out over Normandy without a single transport plane being lost to enemy aircraft.

An eerie stillness blanketed the Bay of the Seine off Normandy. By the faint dawn light, the hulks of thousands of Allied ships were barely visible to the naked eye.

Ears were cocked for the arrival of the Luftwaffe. Even a myopic bombardier could hardly miss, so numerous were the floating targets. But no German plane appeared. By nightfall, some 130,000 troops, together with their accoutrements, had fought their way ashore.

Valor of the assault troops had carried the day for the Allies. But the outcome might have been far different had it not been for the colossal—and mostly unheralded—contributions of British scientists. An official dispatch would state: "The jamming of [German radar] saved the lives of countless soldiers, sailors, and airmen on D-Day."[7]

Schemes to Defeat a Plague of Robots

CONFRONTED BY an onslaught of Adolf Hitler's secret weapons the buzz bombs, sprawling London lived in constant fear and chaos. In desperation—as national survival may have been hanging in the balance—Prime Minister Winston Churchill, on July 13, 1944, proposed the all-out use of poison gas, with all of its hideous consequences, against the citizens of the Third Reich.

British scientists had earlier developed a top-secret bacteriological agent for which there was no known antidote. Using that germ-spreading tactic was finally ruled out: large enough quantities would not be available for at least a year.

Meanwhile, British operational research scientists and Royal Air Force leaders debated among themselves about the most effective way to try to minimize the flying robots' carnage. More than two thousand antiaircraft guns had been rushed to the southern coast of England, but these weapons were largely useless.

After the flying bombs ran a gauntlet of antiaircraft fire, they were chased and attacked by patrolling fighter planes, a formidable challenge for the pilots because the robots flew slightly faster than most of the airplanes.

Among the few British fighters that could overtake a buzz bomb was the Spitfire Mark XIV, with a top speed of more than four hundred miles per hour. On occasion, when a pilot ran out of ammunition, he resorted to a daring tactic that might well have ended in his death. The maneuver was intended to make the robot lose its flight stability by toppling the gyroscopes of its guidance system.

The RAF pilot would approach the flying bomb slowly, make contact as softly as he could by placing his wingtip under the wing of the robot, and then move the control stick gingerly until the robot heeled over into a dive, hopefully exploding harmlessly on the ground.

As the robot carnage continued to plague London, headquarters of RAF Fighter Command was inundated by schemes for defeating the onslaught. These suggestions including tethering lighter-than-air dirigibles firing harpoons, arming fighter planes with bolas (a weapon consisting of two or more iron balls attached to the ends of a cord for hurling at and entangling an animal), using huge butterfly nets, flinging into the sky large containers filled with carbolic acid, and a wide array of airborne hooks and grapples.

One self-described medium offered to post herself in the Fighter Command headquarters and cast a curse on the German robot-launching crews across the English Channel. Another female medium suggested that she detect hidden launching sites by means of an "out-of-body experience."

Suggestions from the British public grew until a staff officer had to be employed on a full-time basis to deal with the flood of correspondence. Each letter received a courteous reply. The category of contributors described as "merely crazy" got form letters. Anxious types were sent reassuring communications. Appreciation was expressed to those sending ideas that operations research scientists and RAF commanders might want to pursue.

In the latter category, a writer had painstakingly analyzed the impact pattern of the flying bombs in a series of tabulating stages of reasoning. Each step was logical and leading to the next step. Clearly, this correspondent was a gifted individual.

In his summation, the writer strongly recommended that the belt of antiaircraft batteries that had been placed along the southern coast of England be removed and that much greater emphasis be placed on fighter planes.

RAF staff officers, who had earlier reached the same conclusion, were delighted by the heavy reinforcement provided by this well-reasoned study. Then it was pointed out to them that the stationery was headed "Kent County Mental Hospital." At the end of the written presentation had been rubber-stamped the wording "The Medical Superintendent accepts no responsibility for the contents of this letter."[8]

A Soviet Plot Fizzles

WITH SOVIET SPEARHEADS charging across Poland and approaching the eastern border of Germany in July 1944, dictator Josef Stalin set up a special technical intelligence committee of scientists under Georgi Malenkov, chairman of the Council of People's Commissars. Aware through his spy network in Germany (called the Red Orchestra by the Gestapo) of successful test firings of thirteen-ton rockets by Nazi experts, Stalin realized that this awesome weapon could revolutionize warfare if perfected.

The Soviets had a minimal missile research and development program, so to close the knowledge gap of perhaps twenty-five years, Malenkov hatched a scheme to gain an edge over the Americans, the British, and the French. He targeted Peenemünde, the German rocket research center, for a cloak-and-dagger operation.

Nine German prisoners of war, all of whom had lived in the Peenemünde region, were removed from Soviet concentration camps and promised their freedom in exchange for participating in the secret mission that Malenkov had in mind. They were given German money, false papers, and shortwave radios. On a dark night, they parachuted near Peenemünde with the task of obtaining as much information as possible about the German missile program.

As soon as the former POWs reached the ground, eight of them shucked their radios, tore up their phony documents, and headed for their homes as rapidly as possible, figuratively thumbing their noses at their Soviet handlers. Only Lieutenant Erwin Brandt, for whatever his reasons, tried to carry out his mission, radioing back to Moscow some trivial information he had picked up from workers living nearby.

After his seventh message, Brandt was tracked down by the highly efficient Funkabwehr (radio intelligence), arrested, and executed.

Commissar Malenkov refused to give up on efforts to steal the German secrets at Peenemünde. But it was months later, on May 5, 1945, with the Third Reich disintegrating, that he focused again on the rocket research center.

A special Soviet commando unit led by Major Anatole Vavilov charged into Peenemünde. Hard on the soldiers' heels, Soviet technical intelligence teams rushed through the front gate, set on collaring the Third Reich's foremost rocket scientists. To the Soviets' dismay, they found that their quarries had flown the coop weeks earlier.

The Soviet scientists then began a frantic search for blueprints, documents, or other related materials about the long-range rockets. All they could turn up was a batch of meaningless memos.[9]

Hitler Counts on Wonder Weapons

TENSION GRIPPED the civilian population of Great Britain during the first week of September 1944. For the past ten days, Josef Goebbels, the Nazi propaganda genius, had been trumpeting over Radio Berlin that Adolf Hitler was nearly ready to launch a frightening wonder weapon against London.

At 6:48 P.M. on September 8, while many Londoners were eating dinner, a terrific blast rocked the suburb of Chiswick-on-Thames. Terrified citizens dashed for their basements. Nineteen homes were demolished. Scores of dead and injured were dug out of the ruins. The explosion had gouged out a thirty-foot-deep crater.

Scientists rushed to the site. They were told by civilians of a thunderclap followed by a rustling sound. British intelligence had long been warning government leaders that the Germans were developing a thirteen-ton rocket (code-named V-2). Because the rocket traveled faster than sound, the blast was heard first and then the missile's approach. The onslaught had begun.

Prime Minister Winston Churchill, to avoid hysteria, clamped a muzzle on any mention of the rocket attacks in the newspapers or on BBC radio. Sixty-four missiles had inflicted colossal carnage and bloodshed before the British public, and the world, would learn details of Hitler's latest *Wunderwaffen* (wonder weapon).

Although powerful Allied armies were pushing up against Germany on three sides in the fall of 1944, Hitler remained optimistic about eventual victory or a stalemate that could result in a negotiated peace with Great Britain, the United States, and France. His confidence was rooted in the knowledge that his scientists were churning out an entirely new range of fantastic weaponry for use on land, at sea, or in the air. There were spectacular technological concepts that would far exceed anything the Allies possessed.

However, Hitler's interference in some projects, especially the revolutionary jet-propelled Me-262 aircraft, proved to be disastrous. The aircraft was designed to be a high-speed interceptor, and it had a maximum speed of 538 miles per hour, far faster than the conventional fighters of the Allies. With its four 40mm cannon and twenty-four air-to-air missiles, the new plane could far outgun American and British aircraft.

When Hitler was told that the Me-262 could carry bombs, he saw the plane as a new revenge weapon to heap destruction on the British Isles. So the speedy Schwalbe (Swallow) became the relatively lumbering Sturmvogel (Storm Bird), loaded with two 550-pound bombs.

The führer's order set back the full development of the Me-262 potential at least four months because the heavy bomb load made the aircraft difficult to handle. When a Sturmvogel was tested in combat, it was slow enough to be pursued and attacked by the Allies' propeller-driven fighters.

Allied intelligence learned that a mammoth underground factory in the Harz Mountains of central Germany would be ready for mass production of engines for jet fighter planes by April 1945, and would turn out twelve hundred of them each month. Then, with a sky armada of five thousand or six thousand jets, the Luftwaffe could drive the Allied air forces from the skies of Europe.

In England, General Carl "Tooey" Spaatz, commander of the U.S. Strategic Air Forces, was deeply concerned about the threat of jet fighter planes. Several of the sleek aircraft had appeared in early 1945 over the Western Front and tangled with Allied bomber streams, shooting down several of the four-engine planes at a time.

Consequently, Spaatz and his staff began investigating ways to destroy the jet factory, which ran for a mile into a mountain. It was a very elaborate layout, a massive, sophisticated, high-tech operation with complicated assembly lines. Thousands of foreign slave laborers were assigned to the operation.

Spaatz and his aides soon determined that even a deluge of two thousand-pound blockbuster bombs would be useless: the plant was too deep underground. So the air baron called in several scientists. Could they come up with a solution to the problem? Indeed they could—a novel scheme to wipe out the jet factory.

Specially equipped Allied bombers would discharge above the Harz Mountains thousands of gallons of a mixture of soap and gasoline, a concoction that could easily be created. This enormous flood of liquid would seep through the ventilation system of the factory and, once inside, it would burst into a raging inferno.

At the same time, swarms of Allied fighter-bombers would plaster all exits with explosives, sealing the factory and preventing workers from escaping and firefighting assistance from entering.

After prolonged discussion with aides, General Spaatz reluctantly scuttled the idea. It may have produced the desired results, but it would have caused the hideous deaths of thousands of slave laborers.

Fortunately for the Allies, the subterranean plant was overrun by American ground forces a few weeks later, just as mass production of the jet engines was ready to begin.

Built at a German shipyard, a manned torpedo called a Neger was lowered into the water from a vessel. The pilot of a Neger sat in a modified torpedo casing and, after using a vertical rod in front of him to sight his target, fired a live torpedo slung below. A Plexiglas dome protected the occupant from ocean waves, but the Negers were not submersible.

Although the fate of the Neger pilot would be a matter of conjecture, navy leaders felt that the odds were in their favor: one "volunteer" lost in return for one Allied ship sunk.

The Biber, a midget submarine, was designed almost identically to a U-boat and could dive ninety feet. But it could not cruise underwater, so the one-man "crew" had to fire its two torpedoes from the surface. Test runs were made of the Biber along the coast of the Netherlands late in the war, and it achieved a degree of success that warranted orders for mass production.

German scientists created an artificial aerial vortex to destroy Allied bombers. A huge amplifier on the ground would project sound waves of high power and low frequency. The noise was intended to kill or disorient Allied aircrews, causing their bombers to crash.

Yet another German creation far ahead of its time was the "Do," a solid-fuel missile that was successfully fired from a submerged submarine. Plans were drawn up for the U-boats to tow 46-foot missiles with one-ton warheads to positions off the United States' eastern coast and fire the weapons at New York City and Washington, D.C., while the submarine was below the surface.

One of the more fantastic ideas of German scientists was a winged rocket proposed by a husband-and-wife team, Eugen Sänger and Irene Bredt. It would be an antipodal bomber 92 feet long and weighing 220,000 pounds. The craft would be launched from a sled driven by rockets developing 1.3 million pounds of thrust.

The sled would send the bomber into the air at 1,000 miles per hour; then its own 200,000-pound-thrust engine would boost it to a speed of 13,700 miles per hour and an altitude of more than 160 miles.

If built, the manned antipodal bomber would skip along the top of the atmosphere (where no human had ever been) like a stone thrown onto a pond, reaching New York City or Washington, D.C., with a bomb load of six tons. Sänger and Bredt calculated that the entire flight, from takeoff to a return landing in Germany, would require only eight minutes.

Sänger and Bredt produced a 409-page report, and 79 copies were distributed by couriers in double envelopes with a return receipt to a list of German airplane production tycoons. An authorized functionary had stamped on the front of each envelope: "This is a top secret. To be kept in locked steel safe in rooms guarded twenty-four hours daily. Any violation of these regulations will be most severely punished."

The list of recipients included Willy Messerschmitt, designer of the Third Reich's foremost fighter planes; Kurt Tank of Focke-Wulf aircraft company; Walther Dornier, manufacturer of bombers; and Julius Mader of Junkers aircraft.

Other German experts were developing a remote-controlled rocket that could be guided to and destroy Allied bombers over the Third Reich. Also in the works were two new types of submarines, both extremely swift, virtually undetectable when submerged, and able to recharge their batteries while underwater. These U-boats would operate without surfacing for weeks at a time.

This manned German rocket was supposed to fire the missiles in its nose when airborne, then crash while the pilot parachuted. (Smithsonian Institution)

Officers and crewmen would be provided with vitamin pills and daily sunlamp treatments to preserve their health.

German scientists were working feverishly on a multistage missile (code-named V-3) that could hit cities on the eastern coast of the United States with one-ton warheads.

Nearly in its final stages and ready to go into production was a jet-powered, futuristic "flying wing" (code-named Horten) that looked like a huge bat in flight. It could attain a speed of six hundred miles per hour and reach a height of forty thousand feet—far faster and higher than any Allied fighter plane could fly or climb.

At a remote locale in Austria, German technicians were testing the rocket-propelled Natter, a startling new concept for a fighter plane that would be used to defend the skies over the Fatherland from the waves of Allied bombers. Natter was of simple construction but had a radically new operational technique.

With a pilot on board, the Natter was catapulted straight up from a launching apparatus. However, it had a maximum range of only thirty-six miles, so the pilot was to fire the twenty-four rockets in the nose at Allied bombers, then detach the forward section, ejecting himself. Pilot and engine would land by separate parachutes, and both would be used again in another Natter.

Because of the wide array of looming wunderwaffen and his deep-rooted conviction (backed by numerous historical precedents) that the brittle and squabbling Allied alliance would yet split apart, Adolf Hitler found grounds for optimism. But Hitler needed time. If there was to be a salvation for the Third Reich, the generals would have to buy the needed time on the battlefield.[10]

Thwarting Japanese Torpedo Planes

AT HIS ORNATE PALACE in downtown Tokyo, Emperor Hirohito, impeccably attired in formal clothing, was ready to receive a delegation of generals, admirals, and top government officials. Formal dress was reserved for special occasions. Hirohito, the father of six, customarily shuffled about the long halls and high-ceilinged rooms of the sprawling palace clad in old casual clothes, scuffed shoes, and in need of a shave. It was October 11, 1944.

Escorted into Hirohito's presence, the visiting delegation, subdued and with hats in hand, confessed their "failures" to the introverted emperor, who for nineteen years had been struggling to make a success of the throne he had inherited at age twenty-five from his father.

Although the Allies were closing in on Japan, the warlords assured Hirohito that the bleak picture would soon be reversed. A high-level official in the Foreign Office of the Soviet Union, supposedly an ally of the United States and Great Britain, had tipped off the Japanese ambassador in Moscow that the Americans were preparing to invade the Philippines. At that time, a plan code-named Sho-Go I (Operation Victory) would inflict a crushing defeat on the fleet and army of General Douglas MacArthur, the delegation told the emperor.

In the early-morning darkness of October 20, a mighty armada of seven hundred U.S. ships slipped into Leyte Gulf in the central Philippines. On board the cruiser *Nashville* was Douglas MacArthur, perhaps America's most popular general on the home front, who had been run out of the Philippines by overwhelming Japanese forces in the spring of 1942.

At 8:00 A.M., warships offshore loosed a thunderous barrage; then assault troops of Lieutenant General Walter Krueger's Sixth Army stormed ashore on Leyte, a large, mountainous island.

Forty-eight hours later, Admiral Soemu Toyoda, chief of the imperial Combined Fleet, was at his headquarters in the Naval War College putting the final touches on Sho-Go I. His planning was aided by a flagrant American security lapse—an uncoded radio message picked up by Japanese monitors gave Toyoda the deployment of the 221 U.S. warships operating in and around the Philippines.

Toyoda was convinced that a new secret radar development by Japanese scientists would result in colossal damage to the invasion fleet. Installed in the cockpits of Japanese torpedo planes and used for aiming the lethal "fish," radar had been created with a frequency below the lowest frequency of the electronic jammers in the U.S. fleet. Therefore the pilot could aim and fire his torpedo unencumbered by the jamming of his radar by the Americans.

Only a few hours after the decisive battle of the Pacific war had erupted at Leyte Gulf, General MacArthur was in a barge returning to the *Nashville* from an inspection ashore. As the little craft burrowed through the green waters, someone shouted, "Look!" and pointed a finger toward the sky. A Japanese torpedo plane flew low over the barge and headed for the light cruiser *Honolulu*. Called the Blue Goose by her crew, the ship was standing by for instructions to bombard targets onshore.

The Blue Goose had led a charmed life. She had been involved in many battles and escaped unscathed each time. Incredibly, she had never lost a man due to accidents or enemy action.

Soon after zooming past MacArthur's barge, the Japanese plane dropped its torpedo into the water; the torpedo raced directly for the *Honolulu*. No American knew that this was one of the aircraft equipped with the low-frequency radar, so the electronic jammers on the ship failed to blur the pilot's aim.

There was an enormous explosion, and the Blue Goose shook violently. Lady Luck had finally turned her back on the cruiser: sixty officers and sailors were killed, and scores of others were wounded.

Japanese torpedo-plane attacks continued and became a menace to the fleet. So an urgent plea was sent to the Pentagon near Washington, D.C., asking for help. The request was promptly turned over to the General Electric Company (GE), whose scientists plunged into the task of developing a countermeasure for the Japanese torpedo-plane radar.

Although a creation of this intricacy, even in wartime urgency, would customarily take many months, in a near-miracle, the GE specialists developed a new low-frequency design within twenty-four hours. Fifty of these devices were turned over to the navy in only a week's time from the original request.

Within hours, the devices were on an airplane bound for the Pacific, where they were installed on ships around the Philippines while what came to be known as the Battle for Leyte Gulf was still raging.

Soon reports began arriving at the Pentagon that told of the success of the equipment. When the ships turned on the new electronic jammers, Japanese torpedo planes often were seen wavering from their courses and finally turning back, unable to find the targets on their blurred radar screens.

American warship skippers authorized operators of the electronic jammers to paint a small Japanese flag on their transmitters after each successful action of this type.

It had been the greatest naval engagement ever fought with regard to the number of ships and airplanes involved on both sides and the magnitude of the ocean surface covered—almost twice the size of the state of Texas. The Japanese Fleet had been virtually destroyed.

Playing a key role in the American victory had been the behind-the-scenes effort of the GE scientists in their amazingly rapid development of a countermeasure against the new-type radar in the Japanese torpedo planes.[11]

A Bizarre Scenario in Zurich

SNOW WAS pelting Zurich, the largest city in neutral Switzerland, on the afternoon of December 14, 1944, when renowned German scientist Werner Heisenberg arrived at the railroad station. He was greeted by a group of Swiss scientists, who had invited the recipient of the 1932 Nobel Prize in physics to give a lecture.

Perhaps only one of the greeting delegation was aware that Heisenberg was the chief theoretician of and moving spirit behind a German project to build an atomic bomb. That Swiss was fifty-two-year-old Paul Scherrer, a professor since 1920 at the Eidgenössische Technische Hochschule (Federal Technical College) in Zurich.

Scherrer was a secret agent for the U.S. Office of Strategic Services (OSS) in Bern, Switzerland. He was the only Swiss scientist who knew that an OSS plan was in the works to kill Heisenberg before he left Zurich, thereby depriving Nazi Germany of his technological know-how.

Scherrer, a friendly, low-key type, was never paid for his services for the OSS, nor did he ever ask for money. He was simply a staunch advocate for the Allied cause. Allen W. Dulles, the OSS chief in Switzerland, gave him the code name Flute.

The unlikely would-be assassin was Morris "Moe" Berg (OSS code name Bemus), a tall, husky man in his early forties who had been mainly a baseball catcher for five major league teams, principally the Chicago White Sox and the Boston Red Sox, for fifteen years. In the jargon of the game, he had been "good field, no hit."

Berg, baseball's only intellectual in the 1930s, could speak seven languages, including German, fluently. Before being sent to Zurich, he had been given a crash course in atomic-bomb theories.

The head of the German atomic-bomb project, Werner Heisenberg, target of an OSS murder plot. (National Archives)

His mission was to take a front-row seat at the lecture hall, and if Heisenberg were to give any indication that he was involved in atomic-bomb development, Berg was to whip a pistol from his pocket and shoot the German dead on the spot.

Berg listened intently as Heisenberg, an affable man in his mid-forties, spoke before a packed house of scientists and students for nearly an hour. He lectured only in general scientific terms, so Berg decided not to kill him.

After the lecture, old friend Paul Scherrer invited the German to his home for dinner and to meet some of the professor's associates and students. It was a convivial affair, with much drinking and scientific talk.

Moe Berg was among the guests at the party, but he was never introduced to Heisenberg, although the German had noticed Berg and thought he was a Swiss. When Heisenberg departed for the ten-minute walk to his hotel, Berg accompanied him through the dark and winding streets.

It was a bizarre scenario. A would-be killer with a loaded pistol in his pocket, strolling alongside the possible target while the two men engaged in friendly conversation. Berg asked persistent questions, trying to extract some hint that his companion was involved in atomic-bomb development. But Heisenberg was not about to disclose his thoughts or activities to a virtual stranger, so he graciously deflected the questions.

At the hotel entrance, the two men shook hands and took leave of one another. Two days later, Heisenberg left Switzerland and spent the last Christmas of the war with his family in southern Germany. Perhaps he had survived his Zurich visit because he had kept mum about his leading role in the German atomic-bomb program.[12]

A Tiny Fuse Balks the Führer

"ADOLF HITLER is *kaputt!*"

The sentiment expressed by a high-ranking intelligence officer in the headquarters of Supreme Commander Dwight Eisenhower echoed the views of other Allied generals nearing the early winter of 1944. U.S., British, and French armies were deployed along the western frontier of the Third Reich. All that was needed was "one more big heave," in the words of an Eisenhower aide, to bring Nazi Germany to its knees.

Suddenly, at 5:28 A.M. on December 16, an eerie silence that had prevailed for several weeks along a sector known as the Ghost Front was shattered by a cacophony of sound and fury. Nineteen hundred pieces of German artillery showered death and destruction on American troops and installations.

When the thunderous barrage lifted, tens of thousands of German assault troops, supported by a thousand panzers, plunged into and through the thin and disoriented American positions and drove into Belgium for fifty miles.

For six weeks, American dogfaces (as GI foot soldiers called themselves) and German stubble-hoppers (infantrymen) fought one another in brutal cold and deep snow. Many on both sides froze to death. No quarter was asked; none was given.

By February 1, 1945, the defeated German armies limped back to their starting positions along the border of the Third Reich. Some eighty thousand German soldiers never returned; seventy thousand young Americans died in the bloody struggle.

Hitler would never know that American scientists had developed a tiny device known as a proximity fuse, which had been fired in combat for the first time during what became known as the Battle of the Bulge. That top-secret innovation had contributed significantly to the outcome of the brutal clash.

The proximity fuse was a miniature radar unit shaped to replace the customary ballistic nose of artillery shells. After a shell had been fired and was on its downward trajectory, the fuse sensed the proximity to a target and exploded the shell it rode.

Because the shell with the proximity fuse burst just above German troops in foxholes and trenches, the jagged shrapnel was sent *downward*, riddling soldiers in the impact area. Conventional shells that exploded on contact with the ground usually sprayed shrapnel *upward*, thereby generally causing no physical harm to soldiers in foxholes or trenches.

An American war plant worker holds in her right hand a subminiature radio tube of the type used in the revolutionary proximity fuse that helped defeat Hitler in the Battle of the Bulge. (U.S. Army)

After the Battle of the Bulge, General George S. Patton Jr., commander of the Third Army, wrote to Major General Levin Campbell, chief of ordnance in Washington, D.C.:

> The new shell with the funny fuse is devastating. One night we caught a German battalion, which was trying to get across the Sauer River, with an [artillery] concentration and killed by actual count 702.
>
> I think that when all our armies get this shell we will have to devise some new method of warfare. I am glad that your [scientists] thought of it first.

For more than two years, scientists at the Carnegie Institution in Washington, D.C., and the Applied Physics Laboratory of Johns Hopkins University in nearby Baltimore had been experimenting with the proximity fuse. On August 11 and 12, 1942, the first field tests under simulated battle conditions were conducted on the cruiser *Cleveland* in Chesapeake Bay, a long arm of the Atlantic Ocean that divides Maryland into two parts.

Drones (radio-controlled planes) flew high above the *Cleveland*, and anti-aircraft shells fitted with fuses were fired. Direct hits were not needed. One after the other the drones were blasted from the sky.

Similar trials with the proximity fuse were conducted on land with dummies placed in foxholes. Shells, with the fuses detonated just overhead, saturated the dummies with fragments.

At the peak of the proximity-fuse development project, more than ten thousand persons had been involved, along with the services of three hundred companies and two thousand industrial plants. All of this activity was cloaked by an intense secrecy that matched that of the atomic-bomb program then in progress.

Gargantuan problems were created by the need for total secrecy. Most of the thousands involved in the fuse program were unaware of precisely what they were working on. Even after contracts were negotiated, only a few top personnel in the companies were given basic information. Military officers charged with security twisted around even these data so that no one executive would have a clear picture of the fuse project.

Fuses shipped by rail from assembly plants were guarded by U.S. Marines, who had orders to shoot to kill if anyone tried to make off with any of the devices. When a shipment of fuses went by ship to ports, armed guards made certain that no one left the vessel until the officer in charge of the secret cargo made sure that every fuse on board had been accounted for and handed over to a designated authority on the dock.

By the spring of 1944, the proximity fuses were being shipped to the various theaters of operation around the world. But the Combined Chiefs of Staff (British and American generals who met in Washington, D.C.) were fearful that duds might be recovered by the Germans and Japanese, whose scientists would copy the devices, so it was decreed that the fuses could be used only over water.

Lieutenant General Ben Lear, the crusty chief of the U.S. Army Ground Forces in the Pentagon, vocally disputed that decision. He regarded the proximity fuse as "the most important innovation in artillery ammunition since the introduction of high explosives," and he called for its release to ground troops.

Finally, in late October 1944, Lear won his battle with the Combined Chiefs of Staff, and they agreed to release the fuse for ground combat effective December 16. Ironically, that was the precise date that Adolf Hitler had set for launching his final roll of the dice in the Battle of the Bulge. Had Lear not been so tenacious in his demands, the führer may have achieved his goal of victory or a stalemate and negotiated peace in the West.[13]

Tactics to Obstruct the Soviets

DURING THE FIRST WEEK of March 1945, General Carl Spaatz, leader of U.S. air forces in Europe, had a visitor from Washington, D.C., Major Frank Smith. Spaatz was handed secret instructions: his bombers were to destroy the sprawling Auer Gesellschaft plant at Oranienburg, north of Berlin. Captured documents had disclosed to Allied intelligence that Auer produced plates and cubes of uranium metal for use in a reactor, a major step in developing an atomic bomb.

Even at this late stage of the war, there remained major concern in Washington and London about the possibility that the Germans might yet develop an atomic bomb. Moreover, leaders of the Western Allies were determined to keep important German manufacturing plants and laboratories out of the hands of the Soviets.

There was ample reason for the aura of secrecy wrapped around the looming raid on the Oranienburg plant. At a meeting of the Big Three—President Franklin D. Roosevelt, Prime Minister Winston S. Churchill, and dictator Josef Stalin—at Yalta, near the Soviet port of Sevastopol, in mid-February 1945, Germany had been carved into four unequal occupation zones. Oranienburg was deep inside the Soviet zone.

On March 15, 1945, a total of 612 U.S. Flying Fortresses flew over the Soviet zone and plastered the Auer Gesellschaft with 1,800 tons of bombs. When Soviet scientists rushed to Oranienburg a short time later, they were furious. The prize factory on which they had set their focus was in ruins and beyond repair.

Although German forces were in disarray, the Americans had met with stubborn resistance and paid a high price. Nine Flying Fortresses had been lost, and sixty-six airmen had gone down with their bombers.

In the meantime, American scientific intelligence teams had been tracking down Germany's supply of uranium, a key ingredient in creating an atomic bomb. The sleuths had discovered some of the ore in Belgium, and prior to that, they had located two railroad cars of the stuff after the Allied invasion of southern France in August 1944.

It was not until April 1945 that twenty-nine-year-old U.S. Major Robert R. Furman found the remaining German uranium stockpile at the Wirtschaftliche Forschungs Gesellschaft, a factory near Stassfurt, in the Soviet zone.

Armed with the information dug up by Major Furman, U.S. Colonel John Lansdale and a top British intelligence official, Charles Hambro, on April 15 strode into the headquarters of the U.S. 12th Army Group in Wiesbaden, Germany. Lansdale was a security officer for the Manhattan Project, which was developing an atomic bomb, and Hambro had been chief of the British cloak-and-dagger organization Special Operations Executive (SOE).

Lansdale and Hambro met with Major General Edwin Siebert, the G-2 (intelligence officer), and briefed him on a plan for an army unit to launch a raid against Stassfurt to "liberate" a stockpile of "vital material." (No one in the U.S. or British armed forces in Europe had even an inkling that an atomic bomb was being developed in America.)

"Impossible!" Siebert replied. At a time when the U.S. Army had tens of thousands of vehicles in Germany and France, the G-2 said that no transport could be spared for a raid. Siebert seemed to think that the proposed operation would be some sort of a wild-goose chase.

Moreover, Siebert declared, the Soviets would be "furious" if they knew the Americans had pilfered this "vital material" from their occupation zone.

Colonel Lansdale, a young lawyer from Cleveland, Ohio, refused to accept the rejection by General Siebert. The G-2 also turned down Lansdale's request to discuss the Stassfurt raid with General Omar N. Bradley, commander of 12th Army Group.

In that case, Lansdale replied, he would have to go back to General Eisenhower's headquarters and explain 12th Army Group's lack of cooperation. Siebert had a sudden change of heart and left the room to consult with his boss.

Known as "Omar the Tentmaker" to American war correspondents, General Bradley was soft-spoken, but his demeanor belied an inner toughness that allowed him to make difficult decisions that affected the course of battles and the lives of his men.

A few minutes later, Siebert returned, telling Lansdale and Hambro that Bradley had brushed aside any diplomatic niceties and said, "The Russians can go to hell!"

Translation: The Stassfurt raid was approved.

A few days later, more than a thousand tons of uranium ore were brought back from Stassfurt and then transferred to Great Britain for safekeeping.

On April 23, General George Marshall in the Pentagon received a terse memo that concluded:

> The capture of this material, which was the bulk of uranium supplies available in Europe, would seem to remove definitely any possibility of the Germans making any use of an atomic bomb.

Omitted from the message was the fact that the crucial uranium had been kept out of the hands of the Soviets. For the first time in four years, top minds were at ease over the specter of a German atomic-bomb threat.[14]

A Polish Janitor Scores a Coup

BY MARCH 15, 1945, large portions of a crumbling Germany had been over-run by the Allies in the East and the West. A great treasure hunt for German scientific booty had erupted, spurred on by intelligence reports confirming colossal German superiority in an entire range of weaponry on land, sea, and air.

There was good reason for this wide-ranging, free-wheeling search for German scientists and their secrets: gigantic and far-reaching rewards would go to the victor in the treasure hunt.

In western Germany alone, the United States had fourteen scientific intelligence teams from the army, navy, and air corps, each independent of one another, skedaddling around to sniff out what they could. Often they competed with teams from the other services—and with their British, French, and Soviet counterparts.

Meanwhile, Adolf Hitler had given orders for all scientific research and development facilities and their documents to be destroyed on the approach of enemy spearheads.

Consequently, on March 18, when elements of the U.S. 1st Infantry Division (the Big Red One) fought their way into Bonn, on the western bank of the Rhine River, scientists at famed Bonn University hastily began to destroy blueprints and documents with regard to the new weapons designs on which they had been experimenting.

Bonn had been badly damaged by bombs and artillery, including a few hits on the university buildings. So when top-secret papers were torn up and flushed down toilets, one commode had not operated properly. With American tanks only a few blocks away, a Polish janitor, who had been forced to work at the university laboratory, fished out a batch of papers from the defective toilet. Later he handed over the scraps to Allied intelligence officers.

When the paper bits were dried and tediously pieced together, it was found that the Pole had scored an intelligence coup. The patched-together sheets contained a digest of all German technological projects, along with the names and addresses of the scientists and technicians who had been involved with each task.

This priceless document was called the Osenberg List by the Allies because it had been assembled during the previous five years by Fritz Osenberg, director of the Planning Office of the Reich Research Council.

Unwittingly, the unheralded Polish janitor had provided the U.S. scientific treasure hunters with an enormous advantage in tracking scores of German scientists in the weeks ahead and offering them jobs in the United States to continue their military research.[15]

Hitler Orders Lethal Gas Assault

ON THE NIGHT of March 23–24, 1945, Allied armies in the West launched Operation Plunder, the assault crossing of the broad, majestic Rhine River, which had been significant in German history since Julius Caesar built a timber bridge over it more than two thousand years earlier. Reinforced after daybreak by history's largest simultaneous parachute and glider attack by the U.S. 17th Airborne and the British 6th Airborne Divisions, the Allies were across the Rhine in strength.

Adolf Hitler's reaction to the shocking news was towering rage. He issued orders for a revolutionary lethal nerve gas (Tabun) to be unleashed against the invading armies in the West and against Great Britain.

Scientists with the German industrial giant I. G. Farben had secretly developed the gas. Neither the Allied armies nor the British civilians had any protection. If Tabun were loaded into the Germans' forty-six-foot missile, the V-2, it could wipe out the entire population of London.

Two years earlier, I. G. Farben's chief chemist, Otto Ambros, had supervised the top-secret construction of a factory in Breslau, Germany, for the mass production of Tabun. Ambros had used the code-name Trilon, the label of an ordinary detergent, to mask the lethal nerve gas being produced. Laboratory tests on animals had proved that Tabun could kill a human being in five minutes or less.

Now, in his fury over the Western Allies being across the Rhine, Hitler ordered the collections of Tabun in the Breslau factory to be loaded onto barges on the Elbe and Danube Rivers. Then a V-2 attack that he hoped would massacre millions of British civilians would be launched.

But at this stage of the war, with mass confusion within the Third Reich, progress was slow on the nerve gas operation. Many containers of Tabun were loaded onto barges at Breslau, but the V-2 missiles would never arrive.[16]

A Trainload of German Brainpower

SOVIET SOLDIERS were within a quarter mile of the Berlin bunker in which Adolf Hitler had been holed up in recent weeks. A day earlier, the führer had married his longtime mistress, Eva Braun, and had instructed his personal surgeon, Professor Wernher Haase, to come to the bunker and give a lethal injection to Hitler's favorite Alsatian dog, Blondi. It was the night of April 30, 1945.

At about 2:30 A.M., Hitler and his wife retired to their bunker suite. Moments later, a single shot was heard. After a few minutes, aides entered the room. Hitler was lying on a sofa, having shot himself through the temple. Frau Hitler was also on the sofa, quite dead. She had swallowed capsules of cyanide.

A week later, on May 7, a delegation of high-ranking German officers arrived at the headquarters of Supreme Commander Dwight Eisenhower in a red brick schoolhouse outside Reims, France. Within an hour, Hitler's war-long military confidant General Alfred Jodl signed an instrument of surrender.

After sixty-eight months of relentless bloodshed and carnage, a shaky peace hovered over Europe.

Although the guns had fallen silent, a Cold War already had erupted—a conflict for the hearts and minds of billions of people around the world. Because the Americans, British, and French on one side and the Soviets on the other realized that German technology was perhaps twenty-five years ahead in some fields, an undercover, no-holds-barred battle was being fought in Germany to corral scientists, chemists, engineers, and technicians.

In this intense scramble, there were charges and countercharges of kidnappings, threats, blackmail, harassment, and intimidation of these skilled German experts and their families.

High on the target list of both the Western Allies and the Soviets were German rocket scientists, headed by thirty-three-year-old Wernher von Braun. A few months earlier, Adolf Hitler had ordered his rocket experts to congregate in the Harz Mountains, a locale in central Germany, where a mammoth underground factory had been constructed.

Inside this mile-deep plant, engines for revolutionary jet fighter planes, a triumph of German scientists, and forty-six-foot V-2 missiles were going to be put into mass production. The experts' task was to make the thirteen-ton rockets more accurate.

In the waning days of the war, the U.S. First Army had overrun and occupied much of the Harz Mountains region, but the territory was in an occupation zone assigned to the Soviets, so the Americans would have to pull back no later than June 1, 1945.

Meanwhile, in Washington, D.C., leaders in the Pentagon decided secretly to import German rocket scientists after U.S. intelligence reported that German technology already had been handed over to the Japanese. The Pentagon veiled the project in the deepest secrecy, fearful of a public outcry against "bringing Nazis into the country." There was an even more compelling reason for the covert status: to keep the Soviets in the dark.

On May 27, 1945, three weeks after the German surrender, U.S. Major Robert Staver, who weeks earlier had been assigned the task of locating German rocket scientists, was handed a daunting mission. Colonel Holger N. "Ludy" Toftoy, chief of U.S. Ordnance Technical Intelligence in Paris, instructed Staver to evacuate all German rocket experts and their families from Thuringia, a region that covers forty-five hundred square miles, including the Harz Mountains.

Colonel (later Major General) Holger "Ludy" Toftoy, master-mind of corraling German rocket scientists. (NASA)

Staver, an energetic and resourceful young man, was stunned by the scope of the order. He felt that the mission was akin to trying to swim up Niagara Falls. Some three million people lived in Thuringia, and even finding the scientists would be tedious and time-consuming. Moreover, Staver had only four days to evacuate this valuable human reservoir of technical know-how before it fell into the hands of the Soviets.

Another enormous difficulty confronted Staver. Washington had handed down no official policy toward German scientists, nor was there an authorization to offer them permanent employment, either elsewhere in Europe or in the United States. It seemed highly unlikely that the rocket experts and their families would want to be uprooted from their homes and spirited away to some unknown locale and to an uncertain future.

On the plus side for Major Staver and his search team, reports of atrocities perpetrated in Berlin and elsewhere in Germany by the conquering Soviet Army already had reached Thuringia, generating great fear and apprehension.

Then Lady Luck smiled on the American search team. Because of high-level wrangling between the recent Allies, the Soviet occupation of Thuringia was postponed for three weeks, until June 21.

Major Staver plunged into his task with customary tenacity. Working with three top German scientists who were eager to join the Americans and escape from the Soviets, Staver drew up a list of scores of rocket experts living in Thuringia. Armed with this compilation, the three cooperative Germans, each with an American driver and a native who knew the men to be contacted, fanned out across Thuringia.

The searchers promptly hit a stone wall. Those contacted were skeptical. What did the United States have to offer them in the future? The only pledge Staver and his men could give was that the rocket men and their families would be whisked out of Thuringia ahead of the Soviet Army, along with a solemn promise that the evacuees would be well fed and comfortably housed in the adjoining American occupation zone.

In desperation, Major Staver brought in Wernher von Braun, who had surrendered to the Americans in southern Germany just before the war in Europe ended, to lend his prestige to the recruiting project. Von Braun's stature proved to be magic: the balky scientists signed up in droves.

Altogether, about 120 experts agreed to be evacuated. But Staver was faced by yet another seemingly unsolvable problem: how to transport these men and their wives and children to the Harz Mountains town of Nordhausen to board a train for the American zone. By begging at assorted U.S. Army head-quarters in the region, however, Staver managed to round up an assortment of 326 vehicles.

Time was running out. The Soviets were to arrive in only three days. A U.S. soldier was assigned to drive each of the fleet of jeeps, trucks, weapons carriers, and staff cars, and an around-the-clock taxi service was put into operation. Dashing about Thuringia, the "taxis" would screech to a halt before a scientist's house; then he and his wife and children would be given fifteen minutes to grab their personal items.

Through superhuman efforts by Major Staver and several junior army officers working with him, all of the recruited rocket experts and their families were gathered at the Nordhausen railroad station at noon on June 20. Thick anxiety hovered over the throng: the Soviet Army was to arrive in fewer than twenty-four hours.

A long line of railroad passenger cars was waiting along the tracks, but the locomotive failed to show up. The clock ticked on: one hour, two hours . . . three . . . four. The Soviets might arrive at any moment. Where was the loco-motive? Suddenly a loud cheer and rousing applause erupted from the nervous crowd: the engine was chugging up to the railroad station.

Just past 6:00 P.M., fewer than six hours before the Soviets were to occupy the region, the long train, crammed with much of Germany's scientific brain-power and their families, rolled westward, crossed the Werra River over a re-paired bridge, and sped on to Witzenhausen, a small town forty miles southwest of Nordhausen in the American zone.

Wernher von Braun (right), who had broken his arm in an automobile mishap, and his brother Magnus surrendered to a group of American GIs. (NASA)

Five months later, on the drab, cold morning of November 16, 1945, the gray-painted U.S.S. *Argentina*, a troop transport, sailed into New York Harbor. On board, along with a few thousand returning American soldiers, were most of the German rocket scientists. Their arrival was cloaked in great secrecy, but the next day, the *New York Herald Tribune* reported that "a group of Reich civilians" had been brought to the United States to drive trucks for the Army Transportation Corps.[17]

Japan's Secret Weapons
Await Invasion

THE WORLD STOOD on the brink of the most horrendous slaughter of the human race since the Mongol warlord Genghis Khan and his armies had swept across northern Asia and eastern Europe in the 1200s. General Douglas MacArthur was preparing to launch Operation Downfall—an American invasion of Japan—history's largest amphibious and airborne operation. It was early July 1945.

Although the Philippines, Okinawa, Iwo Jima, and other outposts of Japan had been lost in recent months, the warlords in Tokyo were feverishly implementing Ketsu-Go (Operation Decision), the last-ditch, fight-to-the-death defense of every inch of the homeland that all Japanese held to be sacred. They believed that the Japanese islands had fallen as drops from the sword of an ancient god.

Defending Japan when MacArthur struck would be 2.4 million veteran soldiers and 250,000 garrison troops, all of them deeply imbued with the warrior's Shintoist code that deemed it to be a sanctified duty and an honor to die in battle for Emperor Hirohito.

Backing up the regulars was a militia, armed with a motley array of weapons (including butcher knives and bamboo spears), and numbering in excess of 32 million civilian men, women, and children. Each had pledged to kill at least one American before his or her own death in battle.

Ten thousand eager *kamikaze tokubetsu kogetika* (suicide pilots) were ready to crash their airplanes into the ships of the American invasion fleet as it approached Japan. Other suicide pilots would ram American transport planes loaded with paratroopers.

The Fukuyuri consisted of hundreds of volunteers who were strong swimmers. Each man would carry a mine on his back, swim to a ship under cover of darkness, and blow up the vessel and himself.

Complementing the suicide groups would be numerous innovative weapons created by Japanese scientists. Two navy lieutenants and a naval architect, Hiroshi Suzukawa, developed a design for the Kaiten (Heaven Shaker), a torpedo launched from a submarine at a distance of forty-eight miles from its target.

Guided by a human, the Kaiten's warhead of 3,340 pounds of dynamite would sink even the largest of U.S. ships. A new training center had been set up in Japan, and 200 recruits began to learn the difficult art of controlling the Kaiten.

In early 1945, a navy pilot, Ensign Mitsuo Ota, came up with a design for a special weapon that would assure the destruction of an American ship by permitting a pilot to crash his bomb directly on the target. Produced with the help of the Aeronautical Section of Tokyo University, Ota's design gained the interest of his superiors, and an emergency program was set up at the Naval Air Research and Development Center outside Tokyo. Known as the Marudai project, it resulted in the Okha (Cherry Blossom), a suicide bomb, of which eight hundred were built.

Carried beneath a Mitsubishi bomber to within twenty miles of its target, the Okha would cut loose from its mother aircraft, and the suicide rider would steer the 2,640-pound warhead, at a speed of 400 miles per hour, into a ship.

The Japanese had high hopes that the Okha bomb (shown hidden in its hangar) and others like it would smash the looming Allied invasion of the home islands. (U.S. Army)

Navy Captain Motoharu Okamura was instructed to recruit and train pilots for the Jinrai Butai (Corps of Divine Thunder), which would operate the Okha.

Despite the enormous scientific ingenuity and effort that had been poured into the development of these secret weapons, a revolutionary American bomb of unprecedented mass destruction would preclude their use against an American invasion of Japan.[18]

Treachery at Los Alamos

ON DARK COMPANIA HILL overlooking the Trinity Test site at remote Alamogordo Air Base in New Mexico, a group of tense scientists put on welders' glasses through which to watch the explosion of history's first atomic bomb. Although the blast would occur twenty miles away, the observers had been instructed not to look directly at ground zero.

Suddenly the eerie silence on Compania Hill was shattered as a clear, measured voice began the countdown as it parceled out the seconds: "Five . . . four . . . three . . . two . . . one . . . zero!" It was 5:29:45 on the morning of July 16, 1945.

Then the sky ignited, silently. A yellow-reddish fireball brighter than the sun, its temperature ten thousand times greater, began an eight-mile ascent, warming the faces of the men on Compania Hill, turning night into day for more than a hundred miles.

Newspapers, wire services, and law enforcement agencies within a radius of three hundred miles were flooded by calls from terrified citizens—including one from a blind woman who said she had discerned the light. To calm the near-hysteria, General Leslie Groves, director of the Manhattan Project, ordered the prompt release of a previously prepared media handout:

> A remotely located ammunition magazine containing a consider-
> able amount of high explosives and pyrotechnics has exploded.
> There was no loss of life or injury.

That false explanation of the atomic bomb explosion was accepted by the American public.

But thousands of miles from ground zero, Soviet dictator Josef Stalin, who was in suburban Berlin meeting with U.S. President Harry Truman and British Prime Minister Winston Churchill, wasn't fooled. He knew the true story.

Stalin's clandestine informant had been thirty-three-year-old Klaus Emil Fuchs, a brilliant scientist who had come to the United States from Great Britain in 1943 to work on the Manhattan Project. Klaus had been one of those on Compania Hill observing the A-bomb explosion.

German-born Klaus had fled from his homeland to escape Nazi oppression in the late 1930s and became a naturalized British citizen. Before coming to the United States, his loyalty presumably had been certified by the government of Great Britain. Actually, the thin, scholarly scientist was a slick Soviet spy.

After his arrival Fuchs had been assigned to the laboratory at Los Alamos in northern New Mexico. Built to carry out research on making an atomic bomb, the laboratory was one of the most closely guarded facilities in the world. Fuchs had made an immediately favorable impression on his superiors. None had known that he had long been deeply involved in the Communist Party in Germany and had continued his activities as a covert agent for the Kremlin while in England.

Fuchs, described by one superior at Los Alamos as possessing amazing versatility and a willingness to volunteer for ever more work, had always been the first on the job in the morning. Chain-smoking, peering owlishly through tortoiseshell eyeglasses, he ground out complicated computations of advanced quality in his ten-foot-by-twelve-foot cubicle.

After being named to head the atomic bomb project in September 1942, General Leslie Groves had conceived an organizational structure he called "compartmentalization." He was obsessed with the technique because he felt it ensured protection against spies. A year later, Groves, in the belief that British security authorities had thoroughly investigated Klaus Fuchs's background (apparently they had not done so), appointed the Soviet spy to be the liaison

Soviet masterspy Klaus Fuchs.
(National Archives)

official among the divisions. That task gave Fuchs an overview of the work being done throughout the entire project.

By the time of the successful atomic bomb test, Fuchs had fed the Soviets voluminous intelligence at least seven times, always through Harry Gold, a courier who reported to Anatoli Yakovlev, whose cover in the espionage ring was vice consul in the Soviet consulate in New York.

Born Heinrich Golodnitsky in Switzerland of Russian parents, Gold had been brought to the United States three years later. A pudgy, swarthy biochemist, he had received a science degree *summa cum laude* from Xavier University in Ohio. During his college days and after his 1935 graduation, he had been a Communist agent for the Soviet Union.

Gold was awed by the quantity and quality of Klaus Fuchs's intelligence productivity. In one consignment, Gold would later state, "There were fifty, sixty, a hundred pages of very close writing on yellow pads. It not only contained a tremendous amount of theoretical mathematics, it contained the [entire] practical setup of [the atomic bomb project]."

During their first six meetings, Fuchs and Gold had rendezvoused while Fuchs was on the East Coast for brief vacations. Their seventh meeting took place, by prearrangement, on the Castillo Bridge at Santa Fe, some twenty-three miles from Los Alamos, late in the afternoon of June 2, 1944. It was Gold's first visit to the southwestern United States, and he had acquired a map so as not to attract attention by having to ask directions.

Gold got into Fuchs's battered old Buick, whose speedometer was broken, and the two spies drove about the region. Progress on developing the A-bomb (as it came to be known) was dramatic, Fuchs declared. Then he turned over a thick sheaf of notes to Gold, and the two men parted on a dark side street in Santa Fe.

The Soviet espionage apparatus also was "compartmentalized," to keep agents from knowing about the activities of other spies. Unknown to Fuchs, Gold, instead of returning to his base in the East, had hopped on a Greyhound bus and checked in at the Hilton Hotel in Albuquerque. On the following morning, he called at the apartment of twenty-three-year-old David Greenglass, a soldier in the U.S. Army who worked at Los Alamos as a draftsman.

When Gold knocked at the door and Greenglass responded, Gold presented half of the side of a Jell-O box, and Greenglass took the matching half out of his wife's handbag. The Jell-O container matchup had been prearranged by Anatoli Yakovlev, the spymaster at the Soviet consulate in New York.

"I have come from Julius," Gold said, a recognition line he had been given by Yakovlev. By coincidence, Julius was the first name of another key member of the Soviet spy network, Julius Rosenberg, the husband of Greenglass's sister, Ethel.

Although Greenglass was a low-level technician at Los Alamos, he was in a sensitive job that permitted him to provide Gold with sketches and descriptions of various patterns of "flat-type lens molds." These lenses involved a combination of high explosives that focused detonation waves as a glass lens focuses light waves, and so touched off the atomic bomb. Greenglass's materials proved to be a bonanza to Soviet scientists.

Julius and Ethel Rosenberg lived in a New York City apartment, and they had been open members of the Communist Party since his graduation from the College of the City of New York with a degree in electrical engineering. Sometime during the war, the couple had shucked their open roles to go underground for the Soviet Union.

When Ethel's brother, David Greenglass, had been drafted and eventually assigned to the supersecret laboratory at Los Alamos, the Rosenbergs sent David's young wife, Ruth Greenglass, to New Mexico to tell him that he must pass along to them all the information he could for Soviet use. Ethel was then twenty-eight and her husband was twenty-six. Both were competent and intelligent persons; David Greenglass had long been devoted to the Rosenbergs.

On August 6, 1945, a lone B-29 Superfortress, piloted by Colonel Paul W. Tibbets, dropped what was later described to an awed world as an atomic bomb on the Japanese industrial city of Hiroshima. When the Japanese war-

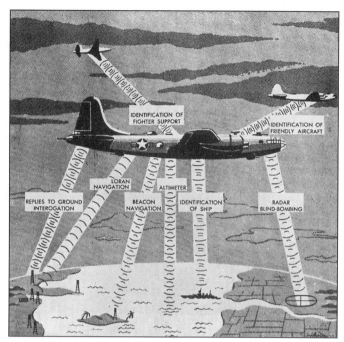

An American B-29 Superfortress was equipped with five types of radar devices for different functions. (U.S. Air Force)

lords ignored a second surrender demand (President Truman had issued the first one before the Hiroshima flight), a second nuclear explosion occurred, over Nagasaki.

Nine days after the first blast, at noon on August 15, diminutive, myopic Emperor Hirohito defied his generals and admirals, took to Radio Tokyo, and announced that the empire was capitulating.

Back in the United States on September 19, about a month after Hirohito's broadcast, Klaus Fuchs and Harry Gold held their eighth and final rendezvous near a church on a road leading out of Santa Fe. Fuchs handed over the remaining atomic secrets. The package he gave Gold contained extensive notes on the precise size of what had become known simply as the Bomb, the dimensions of its parts, and how it was constructed and detonated.

Almost four years later, in August 1949, official Washington was shocked to learn that the Soviet Union had successfully tested an atomic bomb. U.S. scientists had predicted that it would be a decade, or much longer, before the Soviets had the know-how. But these scientists had not been privy to the fact that the Soviets had benefited enormously from the network of American traitors who had stolen all of the nation's atomic energy secrets.[19]

Notes and Sources

Part One—War Breaks Out

1. **German Invention Triggers Global Search**
   Rearguard, Munich, July 15, 1974.
   Anthony Cave Brown, *Bodyguard of Lies* (New York: Harper & Row, 1975), pp. 18–19.
   F. W. Winterbotham, *The Ultra Secret* (New York: Harper & Row, 1974), p. 14.

2. **Stealing America's Radar Secrets**
   Declassified FBI files, 1946, in author's possession.
   Michael Sayers and Albert E. Kahn, *Sabotage!* (New York: Harper & Brothers, 1942), pp. 15, 18.
   Leon Turrou, *The Nazi Spy Conspiracy in the United States* (Freeport, N.Y.: Books for Libraries Press, 1969), pp. 58, 62.

3. **History's Most Important Letter**
   Alan D. Beyerchen, *Scientists Under Hitler* (New Haven, Conn.: Yale University Press, 1977), p. 40.
   Kenneth S. Davis, *FDR: Into the Storm* (New York: Random House, 1993), pp. 483, 510.
   Richard Rhodes, *The Making of the Atomic Bomb* (New York: Viking, 1986), pp. 306, 313.
   Lewis L. Strauss, *Men and Decisions* (New York: Simon & Schuster, 1962), p. 174.
   Geoffrey T. Hellman, "The Contemporaneous Memoranda of Doctor Sachs," *New Yorker*, December 1, 1945.
   Edward Teller, "Energy from Heaven and Earth," *Atomic Science Bulletin*, 1979.
   Leo Szilard, *The Collected Works: Scientific Papers* (Cambridge, Mass.: Harvard University Press, 1972), p. 115.

4. **A U.S. Foundation Funds Nazi Research**
   New York Times, May 5, 1940.
   Author's archives.

5. **"A Bunch of Crazy Scientists"**
   Albert Speer, *Inside the Third Reich* (New York: Macmillan, 1952), p. 197.
   Walter Dornberger, *V-2* (New York: Viking, 1959), pp. 53–54.
   David Irving, *The Mare's Nest* (London: Kimber, 1964), p. 23.

6. **Charles Lindbergh Helps the "Moon Man"**
   Ladislas Farago, *The Game of the Foxes* (New York: McKay, 1971), p. 36.
   Leonard Moseley, *Lindbergh* (New York: Harper & Row, 1976), pp. 344–345.
   Author's archives.

7. **An American Aids Japanese Nuclear Project**
   Author's archives.

8. **Supersecret Station X**
   Ewen Montagu, *Beyond the Secret* (New York: Coward, McCann, & Geoghegan, 1978), pp. 46, 48.
   Author's archives.

9. **Aspirins Foil the Luftwaffe**
   Author correspondence with Professor Reginald V. Jones, Aberdeen, Scotland, March 1991.
   Ronald Lewin, *Ultra Goes to War* (New York: McGraw-Hill, 1978), p. 76.
   George Millar, *The Bruneval Raid* (Garden City, N.Y.: Doubleday, 1975), p. 57.
   R. V. Jones, *Most Secret War* (London: Collins, 1976), pp. 35, 101.

10. **A Plan to Light Up the United Kingdom**
    Robert Watson-Watt, *Three Steps to Victory* (London: Odhams, 1957), p. 117.

11. **Is a Death Ray Feasible?**
    Anthony Cave Brown, *Bodyguard of Lies* (New York: Harper & Row, 1975), p. 32.
    Field Marshal Alan Brooke, *Diaries* (London: Collins, 1957), p. 104.
    Philip Joubert, *The Fated Sky* (London: Hutchinson, 1952), pp. 166–167.
    R. V. Jones, *Most Secret War* (London: Collins, 1976), p. 14.
    Robert Watson-Watt, *Three Steps to Victory* (London: Odhams, 1957), pp. 81, 86.

12. **A Hassle with British Bureaucrats**
    Philip Joubert, *The Fated Sky* (London: Hutchinson, 1952), p. 138.

13. **Conjuring Up Wild Theories**
    Author's archives.

Part Two—Great Britain Stands Alone

1. **A Nation's Survival at Stake**
   R. V. Jones, *Most Secret War* (London: Collins, 1976), p. 126.
   George Millar, *The Bruneval Raid* (Garden City, N.Y.: Doubleday, 1975), p. 108.
   Author correspondence with Professor Reginald Jones, Aberdeen, Scotland, April 1991.

2. **A Little Black Box of Secrets**
   Alan Bullock, *Hitler* (New York: Harper & Row, 1963), p. 304.
   Robert Payne, *The Life and Death of Adolf Hitler* (New York: Popular Library, 1974), p. 401.
   Robert Watson-Watt, *Three Steps to Victory* (London: Odhams, 1957), p. 297.
   Vannevar Bush, *Pieces of the Action* (New York: Morrow, 1970), pp. 33, 36, 107.

3. **A Huge Mousetrap in the Sky**
   Gerald Pawle, *The Secret War* (New York: Sloane, 1957), pp. 102–105.
   Author's archives.

4. **Americans Break the Purple Code**
   David Dilks, ed., *The Missing Dimension* (London: Macmillan, 1984), p. 52.
   "Pearl Harbor and the Inadequacy of Cryptanalysis," *Cryptologia*, vol. 15, 1991.
   Edwin T. Layton, *And I Was There* (New York: Morrow, 1987), p. 81.
   Henry L. Stimson Diary, September 25, 1940. New Haven, Conn.: Yale University Library.
   "Historical Background of the Signal Security Agency" (Washington, D.C.: U.S. Government Printing Office, 1956), part 3, p. 308.
   Bradley F. Smith, *The Ultra-Magic Deals* (Novato, Calif.: Presidio, 1993), pp. 43–44.
   Joint Committee on the Investigation of the Pearl Harbor Attack, part 11, p. 5475. National Archives, Washington, D.C.

5. **The Mystery Truck from Mars**
   John Smyth, *Leadership in War* (New York: St. Martin's Press, 1947), p. 63.
   Author's archives.
   David Irving, *The Trail of the Fox* (New York: Dutton, 1977), p. 207.

6. **Churchill's Agonizing Decision**
   F. W. Winterbotham, *The Ultra Secret* (New York: Harper & Row, 1974), p. 59.
   New York Times, November 10, 1940.
   Royal Air Force, 1939–1945, vol. 1, p. 210.
   Life, December 23, 1940.
   The Times, London, November 16, 1940.

7. **Duel of the Radio Beams**
   R. V. Jones, *Most Secret War* (London: Collins, 1976), pp. 125–126.
   Author correspondence with Professor Reginald V. Jones, Aberdeen, Scotland, June
      1991.

8. **Enigma Betrays the Italian Fleet**
   Author's archives.

9. **Code Names Rebecca and Eureka**
   Author's archives.

10. **A Dying Genius "Sinks" the *Bismarck***
   Donald McLachan, *Room 39* (New York: Athenaeum, 1963), pp. 161, 400.
   Burkard von Mullenheim-Rechberg, *Battleship Bismarck* (Annapolis, Md.: Naval Insti-
      tute Press, 1979), pp. 228, 232.
   Anthony Cave Brown, *Bodyguard of Lies* (New York: Harper & Row, 1975), p. 281.
   Winston S. Churchill, *The Second World War*, vol. 2 (Boston: Houghton Mifflin, 1950),
      pp. 331–332.

11. **Cryptographic Sleuths Silence the Red Orchestra**
   Leopold Trepper, *The Great Game* (New York: McGraw-Hill, 1977), pp. 14, 130, 206.
   Mark M. Boatner III, *The Biographical Dictionary of World War II* (Novato, Calif.: Pre-
      sidio, 1996), p. 697.
   Gilles Perrault, *The Red Orchestra* (London: Barker, 1968), pp. 37, 104, 219.
   Author's archives.

12. **A Miraculous Escape from Denmark**
   Winston Churchill, *The Second World War*, vol. 2 (Boston: Houghton Mifflin, 1950),
      p. 203.
   Ralph Barker, *The RAF at War* (Alexandria, Va.: Time-Life, 1981), p. 83.
   Mark W. Boatner III, *The Biographical Dictionary of World War II* (Novato, Calif.: Pre-
      sidio, 1996), p. 32.
   Author correspondence with Professor Reginald V. Jones, Aberdeen, Scotland, March
      1991.

13. **Bright Ideas for Winning the War**
   Gavin Lyall, ed., *The War in the Air* (New York: Morrow, 1969), pp. 101–102.
   Author's archives.

14. **Operation Jay: An Intricate Hoax**
   Winston S. Churchill, *The Second World War*, vol. 3 (Boston: Houghton Mifflin, 1952),
      pp. 139, 147, 208.
   London Gazette, October 14, 1947.
   Ralph Barker, *The RAF at War* (Arlington, Va.: Time-Life, 1981), pp. 85, 92.
   Robert Watson-Watt, *Three Steps to Victory* (London: Odhams, 1957), pp. 394–395.
   Author's archives.
   R. V. Jones, *Most Secret War* (London: Collins, 1976), pp. 218–219, 221.

15. **England's "Kamikaze" Pilots**
   Gavin Lyall, ed., *The War in the Air* (New York: Morrow, 1969), pp. 235, 236.
   Author's archives.

Part Three—Thrust and Counterthrust

1. **Could Pearl Harbor Have Been Avoided?**
   Author's archives.

2. **The British Invade Washington**
   William L. Shirer, *The Rise and Fall of the Third Reich* (New York: Simon & Schuster, 1960), pp. 896–897.
   Winston S. Churchill, *The Second World War*, vol. 3 (Boston: Houghton Mifflin, 1952), p. 540.
   Henry L. Stimson Diary, December 31, 1941 to January 19, 1942. New Haven, Conn.: Yale University Library.
   Bradley F. Smith, *The Ultra-Magic Deals* (Novato, Calif.: Presidio, 1991), p. 95.

3. **A Scheme to Bomb New York**
   David Irving, *The Rise and Fall of the Luftwaffe* (Boston: Little, Brown, 1973), pp. 341, 356.
   Author's archives.

4. **Five U.S. Scientists Killed**
   Jean Noll, *The Admiral's Wolfpack* (Garden City, N.Y.: Doubleday, 1974), p. 138.
   Ladislas Farago, *The Tenth Fleet* (New York: Obolensky, 1962), p. 46.
   New York Times, June 9, 1942.
   James Phinney Baxter, *Scientists Against Time* (Boston: Little, Brown, 1946), p. 183.

5. **Mystery of the Vanishing U-Boats**
   Author's archives.

6. **The Germans' Four-Poster Beds**
   Janusz Piekalkiewicz, *Secret Agents, Spies, and Saboteurs* (New York: Morrow, 1973), pp. 83–84.
   R. V. Jones, *Most Secret War* (London: Collins, 1976), pp. 221, 265.
   Author's archives.

7. **The Century's Most Audacious Heist**
   Author correspondence with Professor Reginald V. Jones, Aberdeen, Scotland, August 1991.
   James Ladd, *Commandos and Rangers* (New York: St. Martin's Press, 1978), p. 40.
   Hilary St. George Saunders, *Combined Operations* (New York: Macmillan, 1943), p. 63.
   Author correspondence with Major General John D. Frost (Ret.), Aldershot, England, June 1992.

8. **A Secret Move to a Secret Site**
   Author's archives.

9. **Poking Out Britain's "Eyes"**
   Patrick Beesly, *Very Special Intelligence* (Garden City, N.Y.: Doubleday, 1972), p. 124.
   Eddy Bauer, ed., *Illustrated Encyclopedia of World War II*, vol. 6 (London: Cavendish, 1972), pp. 833, 836.
   Janusz Piekalkiewicz, *Secret Agents, Spies, and Saboteurs* (New York: Morrow, 1973), pp. 83, 85.
   The Times, London, February 15, 1942.

10. **A Plan to Turn Hitler Feminine**
    Official History of the Office of Strategic Services, pp. 212–215. Washington, D.C.: National Archives.
    Stanley Lovell, *Of Spies and Stratagems* (Englewood Cliffs, N.J.: Prentice-Hall, 1962), pp. 78–79.

Author's archives.

William Casey, *The Secret War Against Hitler* (Washington, D.C.: Regnery Gateway, 1988), p. 28.

David Stafford, *Camp X* (New York: Dodd, Mead, 1986), pp. 78–80.

11. **Geniuses in a Dungeon**

John B. Lundstrom, *The First South Pacific Campaign* (Annapolis, Md.: Naval Institute Press, 1976), p. 180.

Chichi Nagumo, "The Japanese Story of the Battle of Midway," *ONI Review*, May 1947.

Edwin T. Layton, *Pearl Harbor and Midway* (New York: Morrow, 1985), pp. 428, 436.

Elmer P. Potter, *Nimitz* (Annapolis, Md.: Naval Institute Press, 1976), p. 68.

Samuel Eliot Morison, *Coral Sea, Midway, and Submarine Actions* (Boston: Little, Brown, 1950), pp. 46, 48.

St. Louis Post-Dispatch, April 20, 1942.

12. **A Test Goes Up in Smoke**

Gavin Lyall, ed., *The War in the Air* (New York: Morrow, 1969), pp. 254–255.

Author's archives.

13. **Goering an "Honorary Scientist"**

Louis P. Lochner, ed., *The Goebbels Diaries* (Garden City, N.Y.: Doubleday, 1948), pp. 279–280.

Albert Speer, *Inside the Third Reich* (New York: Macmillan, 1970), pp. 225–226.

David Irving, *The German Atomic Bomb* (New York: Simon & Schuster, 1967), pp. 210, 295.

Der Spiegel, July 3, 1967.

14. **A Nuclear Laboratory Explodes**

Author's archives.

15. **A Gathering of "Luminaries"**

James Phinney Baxter, *Scientists Against Time* (Boston: Little, Brown, 1946), p. 239.

Thomas Powers, *Heisenberg's War* (New York: Knopf, 1993), p. 382.

Richard Rhodes, *The Making of the Atomic Bomb* (New York: Viking, 1986), pp. 420–421.

Part Four—Turning of the Tide

1. **A Spectacular Rocket Feat**

David Irving, *The Mare's Nest* (London: Kimber, 1964), p. 23.

Albert Speer, *Inside the Third Reich* (New York: Macmillan, 1964), pp. 367–368.

New York Times, June 18, 1977.

Arthur Bryant, *The Turn of the Tide* (Garden City, N.Y.: Doubleday, 1957), p. 214.

2. **Stealing German Weather Forecasts**

F. W. Winterbotham, *The Ultra Secret* (New York: Harper & Row, 1974), pp. 89, 92.

Author's archives.

3. **"I Fear We Are in the Soup!"**

Stefan Groueff, *Manhattan Project* (Boston: Little, Brown, 1967), pp. 151, 332.

Leona Libby, *Uranium People* (New York: Scribner's, 1979), p. 95.

Arthur Holly Compton, *Atomic Quest* (London: Oxford University Press, 1956), p. 113.

"All in Our Time," *Bulletin of the Atomic Scientists*, 1974, p. 147.

Leslie Groves, *Now It Can Be Told* (New York: Harper, & Row, 1962), p. 15.

Peter Goodchild, *J. Robert Oppenheimer* (Boston: Houghton Mifflin, 1980), p. 56.
Author's archives.

4. **Fiasco in Chesapeake Bay**
Author's archives.
James Phinney Baxter, *Scientists Against Time* (Boston: Little, Brown, 1946), pp. 69–70.
History of the 2nd Armored Division (privately printed, 1945), pp. 32, 36.

5. **The Soviets' Secret Nuclear Laboratory**
Author's archives.

6. **Prediction: Hitler Will Have A-Bomb**
Otto Frisch, *What Little I Remember* (London: Cambridge University Press, 1979), pp. 127–128.
Arthur Holly Compton, *Atomic Quest* (London: Oxford University Press, 1956), pp. 81–82.
Spencer Weart, *Leo Szilard* (Cambridge, Mass.: MIT Press, 1954), p. 152.
Memo, Leo Szilard to Arthur Compton, record group 227, roll 7. Washington, D.C.: National Archives.
Vannevar Bush interview on atomic-bomb documentary, television History Channel (United States), March 30, 1999.
David Irving, *The German Atomic Bomb* (New York: Simon & Schuster, 1967), p. 151.
Thomas Powers, *Heisenberg's War* (New York: Knopf, 1993), p. 185.

7. **Eavesdropping on Roosevelt and Churchill**
Ladislas Farago, *The Game of the Foxes* (New York: McKay, 1971), p. 588.
Author's archives.

8. **A Burglar Alarm at Gibraltar**
Anthony Cave Brown, *Bodyguard of Lies* (New York: Harper & Row, 1975), p. 424.
Charles Mott-Radclyffe, *The Dictionary of National Biography* (New York: Scribner's, 1981), p. 324.
Albert Speer, *Inside the Third Reich* (New York: Macmillan, 1952), pp. 325–326.
R. V. Jones, *Most Secret War* (London: Collins, 1976), p. 259.

9. **Feuds among Nazi Bigwigs**
The Shadow War (Alexandria, Va.: Time-Life, 1991), pp. 126–128.
Author's archives.
David Kahn, *Hitler's Spies* (London: Hodder & Stoughton, 1978), pp. 113, 118.

10. **A Chess Game in the Atlantic**
"Symbol" Reports and Minutes, January 1943, Modern Military Records. Washington, D.C.: National Archives.
Files of the Office of the Chief of Naval Operations, "Report on Interrogations of U-Boat Survivors," August 1943. Washington, D.C.: National Archives.
S. W. Roskill, *The War at Sea*, vol. 1 (London: Her Majesty's Stationery Office, 1954), pp. 146–147.
Author's archives.
Lothar-Günther Buchheim, *U-Boat War* (New York: Knopf, 1978), p. 112.

11. **History's First Nuclear Spy**
Reader's Digest, March 1946.
David Kahn, *The Codebreakers* (New York: Macmillan, 1978), p. 545.
Anthony Cave Brown, *Bodyguard of Lies* (New York: Harper & Row, 1975), p. 537.
American Magazine, March 1946.

Reader's Digest Association, *Secrets and Spies* (Pleasantville, N.Y.: Reader's Digest, 1964), pp. 233, 285.

Author's archives.

Ladislas Farago, *The Game of the Foxes* (New York: McKay, 1971), pp. 651–653.

12. **A Rain of Metallic Foil**
David Irving, *The Rise and Fall of the Luftwaffe* (Boston: Little, Brown, 1973), p. 247.
Martin Middlebrook, *The Battle of Hamburg* (London: Lane, 1980), p. 95.
Allen Andrews, *The Air Marshals* (New York: Morrow, 1970), p. 48.
Arthur T. Harris, *Bomber Command* (London: Collins, 1947), pp. 165, 179.
Author's archives.

13. **Smuggling a Renowned Scientist**
John Thomas, *The Giant Killers* (New York: Macmillan, 1975), pp. 32–33.
Abraham Pais, *Niels Bohr's Times* (London: Oxford University Press, 1991), p. 486.
Ruth Moore, *Niels Bohr* (New York: Knopf, 1966), pp. 302–303.
Stefan Rozental, *Niels Bohr* (Amsterdam: North-Holland, 1966), pp. 195–196.
Otto Frisch, *What Little I Remember* (London: Cambridge University Press, 1979), pp. 148–149.
Jeremy Bernstein, *Hans Bethe* (New York: Basic Books, 1980), p. 77.
Author's archives.

14. **A Plan to Poison the German Food Supply**
Memo, J. Robert Oppenheimer to Enrico Fermi, May 25, 1943, Oppenheimer papers, box 33. Washington, D.C.: Library of Congress.
Manhattan Engineer District Records, 319.1, Literature, appendix IV, p. 7. Washington, D.C.: National Archives.
Richard Rhodes, *The Making of the Atomic Bomb* (New York: Simon & Schuster, 1968), p. 510.

15. **Bouncing Bombs and Dambusters**
Ralph Barker, *The RAF at War* (Alexandria, Va.: Time-Life, 1981), p. 145.
Paul Brickhill, *The Dam-Busters* (London: Evans, 1951), pp. 174–175.
Gavin Lyall, ed., *The War in the Air* (New York: Morrow, 1969), p. 255.

Part Five—Beginning of the End

1. **Protecting a Sacred Secret**
Author interviews with Lieutenant General James M. Gavin (Ret.), February–March 1989.
Author interview with wartime paratroop chaplain George B. "Chappie" Woods, May 1992.
Author's archives.

2. **A Triumph for German Cryptanalysts**
"The Ploesti Mission," Assistant Chief of Air Staff, Intelligence, U.S. Army Historical Division. Washington, D.C.
General Harold R. L. G. Alexander, "The Conquest of Sicily, Despatch," July 10–August 7, 1943. London: Imperial War Museum.
Dwight D. Eisenhower, *Crusade in Europe* (Garden City, N.Y.: Doubleday, 1948), pp. 160–161.

3. **"You Scare Hell Out of Me!"**
   B. H. Lidell-Hart, *The German Generals Talk* (New York: Morrow, 1948), p. 233.
   "Defensive Measures Taken Against Possible Use by Germans of Radioactive Warfare,"
      Manhattan Engineer District. Washington, D.C.: National Archives.
   Vannevar Bush, *Pieces of Action* (New York: Morrow, 1970), p. 307.
   Author's archives.
   George Martelli, *The Man Who Saved London* (Garden City, N.Y.: Doubleday, 1961),
      p. 214.
   Joubert de la Ferte, *Rocket* (London: Hutchinson, 1957), p. 48.

4. **Snooping on a Japanese Ambassador**
   Gordon A. Harrison, *Cross-Channel Attack* (Washington, D.C.: Office of the Chief of
      Military History, 1951), appendix D.
   Author's archives.

5. **A Rocket Genius Charged with Treason**
   Erik Bergaust, *Reaching for the Stars* (New York: Doubleday, 1960), p. 91.
   Albert Speer, *Inside the Third Reich* (New York: Macmillan, 1952), pp. 172–173.
   Walter Dornberger, *V-2* (New York: Viking, 1958), pp. 169, 171.
   Helen B. Walters, *Wernher von Braun* (New York: Macmillan, 1964), pp. 72–73.
   Author's archives.

6. **German Codebreakers Pinpoint Normandy**
   "Enemy Sources of Information," SHAEF, August 1944. Washington, D.C.: National
      Archives.
   New York Times, March 27, 1944.
   Anthony Cave Brown, *Bodyguard of Lies* (New York: Harper & Row, 1975), pp.
      615–616.
   "Cover and Deception Operations, European Theater of Operations," Informal Report
      to Joint Security Control, May 1944. Washington, D.C.: National Archives.

7. **"Hiding" a Mighty Invasion**
   R. V. Jones, *Most Secret War* (London: Collins, 1976), pp. 401–402.
   London Gazette, January 3, 1947.
   Author's archives.
   Alfred Price, *Instruments of Darkness* (London: Kimber, 1967), pp. 204–205.

8. **Schemes to Defeat a Plague of Robots**
   Peter Wykeham, *Fighter Command* (New York: Putnam, 1960), p. 237.
   Gavin Lyall, ed., *The War in the Air* (New York: Morrow, 1969), pp. 343–344.
   Dwight D. Eisenhower, *Crusade in Europe* (Garden City, N.Y.: Doubleday, 1948),
      p. 302.

9. **A Soviet Plot Fizzles**
   David Dallin, *Soviet Espionage* (New Haven, Conn.: Yale University Press, 1955), p. 268.
   F. H. Hinsley, *British Intelligence in the Second World War*, vol. 3 (London: Her
      Majesty's Stationery Office, 1981), p. 400.
   Author's archives.
   Willy Ley, *Rockets, Missiles, and Man in Space* (New York: Viking, 1968), pp. 222–223.

10. **Hitler Counts on Wonder Weapons**
    Author's archives.

11. **Thwarting Japanese Torpedo Planes**
    Author's archives.
    Courtney Whitney, *MacArthur: His Rendezvous with History* (New York: Knopf, 1956),
       pp. 234–235.

James Phinney Baxter, *Scientists Against Time* (Boston: Little, Brown, 1946), pp. 164–165.

12. **A Bizarre Scenario in Zurich**
Constance Reid, *Hilbert* (Munich: Springer Verlag, 1986), p. 134.
David Irving, *The German Atomic Bomb* (New York: Simon & Schuster, 1967), p. 224.
Louis Kaufman, *Moe Berg* (Boston: Little, Brown, 1974), pp. 213–215.
Neue Zürcher Zeitung (Zurich, Switzerland), February 4, 1960.
Author's archives.

13. **A Tiny Fuse Balks the Führer**
Author's archives.
James Phinney Baxter, *Scientists Against Time* (Boston: Little, Brown, 1946), pp. 230, 232.

14. **Tactics to Obstruct the Soviets**
Leslie Groves, *Now It Can Be Told* (New York: Harper & Row, 1962), pp. 230–231.
David Irving, *The German Atomic Bomb* (New York: Simon & Schuster, 1967), pp. 274–275.
Mark M. Boatner III, *The Biographical Dictionary of World War II* (Novato, Calif.: Presidio, 1996), p. 518.
Thomas Powers, *Heisenberg's War* (New York: Knopf, 1993), p. 417.
John Lansdale Letter to Leslie Groves, February 1, 1960. Groves papers, record group 200. Washington, D.C.: National Archives.
Henry L. Stimson Diary, April 15, 1945. New Haven, Conn.: Yale University Library.

15. **A Polish Janitor Scores a Coup**
Author's archives.

16. **Hitler Orders Lethal Gas Assault**
Author's archives.

17. **A Trainload of German Brainpower**
Author interview with Walter Weisman, Huntsville, Ala., March 1993.
New York Herald Tribune, November 17, 1945.
Author interview with Colonel William A. Castille (Ret.), Austin, Tex., February 1993.
Author interview with Colonel Andrew Barr (Ret.), Washington, D.C., January 1993.
London Daily Express, January 23, 1949.
New York Herald Tribune, November 18, 1945.

18. **Japan's Secret Weapons Await Invasion**
Author's archives.

19. **Treachery at Los Alamos**
Author's archives.

Index